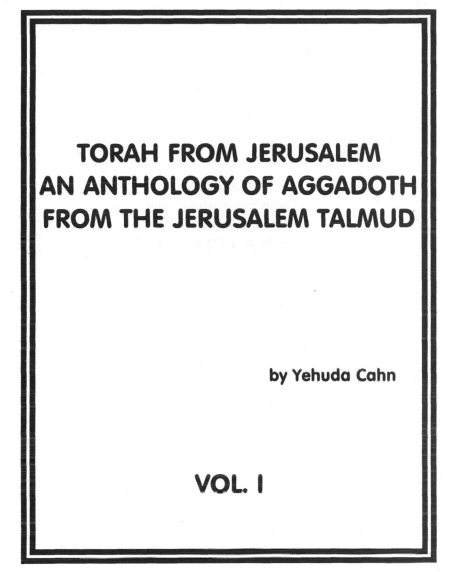

TORAH FROM JERUSALEM
AN ANTHOLOGY OF AGGADOTH
FROM THE JERUSALEM TALMUD

by Yehuda Cahn

VOL. I

ISBN: 0-9707757-1-7 (hardcover)
        0-9707757-2-5 (softcover)

RABBI MOSHE HEINEMANN
6109 Gist Avenue
Baltimore, MD 21215
Tel. (410) 358-9828
Fax. (410) 358-9838

משה היינעמאן
אב״ד ק״ק אגודת ישראל
באלטימאר
טל. 7778-764 (410)
פקס 8878-764 (410)

בס״ד

באתי בשורות אלו להמליץ על ספרו של ידידי ר' יהודה קאן נ״ו שעמד
בעינא פקיחא על האגדות שבתלמוד ירושלמי מסכת ברכות ותרגם אותם
להשפה המדוברת וגם הוסיף להם ביאור נאה ונחמד ודל״ה.
עברתי בין בתרי ספרו הנ״ל ומצאתי בו דברים עתיקים הראוים להעלותם
על שולחן מלכים.
לכן אמינא לפעלא טבא יישר ויזכה שספרו ימצא חן בעיני קוראיו ובזכות
לימוד דברי רבותינו התנאים והאמוראים שהם גופי תורה נזכה לביאת משיח
צדקנו בב״א.
וע״ז באתי עה״ח באחד בשבת לסדר ואת יהודה שלח...להורות לפניו שלושה ימים
לחדש טבת שנת חמשת אלפים ושבע מאות וששים כלבריאת עולם.
משה בהר״ר ברוך גר״ליה כ׳משפחת היינעמאן החונ״פ פה באלטימאר

ACKNOWLEDGMENTS

I would like to thank Rabbi Moshe Heinemann שליט"א, a scholar and leader of rare ability, for taking the time from his busy schedule to read my manuscript and give me a detailed critique which I used to produce the final work.

Rabbi Shaul Abrams, a member of the Kollel at Ner Israel Rabbinical College, also read the manuscript and offered many useful suggestions. In addition, Rabbi Abrams proofread the final draft.

I would also like to acknowledge Mr. David Levy and Mrs. Barbara Mischel who assisted me by providing material for the bibliography which appears at the end of this work.

Finally, I would like to express my gratitude to my wife, Geoula. Besides making sure that I could work on this project without distractions, she used her own vast knowledge of Jewish religious literature to offer several suggestions and insights which I incorporated into the text.

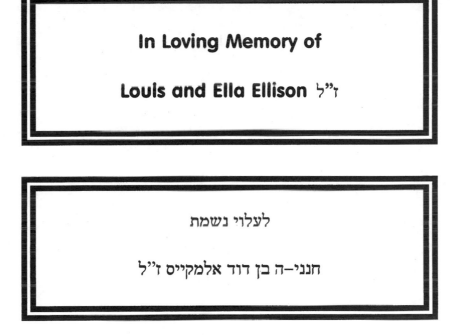

לעלוי נשמות

נסים בן יצחק אלאלוף ז"ל

רפאל בן נסים אלאלוף ז"ל

In Loving Memory of

Louis and Ella Ellison ז"ל

לעלוי נשמת

חנני–ה בן דוד אלמקייס ז"ל

INTRODUCTION

As with most classical Jewish texts, no one person wrote the Jerusalem Talmud. Thus, the Rambam[1] explains in his Introduction to the Mishnah that the Jerusalem Talmud was compiled by Rabbi Yochanan and his disciples, meaning that Rabbi Yochanan established the general outline of the material, but the work did not take final form until about sixty years or so after his death.[2] As the reader will see, Rabbi Yochanan is one of the sages most frequently cited in the Jerusalem Talmud.

Although Medieval Jewish scholars frequently cite the Jerusalem Talmud, it has not received the extensive attention which has been lavished upon the Babylonian Talmud. Indeed, when there is a conflict between the two, the halachic decisors almost always rule according to the Babylonian Talmud. One result of the lack of attention to the Jerusalem Talmud is that there appears to be less certainty as to the correct version of the text. Only one complete manuscript of the Jerusalem Talmud, known as the Leyden manuscript written in 1289, exists. Daniel Bomberg published an edition of the Jerusalem Talmud in Venice in 1523 based primarily on that manuscript and several other manuscripts which have since disappeared.

The present work is based upon the famous Romm

---

[1] **A bibliography and glossary appear at the end of the text.** Rambam is an acrostic for "Rabbi Moshe Ben Maimon," known in English as Rabbi Moses Maimonides. He was born in Spain in 1135 and died in Egypt in 1204.
[2] "Charting the Mesorah," Rabbi Zechariah Fendel (New York, 1994), p. 52.

1

edition first published in Vilna, Lithuania during the 1800's. That edition was based primarily upon an earlier printing in Zhitomir, Poland and includes extensive notes citing the textual variations found in other printed editions and manuscripts.

Despite the fact that several printed editions of the Jerusalem Talmud have been published over the centuries, none has emerged as a standard edition so that specific page numbers can be cited in each tractate. Instead, it is customary to cite references to the Jerusalem Talmud by the chapter and Mishnah (also called "halachah") of the tractate in which they appear and that practice has been followed in the present work.

Because the present work deals with Aggadoth (or, to use the terminology of the Jerusalem Talmud, Haggadoth), one can also find versions of some of the material presented here in Ein Yaakov, a collection of Aggadoth written by Rabbi Yaakov Ibn Chaviv during the 1500's. In addition, many Aggadoth of the Jerusalem Talmud appear in different forms in the Babylonian Talmud or in various Midrashim. While it is not the purpose of this work to perform the scholarly task of comparing the various extant texts of the Jerusalem Talmud or other ancient Jewish literature, cross-references are noted and points of comparison made where helpful to a better understanding of the text.

The renowned Tosafist, Rabbeinu Tam, noted that there were different dialects of Aramaic in use in the Land of Israel and Babylon.[3] For this reason, the vocabulary and the spelling

---

[3] Tosafoth sub verba "Lashon Sursi" (סורסי לשון) on B.T. Baba Kama 93A. See also Rashi sub verba "Lashon Sursi" (סורסי לשון) on B.T. Sotah

of some words found in the Jerusalem Talmud vary from those of the Babylonian Talmud.[4] Although this has discouraged some scholars from a comprehensive study of the Jerusalem Talmud, several excellent Medieval commentaries include translations of the Aramaic text into simple Hebrew so that a clear understanding of the is possible. In addition, several scholars have cataloged some of these linguistic points.

Literal translation of the Talmud, especially the laconic Jerusalem Talmud, is inappropriate and inconsistent with the intent of the original compilers. It is forbidden to write down the oral tradition that God gave Moshe Rabbeinu at Mount Sinai. However, when intense persecution threatened to prevent Jewish scholars from accurately transmitting tradition, the rabbis found themselves forced to record it in the form of the Talmud. However, this meant putting into writing only so much as was absolutely necessary to perpetuate tradition and no more. The resulting work resembles the shorthand notes a university student might take of a professor's lecture. The Talmudic compilers did not mean for later generations to understand the text as it is written. Rather, the intention was that students should add in the words or information necessary

---

49B.

[4] This may have contributed to the difficulty in maintaining the accuracy of the text. Scribes more familiar with the text of the Babylonian Talmud may have occasionally substituted words or spellings with which they were accustomed. For example, in one passage Rabbi Chiya the Great is called רבי חייא רבא and then, only one line later, רבי חייא רבה. (Brachoth 1:1).

3

to have the text make sense. For example, the Talmud often quotes a few words from a Scriptural verse, the idea being that the student would either be familiar with the complete verse or look it up. In the present translation, the full verse is quoted where appropriate.

The abbreviated style of the Jerusalem Talmud also includes the use of specialized terminology. For example, the word "dalemah" דלמא indicates that a story or parable is to follow. Along similar lines, The Talmud sometimes omits words which may be easily implied from the text. For instance, the Talmud may cite the name of a Sage followed by a quotation, but omitting the words, "he said." In these and all similar circumstances, the translation provides the implied words. The Talmud, even in standard printed editions, is written largely without any punctuation. Punctuation has been supplied in the Hebrew excerpts which accompany the translation to assist readers trying to follow along in the original.

In modern English, once a conversation between two speakers is introduced, one usually does not keep identifying who is speaking. Instead, each sentence is a separate paragraph enclosed by quotation marks and the reader understands who is speaking. Because the Talmud uses no punctuation, each sentence of a conversation is often preceded by "He said... ." The instant translation omits many of these redundant phrases, relying instead on the modern convention of using quotation marks.

In an attempt to keep the translation closer to its original meaning, an effort has been made to make it gender neutral where doing so does not destroy the flow of the text. Thus, for example, a literal translation of the beginning of Mishnah 9:5 would read, "A man is obliged to bless God for evil just as he blesses Him for good." The author of the Mishnah obviously did not mean that only men are so obligated and, in former times, anyone studying the Mishnah would have understood that. Unfortunately, in recent times, there are those who insist that such phraseology implies that women are excluded. To avoid this misunderstanding, the translation in the instant work reads, "A person is obliged to bless God for evil just as he or she blesses Him for good." In sentences which repeat the word "he" more than once, however, this type of wording tends to sound awkward. (E.g.: He or she said that if he or she could, he or she would have gone to his or her house, etc.) Accordingly, there are instances where the translation employs the old convention of having the masculine imply both masculine and feminine.

This translation supplies additional information necessary to understand the text in brackets. After each selection, a brief commentary appears in italics designed to further elucidate the concepts presented in the text.

Several commentators have sought to explain why the Jewish sages so often chose to express themselves by means of stories and parables, particularly when these stories tend to contain material which a well-educated person finds difficult to believe. This led the Rambam to explain that certain concepts were too esoteric to be explained in a straightforward manner. Only a parable could make the topic clear. In other cases, the Talmud dealt with matters which the general public may easily misunderstand. Accordingly, the rabbis expressed themselves in parables which only their advanced students could fathom. This permitted them to pass on the information to those capable of understanding it while others could view what was being said as entertaining "stories."[5]

There may be another reason that the sages often expressed themselves with allegories, however. When a rabbi admonishes members of the public to perform religious deeds, the response is straightforward. For instance, a person who hears that he or she should recite a blessing in a certain fashion can easily follow the rabbi's instructions to say the words properly. However, when a rabbi exhorts his followers to improve upon their character traits, the matter is quite different. By way of example, a rabbi might explain that greed is wrong because it leads to strife. When people seek to satisfy their greed, they come into conflict with others who may also be greedy. The result is strife, perhaps even war. In addition, greed is evil because it focuses one's attention on the temporal world and away from God. A person may understand intellectually why greed is wrong, and yet find it difficult to improve, for the change he or she seeks is not merely the outward performance of a religious act but the internal alteration of his or her personality. To change one's character, to alter one's emotions and outlook on life, one needs more than an understanding that such change is right. One needs emotional stimulation. That is where a story comes in. It engages the listener's emotions thereby inducing the change in

---

[5] Introduction to Moreh Nevuchim.

outlook. As the rabbis themselves say, "Aggadah attracts a person's heart."[6]

The Talmud states that "Numerous prophets arose for Israel, twice as many as the number of people who exited Egypt, but a prophecy which was needed for all generations was recorded while that which was not needed was not recorded."[7] If this was the case with prophecy, it is even more true of the Aggadoth because, as with the rest of the Oral Torah, it is forbidden to write down the Aggadoth unless there is a grave danger that they will be utterly forgotten.[8] Accordingly, it is fair to conclude that although myriad homilies and stories may have existed at the time the Talmud was redacted, only the select few which the rabbis thought of essential importance to the Jewish people throughout all generations were immortalized in the Talmud.

In light of the above, the question of whether every detail of the Aggadoth literally occurred is irrelevant. Whether certain Aggadoth represent homiletic exaggeration to impress a point, whether they were sometimes a rabbi's semi prophetic visions or dreams, or whether they were simply cleverly constructed parables is unimportant because their true purpose is to instruct, enlighten and inspire. Their reality is based upon the eternal truths they represent, not the precision of their historical accuracy.

---

[6] B.T. Shabbath 87A and Chagigah 14A.
[7] B.T. Megillah 14A.
[8] J.T. Shabbath 15:1 says that one who writes down Aggadoth has no share in the World to Come.

7

Brachoth 1:1 (Compare B.T. Brachoth 10B)

זהו שעומד ומתפלל צריך להשוות את רגליו. תרין אמורין: רבי
לוי ורבי סימון. חד אמר: כמלאכים וחד אמר ככהנים. מאן דאמר
ככהנים: "וְלֹא תַעֲלֶה בְמַעֲלֹת עַל מִזְבְּחִי..." (שמות כ:כג) שהיו מהלכים
עקב בצד גודל וגודל אצל עקב. ומאן דאמר כמלאכים:"וְרַגְלֵיהֶם רֶגֶל
יְשָׁרָה" (יחזקאל א:ז). רבי חנינא בר אנדריי בשם רבי שמואל בר סוטר:
המלאכים אין להן קפיצין. ומה טעמא? "קָרְבֵת עַל חַד מִן קָאֲמַיָּא..."
(דניאל ז:טז) קיימיא.

One who stands in prayer must keep his legs straight
together. Two Amoraim express opinions as to the reason for
this; Rabbi Levi and Rabbi Simon. One said it is to resemble
angels while one said it is to resemble Kohanim. The one who
said that this stance resembles Kohanim bases it upon the
verse, "You shall not ascend upon steps on my altar,"[9] meaning
that they walked heel to toe. [The Torah commanded the
priests in the Temple to ascend the altar in a dignified fashion.]
The one who said that this stance resembles angels bases it
upon the verse, "Their legs are a straight leg."[10]   Rabbi
Chanina bar Andrai said in the name of Rabbi Shmuel bar Soter
that the angels have no leg joints. [Thus, the angels stand
permanently erect, not able to sit or walk.] How is this known?
The verse says, "I approached one of those who stood."[11]

---

[9] Exodus 20:23.
[10] Ezekiel 1:7.
[11] Daniel 7:16.

The prayer service Jews use today serves as a substitute for the Temple service.[12] However, even in the time when the Temple stood, prayer was viewed as complementary to the Temple service. Thus the Talmud calls the Temple service simply "the Service" (העבודה) while prayer is the "service of the heart" (עבודה שבלב). The above selection of the Talmud makes the point that a Jew should try to approach prayer with the same reverence and devotion as the Kohanim had when they served in the Temple.[13]

What is the significance of angels having straight legs without joints in them? The Talmud teaches that, "In the path a person wishes to walk, so they guide him [from Heaven]."[14] In other words, people have the freedom to choose to do good or its opposite and God helps them carry out their decisions. Angels, by contrast, have no free will. They can only carry out the will of their Creator. In symbolic terms, they have but one straight, unbending leg. They cannot walk.

Angels are intelligent beings, so, in theory, they could choose between good and evil. However, unlike human beings, angels have a full and constant awareness of God's existence and dominion. Having such a recognition prevents them from using their intelligence to do anything but obey His will.

There was a time in history when the entire Jewish people became like the angels. The Talmud states that God

---

12 Hosea 14:3.
13 See Shulchan Aruch, Orach Chaim 98:4 for a similar concept.
14 B.T. Makkoth 10B.

9

held Mount Sinai over the heads of the nation and said, "If you accept the Torah, well and good, but if not, then this will be your grave!"[15] *The idea is that God revealed Himself to the Jewish people with such clarity that although they theoretically possessed the ability to refuse God's will, in practice they could not in the face of such a revelation. It was as though God threatened them with a mountain.*[16]

When a person prays, he or she should try to imitate the angels, to momentarily have such a clear recognition that God exists and rules the world, that one can do nothing else but obey His will. This is the underlying meaning of keeping one's feet together while praying so as to imitate the angels.[17]

---

[15] B.T. Shabbath 88A.
[16] Rabbi Mordechai Shuchatowitz, head of the Baltimore Bais Din.
[17] See Shulchan Aruch, Orach Chaim 95:1.

Brachoth 1:1

רבי חייא רבא ורבי שמעון בן חלפתא הוו מהלכין בהדא בקעת
ארבל בקריצתה וראו איילת השחר שבקע אורה. אמר רבי חייא רבה לרבי
שמעון בן חלפתא בי רבי: כך היא גאולתן של ישראל. בתחילה קימאה
קימאה. כל מה שהיא הולכת היא רבה והולכת. מאי טעמא? "...כִּי אֵשֵׁב
בַּחֹשֶׁךְ ה' אוֹר לִי." (מיכה ז:ח) כך בתחילה: "...וּמָרְדֳּכַי יֹשֵׁב בְּשַׁעַר־הַמֶּלֶךְ..."
(אסתר ב:כא), ואחר כך, "וַיִּקַּח הָמָן אֶת־הַלְּבוּשׁ וְאֶת־הַסּוּס..." (אסתר
ו:יא),ואחר כך, "וַיָּשָׁב מָרְדֳּכַי אֶל שַׁעַר הַמֶּלֶךְ..." (אסתר ו:יב), ואחר כך,
"וּמָרְדֳּכַי יָצָא מִלִּפְנֵי הַמֶּלֶךְ בִּלְבוּשׁ מַלְכוּת..." (אסתר ח:טו), ואחר כך,
"לַיְּהוּדִים הָיְתָה אוֹרָה וְשִׂמְחָה וְשָׂשֹׂן וִיקָר." (אסתר ח:טז).

Rabbi Chiya the Great and Rabbi Shimon ben Chalafta were walking in the valley of Arbel at daybreak. They saw the light of the dawn break forth, whereupon Rabbi Chiya said to Rabbi Shimon, "I swear, master, that thus is the redemption of Israel: It commences little by little and as it continues it gradually increases." What verse shows this? "When I sit in darkness, God is my light."[18] Thus, in the beginning of the Purim story it states that "Mordecai sat in the gate of the king,"[19] then later on, "Haman took the clothing and the horse and dressed Mordecai and rode him through the streets of the city...,"[20] then still further on, "Mordecai returned to the gate of the king and Haman forced himself to his home, mourning and

---

[18] Micah 7:8.
[19] Esther 2:21.
[20] Esther 6:11.

with his head bowed,"[21] then later on, "Mordecai departed from before the king in royal garments...,"[22] and yet still further, "The Jews had light and joy, gladness and honor."[23]

Rabbi Chiya's analogy of the redemption to the dawn helps reassure the Jewish people that just as no matter how dark the night may appear, the dawn shall surely arrive, so too, no matter how dark the exile appears, redemption shall surely come.

This also explains the custom of reciting Slichoth (confessional prayers) early in the morning which is said to be an auspicious time (עת רצון).[24] It is a time that symbolizes the ultimate redemption and, thus, the hope that God will redeem Israel from the darkness of sin.

---

[21] Esther 6:12.
[22] Esther 8:15.
[23] Esther 8:16.
[24] Mishnah Brurah on Shulchan Aruch, Orach Chaim 581:1.

Brachoth 1:1 Compare B.T. Brachoth 3B

בשעה שהיה דוד סועד סעודת מלכים, חצות לילה, ובשעה שהיה
סועד סעודת עצמו, "קִדְּמוּ עֵינַי אַשְׁמֻרוֹת..."(תהלים קיט:קמח). מכל מקום,
לא הוה שחרא אתיא ומשכח לדוד דמיך. הוא שדוד אמר, "עוּרָה כְבוֹדִי
עוּרָה הַנֵּבֶל וְכִנּוֹר אָעִירָה שָּׁחַר." (תהלים נז:ט). איתעיר יקרי מן קומי
איקריה דברייי. איקרי לא חשיב כלום מן קדם איקריה דברייי. "אָעִירָה
שָּׁחַר": אנא הוינא מעורר שחרה; שחרה לא הוה מעורד לי. והיה יצרו
מקטרגו ואומר לו, "דוד, דרכן של מלכים להיות השחר מעוררן, ואת אמר,
'אָעִירָה שָּׁחַר'? דרכן של מלכים להיות ישיניך עד שלש שעות, ואת אמר
'חֲצוֹת לַיְלָה אָקוּם...'?" (תהלים קיט:סב) והוא אומר, "עַל מִשְׁפְּטֵי צִדְקֶךְ"
(שם שם).

[Rabbi Nathan explained that] when King David feasted with other kings, [he would retire late and] arise at midnight. When he feasted privately with his family, [he would retire early and] "my eyes preceded the first watch [i.e., the first third of the night] to recite Your teachings."[25] In any event, the dawn never arrived to find King David sleeping. This is what King David meant when he said, "Awaken my glory! Awaken the harp and lyre! I shall awaken the dawn!"[26] By this he meant, "Let my glory be aroused before the glory of my Creator. My glory is considered nothing before the glory of my Creator."

---

[25] Psalms 119:148.
[26] Psalms 57:9.

13

"I shall awaken the dawn!"[27] By this he meant, "I shall awaken the dawn, but the dawn shall not awaken me." His evil inclination enticed him by saying, "David, the manner of kings is for the dawn to awaken them and you say, 'I shall awaken the dawn!'? The manner of kings is to remain sleeping until three hours after daybreak and you say, 'At midnight I shall arise!'?"[28] To this King David answered with the verse "To thank You for Your righteous statutes."[29]

King David's response to his evil inclination does not seem to be on point. What does thanking God for righteous statutes have to do with arising early to pray and study Torah? The answer is that King David realized that the blandishments of the evil inclination were of no true substance. The real purpose of such impulses was to enable God to reward him for conquering them. Accordingly, King David thanked God for giving humankind an evil inclination, for if people had no such inclination to overcome, there could be no reward and punishment.[30]

---

[27] Psalms 57:9.
[28] Psalms 119:62.
[29] Ibid.
[30] Based on Marei HaPanim ad. loc.

14

Brachoth 1:1 continued

ומה היה דוד עושה? רבי פינחס בשם רבי אלעזר ברבי מנחם:
היה נוטל נבל וכינור ונותנו מראשותיו ועומד בחצי הלילה ומנגן בהם
כדי שישמעו חבירי תורה. ומה היו חבירי תורה אומרים? "ומה אם דוד
המלך עוסק בתורה, אנו על אחת כמה וכמה!" אמר רבי לוי: כנור היה
תלוי כנגד חלונותיו של דוד והיה רוח צפונית מנשבת בלילה ומנפנפת
בו והיה מנגן מאליו. הדא הוא דכתיב, "...וְהָיָה כְּנַגֵּן הַמְנַגֵּן..." (מלכים ב'
ג:טו). "כְּנַגֵּן בַּמְנַגֵּן" אין כתב כאן, אלא "כְּנַגֵּן הַמְנַגֵּן." הכינור היה מנגן
מאיליו.

What did King David do? Rabbi Pinchas, in the name of
Rabbi Elazar bar Menachem, said that he used to take a harp
and a lyre and place them at the head of his bed. He would
arise at midnight to play them so that the Torah scholars should
hear. And what would the Torah scholars say? If King David
occupies himself with Torah at this hour, how much more so
should we!

Rabbi Levi said that a lyre hung opposite King David's
windows. A north wind would blow at night, strumming upon
it so that it played by itself. This is what is meant by the verse,
"It was when the instrument played."[31] The verse does not say,
"It was when playing the instrument," but rather, "It was when
the instrument played," meaning that the lyre played by itself.
[Actually, the verse does not refer to King David at all, but
rather to music played to help Elisha prophesy. However,

---

[31] II Kings 3:15.

15

because the verse mentions "the instrument" without further identification, the Sages took it to refer to the famous lyre of King David.[32]]

What is the significance of a musical instrument awakening King David? The world is full of many sounds which are mere noise until they are organized into a harmonious composition. The warming up of a symphony orchestra sounds like a cacophony of meaningless sounds. Only when the sounds of each instrument are properly arranged and those sounds, in turn, harmonized with the sounds of the other instruments, does beautiful music emerge.[33]

The Maggid of Mezeritch[34] was fond of telling how a barefoot boy once stepped on a splinter. When his father sought to remove it, the child burst into tears and ran away for he knew how painful the procedure would be. Naturally, the father pursued the youngster and successfully removed the splinter, but the boy, far from thanking his father, cried bitterly about what he viewed as "cruelty." He did not realize that leaving the splinter in his foot, while momentarily more comfortable, could have led to painful infection, blood poisoning, possible loss of his foot or even death.

People view many things that happen in the world as evil or at least meaningless because they have the perspective of

---

32 P'nei Moshe and Etz Yosef.
33 For a similar idea, see Rabbi Nosson Scherman, *Artscroll Chumash*, (Mesorah Publications, Ltd., New York, 1994), pp. 375 and 1100.
34 Rabbi Dov Ber of Poland, 18th century.

the child in the parable. Only with the arrival of the Messiah in the era of the final redemption will people see how every event in their lives and every event in history actually worked as a harmonious unit to promote God's benevolent purposes. Just as meaningless noise can be organized into beautifully harmonious music, so, in the future, humankind will see how every apparently meaningless or evil event in history fits into the harmonious plan of the Creator.

The Psalms express a related theme with respect to sleep. "When God returns the captives of Zion, we shall be as dreamers."[35] *Often a person has a frightening dream that appears very real, only to suddenly awaken and realize that "it was only a dream," something utterly devoid of reality. So, too, the Psalmist assures Israel that all of the terrible ordeal of their lengthy exile is nothing more than a dream, something that appears frightening but in the end has no reality.*

The prophets used music to promote the state of ecstasy necessary to achieve prophecy.[36] *King David appears to have used his special lyre for that purpose As forebear of the Messiah, King David, more than any other prophet, had the capacity to perceive the true harmony of the universe, why things happen the way they do, what it all means, and how it will eventually come to a happy ending. Hence King David's lyre awakened him not only physically, but spiritually as well,*

---

[35] Psalms 126:1.
[36] Rabbi Aryeh Kaplan, *Meditation and the Bible*, (New York, Samuel Weiser, Inc., 1978), p. 63.

helping him to realize the true harmony of the universe and how all the vagaries of life are but a dream.

Brachoth 1:1 Compare B.T. Brachoth 9B

אמר רבי יוסי בי רבי בון: ...וכל מי שהוא תוכף גאולה לתפילה
אין השטן מקטרג באותו היום. אמר רבי זעירא: אנא תכפית גאולה
לתפילה ואיתצדית באנגריא מובליא הדס לפלטין. אמרו ליה, "רבי, רבו
היא! אית בני אינשי הבין פריטין מחכים פלטין. אמר רבי אמי: כל מי
שאינו תוכף לגאולה תפילה, למה הוא דומה? לאוהבו של מלך שבא
והרתיק על פתחו של מלך. יצא לידע מה הוא מבקש ומצאו שהפליג.
עוד הוא הפליג.

Rabbi Yossi bar Rabbi Bon said ... "whoever juxtaposes the blessing of redemption to his prayers, the Satan does not confound him that day." Rabbi Z'eira said, "I juxtaposed the blessing of redemption to my prayer, yet I was seized by the king's men and forced to transport myrtle branches to the palace." The students of the academy said to him, "Rabbi, that was good! There are people who pay money to visit the palace!"

Rabbi Ami said, "Anyone who does not juxtapose the blessing of redemption to his prayer, to what may he be compared? To a friend of the king who comes and knocks at the door of the king. The king emerged to see what he wanted and discovered that he departed, so the king also departed."

This passage reflects the normative halachah that one must not interrupt between the blessing of redemption (גאולה) which follows the Shema and the recital of the silent Amidah prayer.[37] In the Babylonian Talmud, Rabbi Yochanan states that one who follows this practice is destined for the world to come. The Talmud there also reports that when Rabbi Bruna once juxtaposed the blessing of redemption to his Amidah prayer, he did not stop smiling the entire day.[38]

It seems strange that the rabbis of the Talmud should place such emphasis on what seems to be the standard order of prayer used by all Jews. What is so exceptionally meritorious about reciting the blessing of redemption immediately prior to the Amidah if that is what everyone does?

Tosafoth raises the above question and suggests that the Talmud means reciting the blessing for redemption immediately before sunrise and the Amidah prayer immediately after sunrise as was the custom of the "pious of old" (ותיקין).[39] This answer does not appear to resolve the difficulty, however, because just as anyone can recite the prayers in their prescribed order, so too anyone can arrange to say his or her prayers at a precise time. Moreover, prayer is "the service of the heart."[40] Accordingly, while there are halachoth regarding the timing, physical setting and formula of the prayers and these must certainly be observed, fulfillment of such mechanical/technical requirements would not appear to justify bestowing exceptional merit upon the worshiper nor

---

[37] Shulchan Aruch, Orach Chaim 61:8 and 111:1.
[38] B.T. Brachoth 9B.
[39] Tosafoth on B.T. Brachoth 9B, sub verba "Kol HaSomech" (כל הסומך).
[40] B.T. Ta'anith 2A.

explain why Rabbi Bruna should get so excited. Thus, the answer Tosafoth offers remains problematic.

The Maharal[41] offers two insights which may explain the importance the rabbis of the Talmud attached to juxtaposing the blessing of redemption to the Amidah prayer. First, the purpose of the redemption from Egypt was to serve God and that service is epitomized by prayer.[42] Secondly, one can only truly serve God when he or she is free of any other control, that is to say, after redemption.[43] Although such redemption can refer to being rescued from the domination of heathen taskmasters as was the case in Egypt, it can also mean liberation from worldly desires and troubles which distract one from God's service. Accordingly, the rabbis of the Talmud were not referring to mere mechanical recitation of prayers in a particular order or at a particular time. Rather, the sages of the Talmud meant that one must struggle to free oneself from any distractions from God's service prior to prayer and develop a keen awareness that any relief God has granted one from worldly troubles is solely to permit such service. Armed with this, one can achieve true union with God through prayer.

An additional point may be that the essence of the idea of redemption is a deep and abiding faith that Hashem controls the universe. Such faith in God's ability and willingness to intervene in human affairs is a prerequisite to successful

---

[41] An acronym for Rabbi Judah Loewy who lived in Prague during the sixteenth century.
[42] Netzach Yisrael, chapter 30.
[43] Nethivoth Olam, Nethiv HaAvodah, chapter 9.

21

prayer for without such faith, why pray? Accordingly, it is the recitation of the blessing about redemption with intense concentration and appreciation of its theme that the rabbis of the Talmud found so praiseworthy.

Furthermore, the symbolism of reciting the blessing of redemption just before sunrise is that one believes not only that God rescued the Jews from slavery in ancient times, but that He will also bring about a redemption in the future just as the sun will surely rise after even the darkest night. Such faith is far more difficult to achieve than is faith in the deliverance from Egypt because it is easier to believe in an established historical fact than in a future redemption the timing and details of which are unknown. In addition, as much as one studies the details of the redemption from Egypt, the fact is that he or she never lived through it. It is far easier to accept that such events occurred in ancient times than it is to have faith that the sufferings and difficulties one actually sees in his or her own generation will soon evaporate.

One who juxtaposes the blessing of redemption to the Amidah prayer in the sense of achieving a full recognition of the above-mentioned concepts merits protection from evil and a share in the world to come, as well as the right to feel truly joyous.

Brachoth 1:2

דרבי שמעון בר יוחאי אמר: אלו הוינא קאים על טורא דסיני
בשעתא דאתיהיבת תורה לישראל, הוינא מתבעי קומי רחמנא דיתברי
לבר נשא תרין פומין; חד דהוי לעי באוריתא וחד דעבד ליה כל צורכיה.
חזר ומר: ומה אין חד הוא לית עלמא יכיל קאים ביה מן דילטוריא
דיליה, אילו הוו תרין על אחת כמה וכמה.

Rabbi Shimon bar Yochai said, "If I had been standing at Mount Sinai at the time when the Torah was given to Israel, I would have requested from the All Merciful One that two mouths be created for people: one with which to discuss Torah and the other for all a person's other needs." He later said, "If with just one mouth the world cannot survive due to evil gossip, how much more so if there were two."

The study of Torah is one of the most important activities in which one can engage. A Torah scholar is greater than a High Priest or king.[44] Moreover, the Talmud teaches that the world would revert to chaos if not for those who study Torah.[45] In additon, one can suffer terrible punishment if he has the opportunity to learn but fails to do so.[46] Thus, initially, Rabbi Shimon bar Yochai says that the world would be better off if people had an extra mouth so that they could engage in Torah

---

[44] Pirkei Avoth 6:5.
[45] B.T. Nedarim 32A.
[46] B.T. Brachoth 5A.

study without the need to interrupt for any mundane matter. Upon further consideration, however, the rabbi realized that this would entail the risk that people might engage in evil speech. Such speech is so harmful that this risk outweighs the possible benefit of increased Torah study, a sobering reminder of the severe nature of evil speech.

It seems peculiar that Rabbi Shimon bar Yochai refers to the time when the Torah was given as the ideal time for asking God to alter the human body. Would not the more appropriate time to ask for a such change be at the time of Creation? The answer is that the world was created only for the sake of the Torah. Thus, the Torah refers to all the other days of Creation as "one day" (יום אחד), "a second day" (יום שני), and so forth, but when God finished Creation, the Torah uses the expression "**the** sixth day" (יום השישי). Rashi[47] explains that this extra "**the**" (ה) hints at the sixth day of the Hebrew month of Sivan when God gave Israel the Torah. Hashem made a stipulation with all Creation: If the Jews accept the Torah in the future, well and good, but if not, everything will revert to nothingness. Since all Creation depended upon Israel's acceptance of the Torah, it was as though Creation actually took place at that later time.[48] Accordingly, the proper time to request a change in Creation would have been then.

A question still remains, however. Rabbi Shimon bar Yochai was no ordinary person. For him, miracles were

---

[47] This is an acrostic for the name of **Rabbi Shlomo Yitzchaki** who lived in France during the 11th century.
[48] Rashi on Genesis 1:31 based on B.T. Shabbath 88A.

commonplace. *As originator of the mystical Zohar, he had knowledge and capabilities far beyond anything people of today can imagine. Why could Rabbi Shimon bar Yochai not have successfully requested a change in man's physical makeup during his own lifetime? Why would it only have been possible at the time of the giving of the Torah?*

The answer seems to be that certain times are more auspicious than others. Even Rabbi Shimon bar Yochai could only perform certain feats or expect to have his prayers answered at those special times. When King Solomon said, "There is a time and season for everything under Heaven. A time to give birth; a time to die. A time to plant; a time to uproot plantings...,"[49] he did not mean it in a poetic sense only. Rather, each moment has a spiritual aspect to it so that what can be accomplished at one time cannot necessarily be accomplished at another.

By extension, this concept teaches that one should be careful to take advantage of every moment that comes along. As the Talmud teaches, "The diligent give priority to mitzvoth."[50] Today's opportunity may disappear tomorrow. For instance, a young man entering yeshiva should not adopt the attitude that applying himself to his studies can wait till later. As Elisha ben Abuyah said, "One who learns as a child, to what may it be compared? To ink inscribed upon fresh paper. And one who learns as an elder, to what may it be compared? To ink inscribed upon paper covered with

---

[49] Ecclesiates 3:1-8.
[50] B.T. Pesachim 4A.

25

erasures."[51] One must be careful to exploit every opportunity to do a mitzvah to the fullest for no amount of wisdom or prayer can help a situation if the timing is wrong.

---

[51] Pirkei Avoth 4:20.

Brachoth 1:4 (compare B.T. 10B-11A)

[The Torah instructs Jews to recite the Shema "when you lie down and when you rise up."[52] The academy of Shammai took this literally to mean that one must lie down when reciting the Shema in the evening and stand up when reciting it in the morning. The academy of Hillel, however, explained that this phrase merely defines the *time* for the recitation, not the manner in which it should be done. The halachah follows the view of Beth Hillel.]

מתנתין: אמר רבי טרפון: אני הייתי בא בדרך והטיתי לקרות כדברי בית שמאי וסיכנתי בעצמי מפני הלסטים. אמרו לו: כְּדַי היית לחוב בעצמך שעברת על דברי בית הלל.

גמרא: חברייא בשם רבי יוחנן: דודים דברי סופרים לדברי תורה וחביבים כדברי תורה; "וְחִכֵּךְ כְּיֵין הַטּוֹב..." (שיר השירים ז:י). שמעון בר ווה בשם רבי יוחנן: דודים דברי סופרים לדברי תורה וחביבים יותר מדברי תורה; "...כִּי טוֹבִים דֹּדֶיךָ מָיָּין." (שיר השירים א:א) רבי בא בר כהן בשם רבי יודה בן פזי: תדע לך שחביבים דברי סופרים מדברי תורה, שהרי רבי טרפון, אלּוּ לא קרא, לא היה עובר אלא בעשה ועל ידי שעבר על דברי בית הלל, נתחייב מיתה על שם, "...וּפֹרֵץ גָּדֵר יִשְׁכֶנּוּ נָחָשׁ." (קהלת י:ח) תני רבי ישמעאל: דברי תורה, יש בהן איסור ויש בהן היתר, יש בהן קולין ויש בהן חומרים. אבל דברי סופרים כולן חמורין הן. תדע לך שהוא כן דתנינן תמן: האומר, "אין תפילין," לעבור על דברי תורה, פטור. "חמש טוטפות," להוסיף על דברי סופרים, חייב. (סנהדרין יא:ג) רבי חנניה בריה דרב אדא בשם רבי תנחום בי רבי חייא: חמורים דברי זקנים מדברי נביאים דכתיב, "אל

---

[52] Deuteronomy 6:7.

27

תִּטְפוּ יַטִּיפוּן לֹא יַטִּפוּ לָאֵלֶּה לֹא יִסַּג כְּלִמוֹת." (מיכה ב:ו) וכתיב, "...אַטֵּף
לְךָ לַיַּיִן וְלַשֵּׁכָר..." (מיכה ב:יא). נביא וזקן, למי הן דומין? למלך ששולח
שני פלמטרין שלו למדינה. על אחד מהן כתב, "אם אינו מראה לכם
חותם שלי וסמנטירין שלי, אל תאמינו לו." ועל אחד מהן כתב, "אף על
פי שאינו מראה לכם חותם שלי, האמינוהו בלא חותם ובלא סמנטירין."
כך בנביא כתיב, "...וְנָתַן אֵלֶיךָ אוֹת אוֹ מוֹפֵת." (דברים יג:ב). ברם הכא,
"עַל פִּי הַתּוֹרָה אֲשֶׁר יוֹרוּךָ..." (דברים יז:י).

Mishnah 4: Rabbi Tarfon said, "I was traveling on the road and lay down to recite Shema according to the ruling of Beth Shammai. I thereby endangered myself due to highwaymen." They said to him, "You deserved to come to harm for transgressing the words of Beth Hillel."

Gemara: The scholars related in the name of Rabbi Yochanan: The rabbinic teachings[53] mirror the words of the Torah and are as precious as the words of the Torah, as the verse says, "Your palate is like fine wine."[54] [The term "your palate" refers to the oral teachings entrusted to the rabbis.[55]]

---

[53] The term דברי סופרים, as used here, refers to the Oral Torah (תורה שבעל פה) which God gave Moses at the same time He gave the Written Torah (תורה שבכתב). Thus דברי סופרים means "rabbinic teachings" in the sense that the Oral Torah was entrusted to the rabbis to preserve and transmit throughout all generations. It most certainly does not mean that the rabbis invented any interpretations or *halachoth* on their own.

[54] Song of Songs 7:10.

[55] P'nei Moshe.

Shimon bar Vava said in the name of Rabbi Yochanan: The rabbinic teachings mirror the words of the Torah and are more precious than the words of the Torah as the verse says, "Your love is better than wine."[56] Rabbi Bo bar Kohen said in the name of Rabbi Yehuda ben Pazzi: You may confirm that the rabbinic teachings are more precious than the words of the Torah for had Rabbi Tarfon not recited the Shema, he would merely have violated a positive commandment [for which one must repent but for which the Torah prescribes no particular punishment]. However, because he transgressed the words of Beth Hillel, he incurred the penalty of death in accordance with the verse, "One who digs a pit shall fall in it and a snake will bite one who breaches a fence."[57] [The same person who creates a hazardous situation by, for example, digging a pit in a public place, will ultimately fall victim to the very danger he has created. Rabbi Tarfon's refusal to follow the normative *halachah* as expounded by Beth Hillel entailed the danger that people who observed him might decide to follow their own opinions in such matters leading to a total rejection of Judaism. Because Rabbi Tarfon created a dangerous situation, he found his own life endangered.]

Rabbi Ishmael explained in a Braitha: The words of the Torah contain prohibited and permitted matters, both leniencies and stringencies, but the rabbinic teachings are all severe in nature. You may confirm that this is so, as we have learned in a Mishnah: **An Elder who says that there is no such Mitzvah**

---

[56] Song of Songs 1:2.
[57] Ecclesiastes 10:8.

29

as Tefillin is exempt from punishment, but if he says that Tefillin have five compartments, thereby increasing the number set by rabbinic teaching, he is punishable.[58]

Rabbi Chanania bar Rav Adda said in the name of Rabbi Tanchum of the academy of Rabbi Chiya: The words of the Sages are to be taken more strictly than those of the Prophets for it is written, "Let prophecy not issue forth, let it not issue forth unto these that they not suffer rebuke."[59] And it is further written, "Were I a man of dissolute spirit and a purveyor of lies, I would prophesy to you to consume wine and liquor..."[60] [The prophet bemoans the futility of prophesying to the evildoers of his generation who, in any event, will ignore the prophecy. It is thus better to forego prophesying altogether. By contrast, the teachings of the Sages are of such vital importance that they must be transmitted even in the face of the possibility that those who hear them will ignore or scoff at them.][61]

To what may a Prophet or a Sage be compared? To a king who sends two of his army officers to a certain province. Concerning one of them, he wrote, "If he does not show you my royal seal, do not trust him." Concerning the other, he wrote, "Even if he does not show you my royal seal, trust him." So, with respect to a Prophet, it is written, "When there shall arise in your midst a Prophet or dreamer of dreams, he shall give you a sign or a wonder,"[62] whereas with respect to a Sage,

---

58 Sanhedrin 11:3. B.T. Sanhedrin 88B.
59 Micah 2:6.
60 Micah 2:11.
61 P'nei Moshe.
62 Deuteronomy 13:2.

30

it is written, "According to the law which they teach you and by the statute which they tell you, you shall do. Do not turn from the thing which they tell you neither to the right nor to the left."[63]

Etz Yosef[64] *explains that the reason the rabbinic teachings must be taken more seriously than the written Torah is that everyone can tell when someone contradicts what is written in the Torah simply by looking at what is actually written there. However, the traditional interpretation of the written Torah must be passed down from generation to generation by word of mouth. If someone corrupts that tradition, those who follow may not be able to detect the error.*

There are several other passages where the Talmud explains that rabbinic scholarship is superior to prophecy. For example, the Talmud discusses a dispute between Rabbi Eliezer the Great and the other Sages as to whether a certain type of oven is susceptible to ritual impurity.[65] *Rabbi Eliezer offered every imaginable logical proof for his position, but his colleagues would not yield. Rabbi Eliezer then said, "If the halachah is as I say, then let this carob tree prove it," whereupon a miracle happened and a nearby carob tree moved one hundred cubits. The other rabbis replied that this was no proof. Rabbi Eliezer then said, "If the halachah is as I say, then let this channel of water prove it." The channel of water*

---

[63] Deuteronomy 17:11.
[64] Rabbi Chanoch Zundel ben Yosef.
[65] B.T. Baba Metzia 59B.

31

near them started to flow backwards, but the Sages insisted that this was no proof. Rabbi Eliezer then said, "If the halachah is as I say, then let the walls of the House of Study prove it." The walls started to fall down, but Rabbi Joshua scolded them, saying, "If scholars argue concerning the halachah, what business is it of yours?" The walls did not fall down completely out of respect for Rabbi Joshua, but did not revert to their upright position out of respect for Rabbi Eliezer. Finally, Rabbi Eliezer said, "If the halachah is as I say, then let Heaven prove it!" A Heavenly voice issued forth and declared, "Why do you argue with Rabbi Eliezer? The halachah is as he says in every situation!" To this Rabbi Joshua retorted, "[Torah] is not in Heaven...,"[66] meaning that the rabbis must not render halachic decisions based upon prophecy or miracles, but rather based upon the reasoned conclusions of scholarly debate.

It seems, however, that the proof adduced in the Jerusalem Talmud to show the superiority of the Sage over the Prophet could actually demonstrate the opposite. For example, one could argue that the Prophet Micah refused to proclaim his prophecy before unworthy people because prophecy is so much more holy than ordinary Torah learning. Dissemination of prophecy to an undeserving public would demean it, but might not necessarily demean Torah learning.

Similarly, the fact that a Prophet must show "credentials" to the public could reflect the superiority of prophecy, mere Torah scholarship not warranting such a

---

[66] Deuteronomy 30:12.

32

requirement. Alternatively, this requirement could simply reflect the practical limitations of trying to verify a person's claim to have experienced prophecy. If one claims to be a scholar, others can readily test his knowledge of Jewish law and tradition. However, a claim to have had a prophetic vision is not subject to independent verification, so the Torah must provide a test. Accordingly, the fact that one may not trust a prophet who has not been tested whereas one may trust a Torah scholar absent such a test is not necessarily proof that one is superior to the other.

This problem grows more complicated when one notes that the Rambam explained that prophecy is only available to one who has reached a very lofty intellectual level and perfected his character traits.[67] Even so, one does not become a prophet if God wills that he should not prophesy.[68] This implies that prophecy is greater than Torah learning which is a mere prerequisite for it.

The resolution of these apparent contradictions is that prophecy and Torah scholarship each have some aspects which are superior to the other. Prophecy is the clear vision of the Divine. Not all merit it, even those who may have achieved a truly exalted intellectual, moral and spiritual stature. Scholarship, however, is available to all. Some may have greater intellectual ability than others, but every Jew can, to a degree, grasp the wisdom of the Torah. If this were not so, there could be no commandment to study Torah, for God does

---

[67] Moreh Nevuchim, Part II, Chapter 36.
[68] Moreh Nevuchim, Part II, Chapter 32.

not give a commandment impossible of fulfillment. By contrast, there is no commandment for all Jews to prophesy because such experiences are not necessarily available to everyone.

This explains why Torah law must be established through traditional logical principles rather than through prophetic visions. All Jews must observe the laws of the Torah. Accordingly, the means to understand those laws must be available equally to all. If Torah law depended on prophecy, then it could not be comprehended by everyone. While the most erudite scholar cannot appreciate the sublime vision of the prophet, the very loftiness of prophecy makes it an unfit vehicle for establishing Jewish law.

From one point of view, the scholar is greater than the prophet because the Jewish nation is in crucial need of the scholar's ability to teach and clarify the halachah. Moreover, one may only derive the halachah from traditional logical principles. From an altogether different perspective, however, it is the prophet who is greater than the scholar because his is a clearer vision of the Divine, a vision which the scholar may never attain.

Brachoth 1:5

מפני מה קורין שתי פרשיות הללו בכל יום? רבי לוי ורבי סימון.
רבי סימון אמר: מפני שכתוב בהן שכיבה וקימה. רבי לוי אמר: מפני
שעשרת הדברות כלולין בהן. "אָנֹכִי ה' אֱ-לֹהֶיךָ..." (שמות כ:ב); "שְׁמַע
יִשְׂרָאֵל ה' אֱ-לֹהֵינוּ..." (דברים ו:ד). "לֹא יִהְיֶה לְךָ אֱלֹהִים אֲחֵרִים עַל פָּנַי"
(שמות כ:ג); "...ה' אֶחָד." (דברים ו:ד). "לֹא תִשָּׂא אֶת שֵׁם ה' אֱלֹהֶיךָ
לַשָּׁוְא..." (שמות כ:ז); "וְאָהַבְתָּ אֶת ה' אֱ-לֹהֶיךָ..." (דברים ו:ה). מאן
דרחים מלכא לא משתבע בשמיה ומשקר. "זָכוֹר אֶת יוֹם הַשַּׁבָּת
לְקַדְּשׁוֹ..." (שמות כ:ח); "לְמַעַן תִּזְכְּרוּ..." (במדבר טו:מ). רבי אומר: זו
מצות שבת שהיא שקולה כנגד כל מצוותיה של תורה דכתיב, "וְאֶת שַׁבַּת
קָדְשִׁי הוֹדַעְתָּ לָהֶם וּמִצְווֹת וְחֻקִּים וְתוֹרָה צִוִּיתָ..." (נחמיה ט:יד), להודיעך
שהיא שקולה כנגד כל מצותיה של תורה. "כַּבֵּד אֶת אָבִיךָ וְאֶת אִמֶּךָ..."
(שמות כ:יב); "לְמַעַן יִרְבּוּ יְמֵיכֶם וִימֵי בְנֵיכֶם..." (דברים יא:כא). "לֹא
תִרְצָח..." (שמות כ:יג); "...וַאֲבַדְתֶּם מְהֵרָה..." (דברים יא:יז). מאן דקטיל
מתקטיל. "...לֹא תִנְאָף..." (שמות כ:יג); "וְלֹא תָתוּרוּ אַחֲרֵי לְבַבְכֶם וְאַחֲרֵי
עֵינֵיכֶם..." (במדבר טו:לט). אמר רבי לוי: ליבא ועינא תרין סרסורין
דחטאה דכתיב, "תְּנָה בְנִי לִבְּךָ לִי וְעֵינֶיךָ דְּרָכַי תִּרְצֶנָה [תִּצֹּרְנָה קרי]."
(משלי כג:כו). אמר הקדוש ברוך הוא, "אי יהבת לי לבך ועיניך, אנא
ידע דאת לי. "...לֹא תִגְנֹב..." (שמות כ:יג); "...וְאָסַפְתָּ דְגָנֶךָ..." (דברים
יא:יד), ולא דגנו של חבירך. "...לֹא תַעֲנֶה בְרֵעֲךָ עֵד שָׁקֶר" (שמות כ:יו);
"אֲנִי ה' אֱ-לֹהֵיכֶם..." (במדבר טו:מא), וכתיב, "וַה' אֱ-לֹהִים אֱמֶת..."
(ירמיה י:י). מהו אמת? אמר רבי אבון: שהוא א-להים חיים ומלך עולם.
אמר רבי לוי: אמר הקדוש ברוך הוא, "אם העדת לחבירך עדות שקר,
מעלה אני עליך כאלו העדת עלי שלא בראתי שמים וארץ." "לֹא תַחְמֹד
בֵּית רֵעֶךָ..." (שמות כ:יד); "וּכְתַבְתָּם עַל מְזֻזוֹת בֵּיתֶךָ..." (דברים ו:ט), ביתך
ולא בית חבירך.

Why do we read the paragraphs of Shema each day? Rabbi Simon and Rabbi Levi each expressed a different view. Rabbi Simon says because it is written in them lying down and rising up. [Since Jews are commanded to recite verses from the Torah upon lying down and upon rising up, those verses should include references to lying down and to rising up.[69]]

Rabbi Levi says it is because they contain the Ten Commandments. "I am the Lord your God"[70] corresponds to "Listen, Israel, the Lord is your God."[71] "You shall have no other gods beside Me,"[72] corresponds to "the Lord is one."[73] "Do not take the name of the Lord your God in vain"[74] corresponds to "You shall love the Lord your God,"[75] for one who loves the king does not swear in his name and then lie. "Remember the Sabbath day to keep it holy"[76] corresponds to "that you remember and do all my commandments."[77] As Rabbi Judah the Prince explains, "all my commandments" refers to the mitzvah of the Sabbath which is equal to all the commandments of the Torah as it is written, "Your holy Sabbath You made known to them; commandments, statutes and law You commanded them through Moses Your servant."[78]

[69] Etz Yosef.
[70] Exodus 20:2.
[71] Deuteronomy 6:4.
[72] Exodus 20:3.
[73] Deuteronomy 6:4.
[74] Exodus 20:7.
[75] Deuteronomy 6:5.
[76] Exodus 20:8.
[77] Numbers 15:40.
[78] Nehemiah 9:14.

The Prophet's singling out of the Sabbath followed by a reference to the entire body of the Torah shows that the two are equal. "Honor your father and your mother that your days may be lengthened upon the land which the Lord your God gives you"[79] corresponds to "that your days and those of your children may increase upon the land which the Lord swore to your forefathers to give them."[80] "You shall not murder"[81] corresponds to "and you shall perish speedily"[82] because one who kills is eventually killed. "You shall not commit adultery"[83] corresponds to "You shall not stray after your heart and after your eyes."[84] Rabbi Levi says that the heart and the eye are two purveyors of sin. It is written, "Give me your heart, my son, and let your eye guard my paths."[85] The Holy One, Blessed be He, says, "If you give me your heart and your eyes, I know that you are truly Mine." "You shall not steal"[86] corresponds to "You shall gather in your grain,"[87] [the term "your"] implying not wrongfully gathering in the grain of your friend. "You shall not testify as a false witness against your neighbor"[88] corresponds to "I am the Lord your God,"[89] as it is

---

[79] Exodus 20:12.
[80] Deuteronomy 11:21.
[81] Exodus 20:13.
[82] Deuteronomy 11:17.
[83] Exodus 20: 13.
[84] Numbers 15: 39.
[85] Proverbs 23:26.
[86] Exodus 20:13.
[87] Deuteronomy 11:14.
[88] Exodus 20:13.
[89] Numbers 15:41.

written, "The Lord is a true God"[90] [who despises false testimony]. What does it mean "true?" Rabbi Avon said that He is a living God and eternal King. Rabbi Levi said that the Holy One, Blessed be He, said, "If you testify falsely concerning your friend, I consider it as though you testified about Me that I did not create heaven and earth." "You shall not desire the house of your neighbor"[91] corresponds to "You shall write them upon the doorposts of your house,"[92] [the term "your"] excluding the house of your friend.

One who does not observe the Sabbath is considered as though he or she denied the entire Torah. Rashi explains that this is because such a person's actions constitute a denial that God rested after Creation.[93] All the commandments of the Torah are guided by the underlying theme of bringing humanity to a recognition of Hashem as Creator and Ruler of the universe. However, while other commandments may do this less directly, Sabbath observance explicitly commemorates God's creation of the world. Accordingly, observance of the Sabbath may be said to equal all the other commandments.

Further on in this selection, Rabbi Avon, describes God as "living." This contrasts to idols which have no power and can neither make nor fulfill a promise. By contrast, Hashem, who is all powerful, can make and fulfill promises.

[90] Jeremiah 10:10.
[91] Exodus 20:14.
[92] Deuteronomy 6:9.
[93] Rashi on B.T. Chullin 5A, sub verba "Ella lav hachi ka'amar" (אלא לאו הכי קאמר).

*Accordingly, idols are called "dead" while God, by contrast, is called "living." However, people do not often see God immediately rewarding, punishing or otherwise executing His will. This is why Rabbi Avon adds that Hashem is an **eternal** King who need not act immediately.*

False testimony may be difficult for a judge to detect, so someone who is inclined to testify falsely must be deterred by respect for God's will. This is why Rabbi Levi emphasizes that one who testifies falsely denies that God created heaven and earth.

The priests in the Temple used to recite the Ten Commandments daily.[94] The Talmud reports that some people wanted to recite the Ten Commandments outside the Temple, but the Sages rejected the idea because certain heretics taught that God gave only the Ten Commandments at Mount Sinai, but not the rest of the Torah.[95] The point of this section of the Jerusalem Talmud is that while Jews do not recite the Ten Commandments outright, they do make reference to them by virtue of their daily recital of the Shema.

---

[94] Tamid 5:1.
[95] J. T. Brachoth 1:5 after this passage and see B.T. Brachoth 12A.

Brachoth 1:6 (compare B.T. Brachoth 12B-13A)

בר קפרא אמר: הקורא לאברהם "אברם" עובר בעשה. רבי לוי
אמר: בעשה ולא תעשה. "וְלֹא יִקָּרֵא עוֹד אֶת שִׁמְךָ אַבְרָם..." (בראשית
יז:ה), הרי בלא תעשה. "...וְהָיָה שִׁמְךָ אַבְרָהָם..." (שם שם), הרי בעשה.
התיבון: הרי אנשי כנסת הגדולה קראו אותו "אברם!" "אַתָּה הוּא ה'
הָאֱ-לֹהִים אֲשֶׁר בָּחַרְתָּ בְּאַבְרָם..." (נחמיה ט:ז). שנייא היא, שעד שהוא
אברם בחרת בו. ודכוותה, הקורא לשרה "שרי" עובר בעשה? הוא נצטווה
עליה. ודכוותה, הקורא לישראל "יעקב" עובר בעשה? שני ניתוסף לו.
הראשון לא נעקר ממנו. ולמה נשתנה שמו של אברהם ושמו של יעקב,
ושמו של יצחק לא נשתנה? אילו אבותן קראו אותן בשמן, אבל יצחק
הקדוש ברוך הוא קראו "יצחק," שנאמר, "...וְקָרָאתָ אֶת שְׁמוֹ יִצְחָק... ".
(בראשית יז:יט)

Bar Kappara said that one who calls Abraham "Abram" violates a positive commandment. Rabbi Levi says both a positive and a negative commandment. A negative commandment as the verse says, "Your name shall no longer be called Abram"[96] and a positive commandment as it continues, "your name shall be Abraham."[97]

They raised an objection: The Men of the Great Assembly called him Abram as it is written, "You are the Lord God who chose Abram."[98]

---

[96] Genesis 17:5.
[97] Ibid.
[98] Nehemiah 9:7.

That is different. The point being made there is that even while he was still Abram, God chose him. [In fact, the end of the verse states that God changed Abram's name to Abraham.]

If this proposition is correct, then one who calls Sarah "Sarai" also violates a commandment [for the Torah states that, "God said to Abraham, Sarai your wife you shall no longer call Sarai, rather Sarah is her name."[99]]

That commandment was directed only to Abraham [whereas "Your name shall no longer be called Abram"[100] applies to everyone.]

Still, if this proposition is correct, then one who calls Israel "Jacob" violates a commandment [for the Torah states, "God said to him, as for your name Jacob, your name shall not be called Jacob any longer, but rather Israel shall be your name... ."[101]]

The second name was merely additional. The first name was never eliminated. [Perhaps the distinction between Abraham and Jacob is as follows. God changed Abraham's name in order to change his fortune (מזל), meaning his spiritual make-up. Abram could not give birth whereas Abraham could be a "father of many nations."[102] By contrast, God did not change Jacob's name to Israel in order to alter his spiritual make-up. Rather the term Israel was a memorialization of the

[99] Genesis 17:15.
[100] Genesis 17:5.
[101] Genesis 35:10.
[102] Rashi on Genesis 15:5 based on B.T. Shabbath 156A-B.

victory of Jacob over the angel of Esau. Thus, while Israel became the main name, it did not replace Jacob.]

Why were the names of Abraham and Jacob altered, but not the name of Isaac? With respect to the former, their parents designated their names whereas the Holy One, Blessed be He, named Isaac as it says, "God said, 'But Sarah your wife will bear for you a son and you shall call his name Isaac...' ."[103]

What is the significance of God Himself naming the Patriarchs? The twelve tribes all received their names from their parents, yet Hashem did not change them.[104] Moreover, the rabbis teach that when parents name a child, they are divinely inspired so that the name reflects the spiritual make-up of the child. If so, why should it be necessary for God to change the names of Abraham and Jacob?

The answer lies in the fact that the Patriarchs were founders of the Jewish nation. The Torah relates how God repeatedly intervened directly in the formation of the Jewish nation. For example, the last plague Hashem sent upon the Egyptians which led to the release of the Jews from slavery was

---

[103] Genesis 17:19. This contradicts the Tanchuma as cited in Yalkut Reuveni sub verba "Shemoth," (שמות) paragraph 8, which states that God also gave Jacob his name before birth, citing verse in Genesis 25:26 which says "he called his name" (ויקרא שמו), evidently hinting that God named Jacob because the verse does not say *who* called the name. By contrast, the prior verse uses the plural form to refer to the naming of Esau, implying that the name came from his parents.

[104] Actually Levi may have been an exception to this rule. Rashi on Genesis 29:34 cites a Midrash that God sent the angel Gabriel to name Levi.

performed "not through an angel, not through a seraph and not through a messenger, rather the Holy One, Blessed be He, in His glory, personally."[105] Likewise, God Himself caused His Presence to appear at Mount Sinai when the Torah was given.

The reason for this direct intervention is because a nation wholly devoted to Hashem's service must have characteristics which are above nature. The Jewish nation has survived for thousands of years despite attempts to destroy it while other nations have disappeared even when not faced with such challenges. While ordinary people can have a name which represents their spiritual essence bestowed through the agency of their parents, only God Himself can name the founders of the Jewish nation thereby bestowing upon the nation a supernatural ability to survive.

---

[105] Haggadah Shel Pesach. Mechilta on Exodus 12:12.

Brachoth 1:6 (continued)

ד' נקראו עד שלא נולדו, ואלו הן: יצחק, וישמעאל, יאשיהו,
ושלמה. יצחק: "...וְקָרָאתָ אֶת שְׁמוֹ יִצְחָק..." (בראשית יז:יט). ישמעאל
דכתיב, "...וְקָרָאת שְׁמוֹ יִשְׁמָעֵאל..." (בראשית טז:יא). יאשיהו: "...הִנֵּה בֵן
נוֹלָד לְבֵית דָּוִד יֹאשִׁיָּהוּ שְׁמוֹ..." (מלכים א' יג:ב). שלמה: "...כִּי שְׁלֹמֹה
יִהְיֶה שְׁמוֹ..." (דברי הימים א' כב:ט). עד כדון בצדיקים, אבל ברשעים:
"...זֹרוּ רְשָׁעִים מֵרָחֶם..." (תהלים נח:ד).

Four were given their names before they were born and
these are they: Isaac, Ishmael, Josiah and Solomon. Isaac as
the Torah says, "you shall call his name Isaac."[106] Ishmael as it
is written, "The angel of the Lord said to her, 'Behold, Hagar,
you are pregnant and shall bear a son and you shall call his
name Ishmael... .'"[107] Josiah as it is written, "Behold a son is
born to the House of David, Josiah is his name."[108] Solomon
as it is written, "Behold a son will be born to you who will be a
man of peace. I shall give him peace from all his surrounding
enemies for Solomon will be his name and peace and quiet I
will give Israel in his days."[109] So it is with the righteous, but
as for the wicked, "The wicked are alienated [from God] from

---

[106] Ibid.
[107] Genesis 16:11.
[108] I Kings 13:2.
[109] I Chronicles 22:9. The name Solomon, Shlomo (שלמה) in Hebrew,
means peace.

the womb... "[110] [indicating that their nature is also fixed before birth].

The Talmud here teaches that the nature of the righteous and the wicked is preordained. Along similar lines, the Torah says that when Rebecca was pregnant, "the sons struggled within her... ."[111] Rashi comments that when Rebecca passed the study hall of Shem and Eber, Jacob struggled to emerge whereas when she passed a place of idol worship, Esau struggled to emerge.[112] However, this does not mean that people do not have free will to choose between good and evil. Everyone's personality is different just as each person's social, economic and other life circumstances differ. However, each person still retains the freedom to overcome any natural inclinations or other obstacles he or she faces to serve Hashem.

Several Midrashim contain statements paralleling this section of the Talmud. However, they list only Isaac, Josiah and Solomon as having been named by God at birth, adding only that "there are those who say also Ishmael."[113] What was so special about these four individuals?

---

[110] Psalms 58:4. This section of the Talmud is set forth in Mechilta Chapter 16 on Parshath Bo.

[111] Genesis 25:22.

[112] Rashi on Genesis 25:22.

[113] Breishith Rabbah 45:8. Mishnath D'Rabbi Eliezer on Breishith Rabbah 45:8 questions how there can be any dispute considering that the verse in the Torah specifically says, "you shall call his name Ishmael." Rashash answers that some hold that the Midrash only counts those who

The Talmud previously taught that it was important for God Himself to name the Patriarchs. Had things worked out ideally, Ishmael, too, may have had a role in the founding of the Jewish people.[114] *That is why Abraham was upset when Sarah demanded that he expel Ishmael from his household, saying, "...for the son of this maidservant shall not inherit with my son, with Isaac."*[115] *Indeed, Abraham did not agree to expel Ishmael until Hashem commanded him to listen to Sarah.*[116] *Evidently, Ishmael would have had a role in passing on Abraham's spiritual legacy if his bad behavior had not precluded it. God named Ishmael at birth to give him the potential to be one of founders of the Jewish nation, but Ishmael did not live up to that potential.*

As far as Solomon goes, Rabbi Moses Maimonides states that the Messiah will be a descendant of "the House of David and the seed of Solomon exclusively."[117] *A dispute exists as to whether the Messiah will perform out and out miracles, or whether he will conduct his activities according to the laws of*

God named prior to their mothers becoming pregnant. Since Hagar was already pregnant when God instructed her concerning Ishmael's name, he is not included. Those who argue interpret the words "Hagar you are preganant" as referring to an earlier pregnancy which ended in a miscarriage, not to Ishmael whose future conception was being predicted.

[114] This is not to suggest that Ishmael would have replaced Isaac, but that the two brothers would have worked together as co-founders of the Jewish nation.

[115] Genesis 21:10.

[116] Genesis 21:12.

[117] Rambam Perush HaMishnayoth on Sanhedrin Chapter 10, Principle 12.

nature.[118] *Even if he accomplishes his task through apparently natural means, however, the fact that all conflict in the world will cease and people will occupy themselves only with striving to contemplate the Divine is so radically different from the present situation of the world that God's supernatural intervention in history will be apparent. As noted above, when Hashem Himself directly names an individual, He thereby bestows upon that person the ability to behave supernaturally. God personally named Solomon, the forebear of the Messiah, in order to grant him and his offspring supernatural talents. This is supported by the Talmudic dictum that the name of the Messiah is one of seven things which were created before the world was created.*[119]

Scripture describes King Josiah as a very unique person, declaring that, "Like him there was none before him; a king who returned to the Lord with all his heart and with all his soul and with all his strength according to all the Law of Moses. And after him none arose like him."[120] *The Talmud applies to him the verse, "The breath of our nostrils, the Messiah of the Lord, was ensnared by their wrongdoing... ,"*[121] *implying that perhaps King Josiah would have become the Messiah had his generation not sinned. Hashem directly named him at birth in order to grant him the supernatural capacity to serve as Messiah*

---

[118] B.T. Sanhedrin 99A.
[119] B.T. Pesachim 54A.
[120] II Kings 23:25.
[121] B.T. Ta'anith 22B. The verse is from Lamentations 4:20.

Brachoth 2:1 (compare B.T. Yevamoth 96B and J. T. Shekalim 2:5)

רבי יוחנן הוה מיסתמיך על רבי יעקב בר אידי והיה רבי אלעזר
חמי ליה ומיטמר מן קדמוי. אמר: הא תרתיי מילין בבלייא עביד
בי. חדא דלא שאל בשלומי וחדא דלא אמר שמועתא משמי. אמר ליה:
כך אינון נהגין גביהן. זעירא לא שאל בשלמיה דרבה, דאינון מקיימין
"רָאוּנִי נְעָרִים וְנֶחְבָּאוּ..." (איוב כט:ח).

מי מהלכין, חמי ליה חד בית המדרש. אמר ליה, "הכא הוה רבי
מאיר יתיב, דרש ואמר שמועתא מן שמיה דרבי ישמעאל ולא אמר
שמועתא מן שמיה דרבי עקיבה."

אמר ליה, "כל עלמא ידעין דרבי מאיר תלמידו דרבי עקיבא."
אמר לו, "כל עלמא ידעין דרבי אלעזר תלמידיה דרבי יוחנן. מהו
מיעבור קומי אהדורי צילמיה?"

אמר ליה, "מה? איתפליג ליה איקר? אלא עבור קומוי וסמי
עיניה!"

אמר ליה, "רבי אלעזר יאות עבד דלא עבר קומיך."

אמר, "רבי יעקב בר אידי, יודע את לפייס!"

Rabbi Yochanan was walking with the assistance of
Rabbi Yaakov bar Iddi. Rabbi Elazar saw him from afar and
hid. Rabbi Yochanan said, "That makes two things that
Babylonian did to me. For one thing, he did not greet me today
and on another occasion he did not quote a teaching in my
name."

Rabbi Yaakov bar Iddi replied, "This is customary
among them. The lesser do not greet the greater so as to fulfill

the verse, "Youths saw me and hid; elders rose and stood."[122] [The idea is that someone of low stature is not worthy to appear before someone of great stature. Thus, Rabbi Elazar meant to show Rabbi Yochanan respect by avoiding him.]

As they continued walking, Rabbi Yaakov bar Iddi saw a study hall whereupon he said to Rabbi Yochanan, "Here Rabbi Meir used to sit lecturing. He would recite teachings in the name of Rabbi Ishmael but not recite teachings in the name of Rabbi Akiva [so you need not feel slighted that Rabbi Elazar did not quote teachings in your name]."

Rabbi Yochanan answered, "The whole world knows that Rabbi Meir was the student of Rabbi Akiva [and so assume that whatever he said he learned from Rabbi Akiva]."

"The whole world knows that Rabbi Elazar is the student of Rabbi Yochanan," said Rabbi Yaakov bar Iddi. "Is it permitted to pass before an idol?"

"What is the problem? Would you be showing respect for it? Rather, pass before it and ignore it." [You thus disgrace the idol by walking by without bowing or otherwise acknowledging it.]

"So Rabbi Elazar acted properly not to pass before you!"

"Rabbi Yaakov bar Iddi, you indeed know how to pacify."[123]

---

122 Job 29:8.
123 Shulchan Aruch, Yoreh Deah 242:16 states that one should not greet his teacher in the same fashion he greets others. Rabbi Moshe Isserles states in a gloss that some say one should not greet a teacher at all, evidently referring to this section of the Talmud.

When Rabbi Yaakov bar Iddi pointed out that Rabbi Meir used to teach without citing Rabbi Akiva, Rabbi Yochanan explained that everyone knew about their student/teacher relationship and would assume that whatever Rabbi Meir said was derived from Rabbi Akiva. Accordingly, it appears that such behavior was customary in Talmudic times and that Rabbi Yochanan was well aware of this.[124] If so, why was Rabbi Yochanan upset with Rabbi Elazar in the first place?

Rabbi Yosef Hayyim[125] explains that, indeed, Rabbi Yochanan's primary complaint against his student was that he did not greet him for if Rabbi Elazar had offered him the traditional, "Peace be upon you, my Master and Teacher," then everyone would know about their student/teacher relationship and assume that whatever Rabbi Elazar said came from Rabbi Yochanan. By failing to greet Rabbi Yochanan, Rabbi Elazar gave the impression to onlookers that Rabbi Yochanan was not his teacher.[126]

---

[124] B.T. Yevamoth 96B and J. T. Shekalim 2:5 report that Rabbi Ammi and Rabbi Assi pointed out to Rabbi Yochanan that when Joshua taught the people, he did not constantly state that he was quoting Moses, rather this was self-understood. Rabbi Yochanan agreed but did not feel consoled.

[125] Popularly known as Ben Ish Chai, he flourished in Baghdad during the 19th century.

[126] Ben Yehoyada ad. loc.

Brachoth 2:1 continued (Compare B.T. Yevamoth 96:B and J. T. Shekalim 2:5)

ורבי יוחנן בעי דייימרון שמועתא מן שמיה. אף דוד ביקש עליה
רחמים: "אָגוּרָה בְאָהָלְךָ עוֹלָמִים..." (תהלים סא:ה). רבי פינחס ורבי
ירמיה בשם רבי יוחנן: וכי עלת על לב דוד שהוא חי לעולם? אלא
אמר דוד, "אזכה שיהו דברי נאמרין על שמי בבתי כנסיות ובבתי
מדרשות." מהניא ליה? לוי בר נזירא אמר: כל האומר שמועה משם
אומרה, שפתותיו רוחשות עמו בקבר. מה טעם? "...דוֹבֵב שִׂפְתֵי יְשֵׁנִים,"
(שיר השירים ז:י) ככומר הזה של ענבים שהוא זב מאיליו. רבי חנינא בר
פפאי ורבי סימון: חד אמר: כהדין דשתי קונדיטון, וחרנה אמר: כהדין
דשתי חמר עתיק; אף על גב דהוא שתי ליה, טעמיה בפומיה.

Rabbi Yochanan wanted his disciples to recite teachings in his name just as King David prayed, "May I dwell in Your tent forever... ."[127] Rabbi Phinehas and Rabbi Jeremiah said in the name of Rabbi Yochanan: Did David suppose that he would live forever? Rather, David meant, "May I merit that my words should be recited in my name in synagogues and study halls."

What benefit does he have from this? Levi bar Nezira said: Whoever recites a teaching in the name of the one who said it causes the latter's lips to whisper along with him in the grave. What Scriptural verse supports this? "Your palate is like fine wine which brings forth true love and causes the lips

---

[127] Psalms 61:5.

51

of the sleeping to murmur."[128] It is similar to a hopper of grapes which oozes juice of its own accord. Rabbi Chanina bar Papa and Rabbi Simon each offered an explanation of this. One said that it is similar to one who drinks spiced wine while the other said that it is similar to one who drinks old wine; even though he already drank it, its flavor remains in his mouth.

The idea here is that just as a strong drink leaves a flavor in one's mouth, so a great rabbi's teachings leave an impression on his soul when repeated after his death.[129] *The Maharal notes that, of course, the lips of a dead person cannot move. The reference here is to a spiritual benefit to the soul of the deceased. King Solomon referred to Torah as, "a tree of life to those who take hold of it."*[130] *Thus, one who recites Torah teachings in the name of the deceased connects that person's soul to the source of all life.*[131]

Why was Rabbi Yochanan so particular about having his student recite his teachings in his name? This does not appear to have been a major concern for other rabbis of the Talmud. Etz Yosef explains that Rabbi Yochanan had no sons to survive him.[132] *Thus, if his students did not recite teachings in his name, no one else would.*[133]

---

[128] Song of Songs 7:10.
[129] Rabbi Yaakov Ibn Chaviv (HaKothev), author of the "Ein Yaakov" collection of Aggadoth who lived in Spain and Turkey from 1445-1516, on J. T. Shekalim 2:5.
[130] Proverbs 3:18. See also, VaYikra Rabbah 35:5.
[131] Maharal on B.T. Yevamoth 96B.
[132] He bases this on B.T. Brachoth 5B where Rabbi Yochanan displayed

Brachoth 2:1 continued (Compare B.T. Makkoth 10B and J. T. Shekalim 2:6)

אין דור שאין בו ליצנים. מה היו פריצי הדור עושין? היו הולכין אצל חלונותיו של דוד ואומרים לו, "דוד, אימת יבנה בית המקדש? אימתי בית ה' נלך?" והוא אומר, "אף על פי שמתכונין להכעיסני, יבא עלי שאני שמח בלבי." "שָׂמַחְתִּי בְּאֹמְרִים לִי בֵּית ה' נֵלֵךְ." (תהלים קכב:א).

"כִּי יִמְלְאוּ יָמֶיךָ [וְשָׁכַבְתָּ אֶת אֲבֹתֶיךָ וַהֲקִימֹתִי אֶת זַרְעֲךָ אַחֲרֶיךָ אֲשֶׁר יֵצֵא מִמֵּעֶיךָ וַהֲכִינֹתִי אֶת מַמְלַכְתּוֹ. הוּא יִבְנֶה בַּיִת לִשְׁמִי וְכֹנַנְתִּי אֶת כִּסֵּא מַמְלַכְתּוֹ עַד עוֹלָם]." (שמואל ב' ז:יב-יג) אמר רבי שמואל בר נחמני: אמר הקדוש ברוך הוא לדוד, "דוד! ימים מלאים אני מונה לך. איני מונה לך ימים חסירים. כלום שלמה בנך בונה בית המקדש לא להקריב בו קרבנות? חביב עלי משפט וצדקה שאתה עושה יותר מן הקרבנות." ומה טעם? "עֲשֹׂה צְדָקָה וּמִשְׁפָּט נִבְחָר לַה' מִזָּבַח." (משלי כא:ג).

There is no generation which does not have scoffers. What did the shameless of that generation do? They would go next to the windows of King David and say, "David, when will the Temple be built? When will we go to the House of the Lord?" [This was their way of wishing that King David die for they knew that God had told him that the Temple could only be built after his death.[134]]

---

the tooth of his tenth son who had died.

[133] Etz Yosef on B.T. Yevamoth 96B.

[134] II Samuel 7:12-13.

King David would say, "Even though they intended to anger me, may retribution strike me if I did not rejoice in my heart," as the verse says, "I rejoiced when they said to me, 'We will go to the House of the Lord.'"[135]

"When your days will be filled and you shall lie with your ancestors, I will raise up your seed after you that shall go forth from your innards and I shall establish his kingdom. He shall build a house for My Name and I shall establish the throne of his kingdom forever."[136] Rabbi Shmuel bar Nachmeni said: The Holy One, Blessed be He, said to David, "David, I count full days for you, not incomplete ones. Does not your son Solomon build the Temple only for the purpose of offering sacrifices? The justice and righteousness which you perform are more dear to me than offerings." What is the Scriptural basis for this? "Performance of righteousness and justice is more preferable to the Lord than sacrifice."[137]

In the time of King David, the Tabernacle had been in use for hundreds of years. All the sacrificial services which were performed in the Temple were also performed in the Tabernacle. Why, then, was King David so anxious to have the Temple built that he felt that his own life was unimportant? What crucial element of service did he see as missing?

The key here is to understand the distinction between something temporary and something permanent. Although the

---

[135] Psalms 122:1.
[136] II Samuel 7:12-13.
[137] Proverbs 21:3.

Jews used the Tabernacle for their worship for centuries, they always understood that it was only a temporary structure which would only serve until a permanent Temple would be built. As King Solomon said, "I have indeed built You a glorious house, an abode for Your habitation unto all eternity."[138] *The advantage of the permanent over the temporary is so great that King David was happy to die if his death would mean having a permanent Temple.*

The importance of permanency is reflected in the Mishnah which says, "Make your Torah permanent,"[139] *meaning that one should view Torah study as his chief occupation and constantly review his studies.*[140] *Similarly, the Talmud teaches that one of the first questions the Heavenly Court asks a man when he dies is, "Did you have fixed times for learning Torah?"*[141] *The reason for all this is that God wants people to serve Him with constancy. One does not discharge one's duty by displaying exceptional devotion on special occasions such as, for example, Yom Kippur. Rather, a person must serve God daily. While one who contributes a large sum to charity on a certain occasion has done a great deed, one who contributes a little each day accomplishes more because constant service trains a person to an awareness of Hashem, making it the centerpoint of his or her life.*

---

[138] I Kings 8:13.
[139] Pirkei Avoth 1:15.
[140] Rabbi Pinchas Kehati ad loc.. citing Rambam and Pirkei D'Rabbi Nathan.
[141] B.T. Shabbath 31A.

The Book of Esther says that "For Mordecai the Jew was a viceroy to King Ahasuerus and great among the Jews and pleasing to most of his brothers... ."[142] The Talmud notes that Mordecai was pleasing to "most of his brothers," but not all of his brothers. Some of Mordecai's colleagues criticized him because he abandoned Torah study to save the Jewish people.[143] What a strange criticism! Torah law clearly mandates that a person must set aside his Torah studies to save a life. Surely, Mordecai did nothing wrong.

What bothered some of Mordecai's associates was the very issue raised here. Most people have it within themselves to rise to a momentous occasion. When a nation is threatened with genocide, when heroism is required, people find the wherewithal to act heroically. But what about daily devotion, the kind that does not earn the recognition and gratitude of an entire nation? The consistent effort to serve God, to imitate His ways and obey His will on a day to day basis is much greater. Thus Mordecai's colleagues did not, God forbid, criticize him for setting aside his Torah studies to save the Jewish people. Rather, they pointed out that Mordecai would have achieved even more had circumstances not required him to interrupt his constant Torah learning.

King David viewed this concept of permanent, continual service as being of such great importance that he would have preferred an early death if it meant that the permanent Temple might be built that much earlier. To this Hashem replied that

---

[142] Esther 10:3.
[143] B.T. Megillah 16B.

56

King David's personal service was of even greater importance because it had an aspect of permanency of its own. This is because King David arranged the Book of Psalms which became a permanent part of the Holy Scripture of the Jewish people. Long after the destruction of the Temple, Jews recite the Psalms daily during every prayer service so King David's Psalms are even more permanent than the Temple.[144]

---

[144] Rav comments that the world was only created for the sake of King David who would one day write songs and praises to Hashem. (B.T. Sanhedrin 98B with Rashi's commentary.)

57

Brachoth 2:3   (Compare B. T. Sotah 13A and Mechilta on
Exodus 13:19)

[When the bathhouse attendant brought Rabbi Yochanan
his Tefillin after he finished bathing, Rabbi Yochanan used to
say the following:]

שני ארונות היו מהלכין עם ישראל במדבר: ארונו של חי
העולמים וארונו של יוסף. והיו אומות העולם אומרים, "מה טיבן של
שני ארונות הללו?" והיו ישראל אומרין להן, "זה ארונו של יוסף עם
ארונו של חי העולמים." והיו אומות העולם מונין את ישראל ואומרים,
"וכי איפשר לארון המת להיות מהלך עם ארונו של חי העולמים?" והיו
ישראל אומרים, "על ידי ששימר זה מה שכתָב בזה."
ולמה הוא אמר דא מילתא? אמר רבי חנינא: בגין מימר מילא
דאוריא.
אמר ליה רבי מנא: והכין לא הוה ליה מילא דאוריא חורי למימר
אלא דא? אלא קינתודין הוון לומר, "יוסף לא זכה למלכות אלא על ידי
ששימר מצותיו של הקדוש ברוך הוא ואנו לא זכינו לכל הכבוד הזה
אלא על ידי ששמרנו מצותיו של הקדוש ברוך הוא ואתון בעיי מבטלה
מצוותא מינן?!?!"

Two chests accompanied Israel in the desert: The chest
of the One Who Lives Eternally [containing the stone tablets
inscribed with the Ten Commandments] and the chest which
bore Joseph's corpse.

The nations of the world inquired, "What is the nature of
these two chests?"

Israel responded to them, "This is the chest which bears Joseph's corpse and this is the chest of the One Who Lives Eternally."

The nations of the world taunted Israel and said, "Is it possible that the chest of a corpse can accompany the chest of the One Who Lives Eternally?"

Israel explained, "Because he observed what is written in this, [Joseph deserves this honor]."

Why did Rabbi Yochanan talk about this topic [when he received his Tefillin upon emerging from the bathhouse]?

Rabbi Chanina says: Because he wanted to speak a word of Torah. [One is forbidden to speak words of Torah in the part of the bathhouse where people are undressed.[145] Rabbi Yochanan was so anxious to resume his studies, that as soon as he dressed and emerged, he would mention this topic.]

Rabbi Manna said to him: Did he indeed have no other word of Torah to say? Rather, this was a criticism [of the attendant] by which he meant to say that Joseph did not merit royalty except by virtue of his observing the commandments of the Holy One, Blessed be He, and we have not merited all of this honor except by virtue of our observing the commandments of the Holy One, Blessed be He, yet you seek to keep us idle from the commandments [by not bringing the Tefillin more quickly].

---

[145] Rabbi Moshe Isserles and Rabbi Yisroel Meir Kagan (Mishnah Brurah) on Shulchan Aruch, Orach Chaim 84:1.

Rabbi Manna raises a valid point. If Rabbi Yochanan simply sought to recite a "word of Torah" upon exiting the bathhouse, why was it his custom to choose this one in particular? Perhaps Rabbi Chanina meant as follows:

The Mechilta teaches that besides the coffin of Joseph, the Jewish People also brought out of Egypt the coffins of Joseph's brothers.[146] However, they carried those coffins outside the camp whereas they carried Joseph's next to the Ark of the Covenant.[147]

The Mishnah states that Abraham observed the tenets of the Torah even before it was given.[148] Most authorities maintain that this was true of the other ancestors of the Jewish People as well and this is supported by the statement in the text under consideration that Joseph merited to have his coffin borne near the Ark of the Covenant because he fulfilled the commandments of the Torah.[149]

Why did only Joseph merit to have his coffin borne alongside that of the Ark of the Covenant while his brothers, who also fulfilled the commandments, did not? The answer has to do with the unique events of Joseph's life. Joseph's brothers sold him into slavery from which he later rose to become second to the king. He maintained strong faith in Divine Providence even as a slave, never forsaking hope for his eventual redemption. More importantly, when he rose to

---

[146] Mechilta on Exodus 13:19.
[147] Maharsha (Rabbi Shmuel Eliezer Eidels of Poland, 1555-1632) on B.T. Sotah 13A-B.
[148] Kiddushin 4:14 and see B.T. Yoma 28B.
[149] See also Ramban on Genesis 26:5.

power and had the opportunity to take revenge against his brothers, he declined to do so insisting that "Behold, do not be upset nor let it appear wrong in your eyes that you sold me here, for as a sustainer God sent me before you... Behold, you did not send me here, but rather God, and He made me chief advisor to Pharaoh, lord over all his household and ruler of all the Land of Egypt."[150]

Joseph's experience closely paralleled that of the entire Jewish People which became enslaved in Egypt but never lost faith in the eventual redemption and eventually departed "with the upper hand,"[151] carrying off all the riches of Egypt.[152] Thus, Joseph had an experience during his lifetime which closely mirrored the Exodus from Egypt while his brothers did not. In this sense, one can say that Joseph fulfilled what was written in the Torah in a way that his brothers did not since the Torah contains a full account of the Exodus from Egypt as well as the many commandments Jews observe to commemorate that event.[153]

The Torah sets forth the commandment to wear Tefillin in four places, two of which refer to the Exodus from Egypt.[154]

---

[150] Genesis 45:5 and 8.
[151] Exodus 14:8
[152] Exodus 12:36.
[153] Mechilta on Exodus 13:19 goes into detail to show how Joseph fulfilled each of the Ten Commandments. Rabbi Yosef Hayyim in Ben Yehoyada on B.T. Sotah 13A points out that Joseph more than his brothers showed respect for his father by traveling to the Land of Israel to bury him. He also was tempted by Potiphar's wife to commit adultery but resisted.
[154] Exodus 13:2-10 and 13:11-16.

*These four sections of the Torah are written on the parchments
inside the boxes of the Tefillin. The principal lesson of the
Exodus from Egypt is that God alone rules the universe
controlling every aspect of human destiny.[155] In ancient times,
people, especially great rabbis, wore Tefillin throughout the
day, not just during morning prayers as they do today. The
Torah states that Joseph's brothers failed to recognize him
before he revealed his identity to them,[156] yet if Joseph wore
Tefillin, this could not have been the case. Thus, one must
conclude that Joseph did not wear Tefillin at all times. In fact,
he may not have worn them at all because, according to the
Ramban, the ancestors of the Jewish people only observed the
laws of the Torah while residing in the Land of Israel.[157]
Instead, Joseph must have fulfilled the commandment primarily
in a spiritual sense by recognizing and acting upon the central
principle they represent.[158]*

*Rabbi Yochanan could not wear his Tefillin inside the
bathhouse nor could he discuss or think about Torah concepts
there.[159] When he emerged and waited for the attendant to
bring his Tefillin, however, he recalled how Joseph, though not*

---

[155] See, for example, Sefer Meirath Einayim on Shulchan Aruch, Choshen
Mishpat 231:19, note 35.
[156] Genesis 42:8.
[157] Ramban on Genesis 26:5.
[158] Indeed, Rabbi Shneur Zalman of Liadi writes in Torah Ohr, Parshath
Lech L'cha, 11D that the forefathers of the Jewish people did not literally
wear Tefillin at all. Instead, Tefillin and all mitzvoth have both a physical
outer aspect and an inner spiritual aspect. The Jewish forefathers fulfilled
the mitzvah of Tefillin in its inner spiritual aspect only.
[159] Shulchan Aruch, Orach Chaim 45:2.

actually donning Tefillin at all times, is nonetheless viewed as having fulfilled the commandment by virtue of his keen awareness of God's Providence. By citing this fact, Rabbi Yochanan hoped that he, too, might merit to be viewed as fulfilling the commandment of Tefillin even before he actually put them on.

Rabbi Manna argues with the view of Rabbi Chanina. As true as it may be that Joseph fulfilled the commandment of Tefillin in a spiritual sense, that was because the Torah had not yet been given and the observance of its commandments would, in any event, have been purely voluntary. Now that Hashem gave the Torah, however, actual physical performance of the commandment is essential. Mere recognition of the ideas it symbolizes does not help. Thus, Rabbi Yochanan would not have been content with merely comparing his situation to that of Joseph. Rather, he craved to actually perform the commandment and criticized the bathhouse attendant for his laxity.

Brachoth 2:4 (Compare B.T. Sanhedrin 98B-99A and Eichah Rabbah 1:51)

רבנן אמרי: אהן מלכא משיחא אין מי חייא הוא, דוד שמיה. אין
מי דמכייא הוא, דוד שמיה. אמר רבי תנחומא: אנא אמרית טעמא:
"וְעֹשֶׂה חֶסֶד לִמְשִׁיחוֹ לְדָוִד..." (תהלים יח:נא). רבי יהושע בן לוי אמר:
צמח שמו. רבי יודן בריה דרבי אייבו אמר: מנחם שמו.

אמר חנינה בריה דרבי אבהו: ולא פליגי. חושבניה דהדין
כחושבניה דהדין. הוא צמח הוא מנחם.

ודא מסייעא להו, דמר רבי יודן בריה דרבי אייבו: עובדא הוה
בחד יהודאי דהוה קאים רדי. געת תורתיה קומוי. עבר חד ערביי ושמע
קלה. אמר ליה, "בר יודאי! בר יודאי! שרי תורך ושרי קנקנך דהא
חריב בית מוקדשא!"

געת זמן תניינות. אמר ליה, "בר יודאי! בר יודאי! קטור תוריך
וקטור קנקניך דהא יליד מלכא משיחא!"

אמר ליה, "מה שמיה?"

"מנחם."

אמר ליה, "ומה שמיה דאבוי?"

אמר ליה, "חזקיה."

אמר ליה, "מן הן הוא?"

אמר ליה, "מן בירת מלכא דבית לחם יהודה."

אזל, זבין תורוי וזבין קנקנוי ואיתעביד זבין לבדין למיינוקא
והוה עייל קרייה ונפקא קרייה עד דעל להההוא קרתא והויין כל נשייא
זבנן ואימה דמנחם לא זבנה. שמע קלן דנשייא אמרין, "אימיה דמנחם!
אימיה דמנחם! איתיי זובנין לברך!"

אמרה, "בעייא אנא מיחנקוניה סנאיהון דישראל דביומא
דאיתיליד איחרוב בית מוקדשא."

אמר לה, "רחיציא אנן דברגליה חריב וברגליה מתבניי."

אמרה ליה, "לית לי פריטין."

אמר לה, "והוא מה איכפת ליה. איתיי זובנין ליה. אין לית
קומך יומא דין, בתר יומין אנא אתי ונסיב."
בתר יומין, עאל להההיא קרתא. אמר לה, "מהו מיינוקא עביד?"
אמרה ליה, "מן שעתא דחמיתני, אתון רוחין ועלעולי וחטפיניה
מן ידיי."
אמר רבי בון: מה לנו ללמוד מן הערבי הזה? ולא מקרא מלא
הוא? "...וְהַלְּבָנוֹן בְּאַדִּיר יִפּוֹל." (ישעיה י:לד). מה כתיב בתריה? "וְיָצָא
חֹטֶר מִגֵּזַע יִשָׁי..." (ישעיה יא:א).

The rabbis say: The King Messiah, if he is among the
living, his name is David and if he is among the dead, his name
is David [meaning that if he is among the dead, King David
himself will be the Messiah[160]]. Rabbi Tanchuma said: I can
cite a Scriptural basis for this: "...He does kindness to his
Anointed One [his Messiah], to David..."[161] [implying that, one
way or another, the Messiah's name will be David[162]].

Rabbi Joshua ben Levi said: His name is Tzemach
["sprouting forth"]. Rabbi Yudan the son of Rabbi Aibbo said:
His name is Menachem ["comforter"]. Rabbi Chanina the son
of Rabbi Abahu said: Actually, they are not arguing, for the
numerical value of this one is the same as the numerical value
of that one. Thus Tzemach צמח and Menachem מנחם are
identical.[163]

---

[160] P'nei Moshe.
[161] Psalms 18:51.
[162] P'nei Moshe. See also Ezekiel 37:24 which says, "My servant David
will rule over them... ."
[163] צמח: צ = 90; מ = 40; ח = 8, totaling 138. מנחם: מ = 40; נ = 50; ח = 8; ם =

65

And the following supports their view [that Messiah is named Menachem and Tzemach]: Rabbi Yudan the son of Rabbi Aibbo said: There was an incident involving a certain Jew who was plowing when his ox bellowed before him. A passing Arab who heard the sound said to him, "Jew! Jew! Unfasten your ox! Unfasten your plow! Behold, the Temple has been destroyed!" The ox bellowed a second time whereupon the Arab said, "Jew! Jew! Hitch up your ox! Hitch up your plow! Behold, the King Messiah has been born!"

The Jew said, "What is his name?"

"Menachem."

"What is his father's name?"

"Hezekiah."

"Where is he?"

"In the royal capital of Bethlehem in Judah."

The Jew sold his ox and plow and became a seller of velvet stuffs for babies. He traveled in and out of various towns until he entered a certain village. There he sold his wares to all the women, but the mother of Menachem did not buy. He heard the voices of the other women calling, "Mother of Menachem, mother of Menachem, come buy for your son!"

She answered, "I would like to choke that enemy of Israel for upon the day he was born, the Temple was destroyed."[164]

40, totaling 138.

[164] She was not suggesting that the baby somehow bore responsibility for the destruction of the Temple. Rather, the coincidence of the two events showed that he had a bad Mazal (fortune). See Eichah Rabbah 1:51.

The seller said, "I am certain that just as it was destroyed at its appointed time, it shall be rebuilt at its appointed time."

She said, "I have no money."

"What do I care? If you have no means today, I will come later and take payment."

After many days passed, he again visited that village and said to her, "How is that child doing?"

"After the moment you saw me, a whirlwind came which lifted him and snatched him out of my hands."

Rabbi Bon said: What do we learn from this Arab? Is it not explicitly set forth in a Scriptural verse? "The tangle of the forest shall be cut with iron and the Lebanon fall with great force."[165] [The Temple is called "Lebanon."[166]] What is written afterwards? "A branch shall issue forth from the trunk of Jesse and a shoot from his roots flourish."[167] [Jesse was the father of King David so the implication is that immediately after the Temple would fall, the Messianic king who descends from David would flourish.]

Y'feh Anaf[168] explains why the Talmud says that if the Messiah is among the living his name is David and if from among the dead, also David. There is a dispute as to whether the resurrection of the dead will occur before or after the

---

[165] Isaiah 10:34.
[166] B.T. Yoma 39B. Lebanon derives from the word "lavan," לבן, white, because the Temple service "whitens," i.e., atones for sins.
[167] Isaiah 11:1.
[168] Rabbi Shmuel Yafeh Ashkenazi who lived in Turkey during the sixteenth century.

advent of the Messiah.[169] *If it occurs before the advent of the Messiah, then King David himself, having been revived, will be the promised Redeemer. If the resurrection is to occur later, then a descendant of King David will be the Messiah.*[170]

Identifying the Messiah's name appears to have had special importance to the rabbis who compiled the Talmud. In the Babylonian Talmud and in the Midrash Rabbah[171] *other names are suggested. The Talmud even states in one place that the Messiah will have God's name!*[172] *Of course, the Messiah could have more than one name as was the case with other historical figures such as Moses*[173] *and Jethro.*[174] *Still, what is the significance of trying to identify the Messiah's name or names? Why not focus attention on more practical issues and let the Messiah's name become known whenever he appears? Why speculate on the subject?*

The Rambam states that it is a religious duty incumbent upon every Jew to believe in and to await the coming of the Messiah.[175] *If the name or names of the Messiah teach something about the nature of this commandment, then they have a practical significance now.*

[169] See, for example, B.T. Sanhedrin 99A.
[170] Y'feh Anaf on Eichah Rabbah 1:51.
[171] B.T. Sanhedrin 98B and Eichah Rabbah 1:51.
[172] B.T. Baba Bathra 75B.
[173] B.T. Megillah 13A.
[174] Rashi on Exodus 18:1 based on Mechilta ad loc.
[175] Rambam, Hilchoth Melachim 11:1.

Hebrew names always mirror the spiritual essence of the things to which they refer.[176] *Even God's Name teaches something about Him. For example, the name YHVH* י-ה-ו-ה *derives from "was, is, will be," reflecting God's eternal nature.*[177] *The names of the Messiah also reflect the essence of his role in the course of history and what Jews are required to believe about him.*

The name Menachem means "comforter" alluding to the comfort Jews will derive from the restoration of the Davidic monarchy and of the sacrificial service in the Temple. However, the role of the Messiah extends beyond mere restoration. When the Messiah arrives, all humankind will recognize the truth of the Torah.[178] *As the Rambam writes, "At that time there will be neither hunger nor war nor jealousy nor competition, for goodness will radiate forth exceedingly. All desirable things will be as readily available as dust. There will be no other occupation for the world except to know God alone. Accordingly, Jews will be great sages, knowing hidden matters. They will achieve knowledge of their Creator to the fullest extent human beings can, as it says, 'For the Earth shall be as full of knowledge of the Lord as water covers the ocean.'*[179]*"*[180] *The name Tzemach, meaning "sprouting forth," reflects the idea that recognition of Hashem will both be*

---

[176] Rabbi Shneur Zalman MiLiadi, Sha'ar HaYichud, chapter 1, et. seq.
[177] Shulchan Aruch, Orach Chaim 5:1.
[178] B.T. Brachoth 57B.
[179] Isaiah 11:9.
[180] Rambam, Hilchoth Melachim 12:5.

restored through reinstatement of the Temple service and also enhanced and extended to all humanity.

Both names, Menachem and Tzemach, have the same numerical value because the concepts of restoring ancient Jewish practice and spreading the truth of the Torah are complementary to one another. A full, permanent restoration can only be secure when all people throughout the world recognize the truth of the Torah. Only then can there be any assurance that the Temple will not be destroyed yet again and the Jewish people exiled once more from their homeland. On the other hand, what will cause all people to acknowledge the truth of the Torah will be witnessing the great deeds of the Messiah in rebuilding the Temple, gathering all Jews into the Land of Israel and inspiring their full return to their ancestral faith.

This section of the Jerusalem Talmud states that the name of the Messiah's father is Hezekiah. The Babylonian Talmud relates that when King Hezekiah became deathly ill, Isaiah visited him. The prophet warned the king that he would die both in this world and in the next because he failed to marry and produce children. King Hezekiah explained that he did not wish to marry because he knew prophetically that some of his offspring would become evildoers. To this Isaiah replied, "What have you to do with the schemes of the All Merciful One? You must do as you are commanded to do and what is pleasing to the Holy One, Blessed be He, He will do."

King Hezekiah then married Isaiah's daughter and recovered from his illness.[181]

That the name of the Messiah's father is Hezekiah suggests that one must not delve too deeply into the exact details of when and how the Messiah will arrive. A simple belief in the general concept of Messianic redemption is sufficient. It is not for human beings to inquire into the precise nature of how this will happen just as King Hezekiah had no right to delve into God's plans for his offspring. As Rabbi Samuel bar Nachmeni said in the name of Rabbi Yochanan, *"May the spirit of those who calculate the end be blasted for they are led to say that since the destined time arrived and he did not come, he will never come. Rather, wait for him!"*[182] Moreover, the Rambam writes, *"As to all these matters and all similar matters, no person knows how they will occur until they occur for these things are not explained by the Prophets and the later Rabbis also had no tradition concerning such matters."*[183]

Thus the Talmud here teaches that Menachem, the Messiah, is the son of Hezekiah, meaning that he derives from the principle expounded concerning King Hezekiah. The Messiah will come as a result of maintaining a simple faith in God's promise to send him without inquiring into the specific fine points as to when and how this will happen. This idea is emphasized by the story which follows where inquiring after

---

[181] B.T. Brachoth 10A.
[182] B.T. Sanhedrin 97B.
[183] Rambam, Hilchoth Melachim 12:2.

71

the Messiah results in his being whisked away by a whirlwind. Delving into such esoteric matters is counterproductive.[184]

The point of the story about the Messiah being born on the very day the Temple was destroyed is that such destruction and suffering are actually a prerequisite for the final redemption. No one truly knows why suffering occurs in the world. As Rabbi Yannai said, "It is not within our power to understand the prosperity of the wicked nor the troubles of the righteous."[185] *Nonetheless, perhaps it is possible to grasp in some small measure how suffering leads to redemption by analyzing the Exodus from Egypt which is the paradigm for all future exiles of the Jewish people.*

Hashem told Abraham "...know for a certainty that your seed shall be a stranger in a land which is not theirs where they shall enslave them and torment them for four hundred years. Also that nation which enslaves them shall I judge and afterwards they shall go forth with great wealth."[186] *This verse shows that the Egyptian exile was a preordained segment of a Divine master plan. Surely God could have created the Jewish nation and given it the Torah in the Land of Israel. Why was it necessary to do all this by means of exile and slavery?*

The purpose of all existence, to the extent people are capable of understanding it, is to recognize the existence and dominion of God in the universe. To create a lasting, striking

---

[184] Compare B.T. Chagigah 11B, et. seq.
[185] Pirkei Avoth 4:15.
[186] Genesis 15:13-14.

recognition sufficient to become a special people dedicated to Hashem's service and capable of receiving the Torah required an extraordinary revelation which could only be brought about through Egyptian slavery. The Torah says that when Moses and Aaron first visited Pharaoh and told him that God wanted him to free the Jews, his answer was, "...who is the Lord that I should listen to His voice to send forth Israel? I do not recognize the Lord and also Israel I shall not send forth."[187] Pharaoh knew that God existed, but refused to recognize Him in the sense that he did not believe that God takes cognizance of or in any way influences human affairs.[188] Pharaoh's denial of God was based on the idea that the affairs of the physical world are utterly separate from God.

The Torah relates that when Moses and Aaron produced miraculous signs to prove the authenticity of their mission, Pharaoh had his magicians perform similar feats[189] for the Egyptians were thoroughly steeped in witchcraft. As the Talmud states, "Ten measures of witchcraft descended to the world. Egypt took nine of them."[190] The Rambam maintains that witchcraft is sleight of hand and that there is no supernatural force of witchcraft. He writes: "...whoever believes in these or similar things and thinks in his heart that they are true and a matter of wisdom but that the Torah forbade them is but among those who are foolish and

---

[187] Exodus 5:2.
[188] Rambam, Hilchoth Avodah Zarah 1:1-2.
[189] See, for example, Exodus 7:11, 7:22 and 8:3.
[190] B.T. Kiddushin 49B.

ignorant... ."[191] *Rather, the Egyptian magicians were masters of illusion. This epitomizes the attitude of Pharaoh; he preferred to deny the truth of Hashem's omnipresence and omnipotence, to live by an illusion, rather than acknowledge the truth even when faced with the threat of severe plagues.*

It is one thing to speak theoretically about God creating and controlling the universe. It is quite another to experience it, to see the deliberate self-delusions of a Pharaoh utterly shattered before one's eyes; to be subjected to the most degrading bondage, to almost lose hope and then to participate in sudden and explicit salvation through direct Divine intervention. These experiences were necessary to create a Jewish people both worthy and capable of receiving the Torah.

The same type of radical experience is necessary if all humankind is to achieve an exalted level of recognition of God in Messianic times. Thus, the destruction of the Temple, the seemingly endless exile and suffering of the Jewish people is a necessary prerequisite to a miraculous salvation which can and will transform the thinking and attitude of humanity in a fundamental and radical way when the Messiah arrives. (May he come speedily and in our days.)

---

[191] Yad HaChazakah, Hilchoth Avodah Zarah 11:16 and see Rabbi David Kimchi on I Samuel 28:24. Not all great rabbis agree with the Rambam. Some maintain that a supernatural force of witchcraft indeed existed in the past. However, that force only existed because God willed it, just like any other creation. Those who abandoned faith in God to follow witchcraft had deluded themselves into believing that such forces existed independently of God. Thus, according to these rabbis as well, Pharaoh and his people were guided by self-delusion.

Brachoth 2:8 (Compare B.T. Brachoth 16B)

מעשה שמתה שפחתו של רבי אליעזר ונכנסו תלמידיו לנחמו
ולא קיבל. נכנס מפניהם לחצר ונכנסו אחריו, לבית ונכנסו אחריו. אמר
להן, "כמדומה הייתי שאתם נכוין בפושרין ואי אתם נכוין אפילו
ברותחין. והלא אמרו: **אין מקבלין תנחומין על העבדים**...?"

An incident took place where the maidservant of Rabbi
Eliezer died. His disciples entered his house to comfort him
but he refused to receive them. He entered the courtyard [to
avoid them]. They entered after him so he went into the house.
They followed after him there as well. He said to them, "It
appeared to me that you would be scalded with lukewarm
water, but you are not scalded even with boiling water. Have
not the Sages said, 'We do not accept condolences for
slaves...?'"

*Rabbi Eliezer should have simply told his disciples that
the halachah forbids one to accept condolences for the death of
a slave. Why did he avoid his disciples at first rather than
simply telling them this halachah?*

*The Mishnah reports that Rabban Gamliel accepted
condolences when his slave, Tavi, died because Tavi was
exceptional.[192] This was true to such a degree that elsewhere*

---

[192] Brachoth 2:7.

75

Rabban Gamliel calls Tavi a scholar[193] and the Talmud declares that he was worthy of rabbinic ordination.[194]

Jews are forbidden to marry slaves just as they are forbidden to marry any other non-Jews. Tosafoth explains that the Rabbis forbade accepting condolences for slaves because onlookers might think that the deceased slave was a relative of the mourner. Such confusion could lead Jews to marry relatives of the deceased slave thinking them to be Jews.[195]

It may be that because Tavi was so widely renowned as a scholar, this concern did not apply to him for everyone knew about his status as a slave. In any event, the exception made for Tavi did not apply to Rabbi Eliezer's maidservant so he was halachically bound to reject any condolences for her. However, this did not mean that Rabbi Eliezer had no respect for his maidservant's feelings. True, he could easily have come straight out and told his disciples the halachah, but that would mean pointing out the low status of the deceased maidservant who did not merit that her master accept condolences for her. So sensitive to the feelings of others was Rabbi Eliezer that it was unthinkable to him to say something negative about another human being even after that person died. Only when circumstances absolutely forced him to do so, did he openly explain the halachah to his disciples.

---

[193] Sukkah 2:1.
[194] B.T. Yoma 87A.
[195] Tosafoth on B. T. Brachoth 16B sub verba "Ain Omdim" (אין עומדים).

76

Brachoth 2:8 (Compare Shir HaShirim Rabba on verse 6:2 and Koheleth Rabba on verse 5:11)

כד דמך רבי חייא בר אדא, בר אחתיה דבר קפרא...רבי שמעון
בן לקיש...עאל ואיפטר עילוי, "דּוֹדִי יָרַד לְגַנּוֹ לַעֲרוּגוֹת הַבֹּשֶׂם לִרְעוֹת
בַּגַּנִּים [וְלִלְקֹט שׁוֹשַׁנִּים]." (שיר השירים ו:ב). לא צורכה אלא "דודי ירד
לגנו לרעות בגנים." "דּוֹדִי," זה הקדוש ברוך הוא. "יָרַד לְגַנּוֹ," זה
העולם. "לַעֲרוּגוֹת הַבֹּשֶׂם," אֵילּוּ ישראל. "לִרְעוֹת בַּגַּנִּים," אֵילּוּ אומות
העולם. "וְלִלְקֹט שׁוֹשַׁנִּים," אֵילּוּ הצדיקים שמסלקן מביניהן.

משלו משל: למה הדבר דומה? למלך שהיה לו בן והיה חביב
עליו יותר מדאי. מה עשה המלך? נטע לו פרדס. בשעה שהיה הבן
עושה רצונו של אביו, היה מחזר בכל העולם כולו ורואה אי זו נטיעה
יפה בעולם ונוטה בתוך פרדיסו. ובשעה שהיה מכעיסו, היה מקצץ כל
נטיעותיו. כך בשעה שישראל עושין רצונו של הקדוש ברוך הוא, מחזר
בכל העולם כולו ורואה אי זה צדיק באומות העולם ומביאו ומדבקו
לישראל. כגון יתרו ורחב. ובשעה שהן מכעיסין אותו, היה מסלק
הצדיקים שביניהן.

דלמא: רבי חייא בר אדא וחבורתיה, ואית דמרין רבי יוסי בי
רבי חלפתא וחבורתיה, ואית דמרין רבי עקיבה וחבורתיה, הוו יתבין
לעיי באוריתא תחות הדא תאינה והוה מרא דתאינתא קריץ ולקיט לה
בכל יום. אמרין שמא הוא חושדינו. נחלוף את מקומינו.

למחר, אתיא מרה דתאינתא גבון. אמר לון, "מריי אף חדא
מצוה דהויתן נהיגין ועבדין עמי מנעתונה מיני."

אמרון ליה, "אמרין, 'דלמא דאחשד לן.'"

בצפרא, אתי מודעא יתהון. זרחה עליו החמה והתליעו
תאינותיה. באותה שעה אמרו, "בעל התאנה יודע אימתי עונתה של
תאינה ללקוט והיה לוקטה."

כך הקדוש ברוך הוא יודע אימתי עונתן של צדיקים לסלק מן
העולם והוא מסלקן.

When Rabbi Chiya bar Adda, the nephew of Bar Kappara, died, Resh Lakish...eulogized him with the verse, "My beloved descended to his garden, to the spice patch, to roam in the gardens, to gather lilies."[196] The verse did not need to say anything but "My beloved descended to his garden, to roam in the gardens." [The words "to the spice patch" are unnecessary, so the following interpretation of the verse is suggested:] "My beloved" means the Holy One, Blessed be He; "descended to his garden" means the world; "to the spice patch" means Israel; "to roam in the gardens" means the [non-Jewish] Nations of the World; "to gather lilies" means the righteous ones whom He removes from among them.

Behold, a parable: To what may the matter be compared? To a king who had a son who was exceedingly precious to him. What did the king do? He planted him an orchard. When the son performed the will of his father, the father would search throughout the entire world to see which beautiful plants were available and plant them in his orchard. If the son angered him, the king would cut down all his plants.

So, when Israel performs the will of the Holy One, Blessed be He, He searches throughout the entire world and sees which righteous person exists among the Nations of the World. He brings that person and attaches him to Israel. Such were Jethro and Rahav [who were converts]. When Israel angers Him, He removes the righteous among them.

An incident took place involving Rabbi Chiya bar Adda and his academy, some say it was Rabbi Yossi of the academy

---

[196] Song of Songs 6:2.

of Rabbi Chalafta and his academy, and some say it was Rabbi Akiva and his academy. They would sit and discuss Torah beneath a certain fig tree. The owner of the tree used to arise early each day and harvest the figs. The students said, "Perhaps he suspects us [of stealing his figs. This is why he hurries to harvest them.] Let us change our place."

The following day, the owner of the fig tree came them and said, "My Masters, the meritorious deed you were accustomed to do with me, you now withhold from me."

They replied, "We figured that perhaps you suspected us [of theft]."

In the morning, the owner of the fig tree said to himself, "I will make known to them [that I bear no suspicion towards them]." The sun shone forth and his figs became wormy.

At that moment, the students said, "The owner of the fig tree knew when the proper time to harvest was and did so." [The owner used to harvest the figs early in the morning only to avoid their becoming wormy and not because he suspected us of stealing his figs.]

So the Holy One, Blessed be He, knows when is the proper time for the righteous to depart from the world and He removes them.

There seems to be a contradiction here. On the one hand, the Talmud appears to teach that God punishes the Jewish people by taking away its righteous members. On the other hand, the Talmud says that Hashem knows when the right time is for them to die, suggesting that their death has nothing to do with punishment of anyone else. In addition, a fundamental tenet of the Jewish religion is that people are judged only for their own actions. It is manifestly unjust, and not God's way, to kill a righteous person as a punishment for others who have sinned.

Y'feh To'ar[197] explains that sometimes Hashem brings about the death of righteous individuals to preserve their righteousness. In other words, God knows that if such people continue to live, they will not be able to withstand temptation and will sin. It is actually a reward for their righteousness that they die at any early age before that can occur. Alternatively, God foresees great misery in the life of the righteous person and causes him die to spare him that misery.[198]

Accordingly, the two apparently contradictory aspects of the righteous person's death are actually two complementary perspectives of the same phenomenon. When Hashem sees wickedness in a generation, he causes the righteous to die to spare them from either (a) negative influences which may cause them to stray, or (b) the pain they will experience from witnessing such wickedness (or which wicked people may inflict upon them). Thus, God acts justly and mercifully when he causes a righteous person to die. On the other hand, what is beneficial for the righteous person is actually a punishment for the wicked generation which is deprived of the guidance and merit of that person.

---

[197] Rabbi Shmuel Yafeh Ashkenazi who lived in Turkey during the sixteenth century.

[198] Y'feh Toar on Koheleth Rabbah on verse 5:11.

This passage of the Talmud states that when Israel is righteous, Hashem rewards the nation by having the righteous of other nations join it as converts, implying that it is highly beneficial for Israel to accept converts. However, the Babylonian Talmud teaches that "converts are as troublesome to Israel as a leprous scab,"[199] implying that converts are extremely detrimental to Israel. How can these statements be reconciled?

The Talmud teaches that all Jews have a basic desire to observe the Torah and behave properly. However, the evil inclination and corrupting influences of other cultures lead them astray.[200] One opinion in Tosafoth explains that converts are troublesome to Israel because they are more scrupulous in observing the Torah than native-born Jews.[201] This may be because they contradict Israel's justification for sinning. When Jews say they would have obeyed the Torah but corrupting influences led them astray, the Heavenly tribunal can point to converts who were far more immersed in non-Jewish culture than anyone born Jewish, yet they converted and now follow the precepts of the Torah.

The apparent contradiction between the Talmud's positive and negative views of converts can be explained by distinguishing between Jews as individuals and as a nation.

---

[199] B.T. Yevamoth 47B.
[200] B.T. Brachoth 17A.
[201] Tosafoth sub verba "Kashim Gerim" (קשים גרים) on B.T. Kiddushin 70B and Tosafoth Yeshanim sub verba "Kashim Gerim" (קשים גרים) on B.T. Yevamoth 47B.

Rabbi Moshe Chaim Luzzatto[202] taught that after Adam sinned, humankind sank to a very low spiritual level. Adam's descendants, who were the forebears of all the nations of the world, had an opportunity to rectify this problem and regain the original lofty spiritual status God intended people to have. The only individual who actually proved worthy, however, was Abraham. The selection of Abraham's descendants as God's chosen people became final when the Torah was given. After that, no nation could ever replace Israel or match its level of spiritual achievement. However, individual members of any nation through their own efforts can still rise to a high spiritual level and join the Jewish people by converting.[203]

That Israel's role as Hashem's special nation is permanent is confirmed by the Talmud which teaches that God granted Moses's request that He cause His Presence to dwell exclusively on Israel.[204] This explains why the passage of the Jerusalem Talmud under review deems the addition of converts to Israel as highly positive. The merit of such people contributes to the spiritual preeminence of the Jewish nation. When the Talmud talks about converts proving troublesome, however, it refers to the way in which the behavior of those righteous individuals contrasts with that of certain individual Jews causing Heaven to judge the latter unfavorably.

---

[202] Italy, 18th century.
[203] Derech HaShem, Part II, Chapter 4. "The Way of God," translated and annotated by Rabbi Aryeh Kaplan (New York, Feldheim 1977) pp. 130-143.
[204] B.T. Brachoth 7A.

Brachoth 2:8 continued

כד דמך רבי בון בר רבי חייא, על רבי זעירא ואפטר עילוי,
"מְתוּקָה שְׁנַת הָעֹבֵד [אִם מְעַט וְאִם הַרְבֵּה יֹאכֵל וְהַשָּׂבָע לֶעָשִׁיר אֵינֶנּוּ
מַנִּיחַ לוֹ לִישׁוֹן.] (קהלת ה:יא). "יָשָׁן" אין כתיב כאן, אלא, "אִם מְעַט וְאִם
הַרְבֵּה יֹאכֵל." לְמה היה רבי בון ברבי חייא דומה? למלך שׁשׂכר פועלים
הרבה והיה שם פועל אחד והיה משׁתכר במלאכתו יותר מדאי. מה עשה
המלך? נטלו והיה מטייל עמו ארוכות וקצרות. לעיתותי ערב, באו
אותם פועלים ליטול שכרן ונתן לו שכרו עמהן מִשָׁלֵם.
והיו הפועלים מתרעמין ואומרים, "אנו יגענו כל היום וזה לא יגע
אלא שתי שעות, ונתן לו שכרו עמנו מִשָׁלֵם."
אמר להן המלך, "יגע זה לשתי שעות יותר ממה שלא יגעתם
אתם כל היום כולו."
כך יגע רבי בון בתורה לעשרים ושמונה שנה מה שאין תלמיד
ווֹתיק יכול ללמוד למאה שנה.

When Rabbi Bon bar Chiya died, Rabbi Z'eira eulogized him with the verse, "Sweet is the sleep of the worker whether he eats little or much... ."[205] "Sleep" is not written here, but "whether he eats little or much." [Since the verse starts off discussing sleep, it should also conclude "whether he sleeps little or much."] What did the life of Rabbi Bon bar Chiya resemble? A king hired many workers. There was a certain worker who performed his labor exceedingly well. What did the king do? He took that worker and strolled with him through the length and breadth of his kingdom.

---

[205] Ecclesiastes 5:11.

In the evening, when all the workers came to collect their payment, the king paid that worker his full wages the same as the others. The other workers grumbled and said, "We toiled the whole day while he toiled but two hours and he gives him his full wages the same as he gives us."

The king answered them, "This one accomplished in two hours what you did not accomplish in an entire day."

So did Rabbi Bon accomplish in learning Torah during twenty-eight years what an experienced student could not accomplish in a hundred years.

[When reading the full verse, "Sweet is the sleep of the worker whether he eats little or much, but the plenty of the rich man does not permit him to sleep,"[206] the term "sleep" denotes the reward one receives in the hereafter for studying Torah while "eating" denotes "living." The reward of one who strives mightily in his Torah studies, accomplishing much, is great whether he lives long or not, whereas "the plenty of the rich man," the long life of one who lives at ease without struggling over his studies, "does not permit him to sleep," meaning that it yields no reward in the next world.]

A number of commentators question the premise of this passage. True, Rabbi Bon bar Chiya achieved a great deal during his brief lifetime, but would it not have been even better had he lived longer and been able to accomplish even more?[207]

---

[206] Ecclesiastes 5:11.
[207] Rabbi Yosef Chaim in Sefer Benyahu on this passage and Y'feh Kol

The silent prayer Jews recite each Sabbath includes the following: "Our God and God of our fathers, be pleased with our rest, sanctify us with Your commandments and grant us our share in Your Torah... ." Why does the prayer request "our share" in the Torah rather than simply "a share" in the Torah? The answer is that each person has his or her own special portion in the Torah, something unique which he or she is supposed to learn and accomplish.[208] *Accordingly, each person prays that he or she be granted the ability and opportunity to carry out his or her special mission in life; "our share" as opposed to "a share." Perhaps Rabbi Bon bar Chiya completed his earthly task at a very young age. It would not have been possible for him to accomplish more even if he had lived longer.*

on Shir HaShirim Rabbah on verse 6:2. Each suggests a different answer than the one offered here.

[208] Kabbalistic literature refers to this as a Tikkun (תיקון) or Rectification.

Brachoth 2:8 continued (compare J.T. Horayoth 3:5)

כד דמך רבי סימון בר זביד, עאל רבי לַיָא ואפטר עילוי: ארבעה
דברים תשמישו של עולם וכולן אם אבדו, יש להן חליפין. "כִּי יֵשׁ לַכֶּסֶף
מוֹצָא וּמָקוֹם לַזָּהָב יָזֹקּוּ. בַּרְזֶל מֵעָפָר יֻקָּח וְאֶבֶן יָצוּק נְחוּשָׁה." (איוב
כח:א-ב). אֵילּוּ, אם אבדו, יש להן חליפין, אבל תלמיד חכם שמת, מי
מביא לנו חליפתו? מי מביא לנו תמורתו? "וְהַחָכְמָה מֵאַיִן תִּמָּצֵא וְאֵי זֶה
מְקוֹם בִּינָה." (איוב כח:יב). "וְנֶעֶלְמָה מֵעֵינֵי כָל חָי..." (איוב כח:כא).
אמר רבי לוי: מה אם אחי יוסף על שמצאו מציאה יצא לבם,
דכתיב "[וַיִּפְתַּח הָאֶחָד אֶת שַׂקּוֹ לָתֵת מִסְפּוֹא לַחֲמֹרוֹ בַּמָּלוֹן וַיַּרְא אֶת
כַּסְפּוֹ וְהִנֵּה הוּא בְּפִי אַמְתַּחְתּוֹ. וַיֹּאמֶר אֶל אֶחָיו הוּשַׁב כַּסְפִּי וְגַם הִנֵּה
בְאַמְתַּחְתִּי] וַיֵּצֵא לִבָּם וַיֶּחֶרְדוּ אִישׁ אֶל אָחִיו לֵאמֹר מַה זֹּאת עָשָׂה
אֱ-לֹהִים לָנוּ.]" (בראשית מב:כז-כח), אנו שאבדנו את רבי סימון בר זביד,
על אחת כמה וכמה.

When Rabbi Simon bar Zavid died, Rabbi Laya entered
and eulogized him, saying: Four types of metal are the principal
ones used by the world and any of them which are lost may be
replaced as the verse says, "Because there is for silver a source
and a place for gold to flow. Iron from ore is extracted and
stone pours forth copper."[209] For these, if they are lost, there
are replacements. However, when a scholar dies, who will
bring us a replacement? Who will bring us his substitute? As
the verse says further on, "Wisdom from where will it be
produced and where is the origin of understanding?[210]...It is

---

209 Job 28:1-2.
210 Ibid. 28:12.

hidden from the eyes of all the living and from the fowl of the heavens it is concealed."[211]

Rabbi Levi said: When the brothers of Joseph made a [beneficial] discovery, their hearts leapt, as it is written, "One of them opened his sack to give provisions to his donkey at the inn and he saw his money; behold, it was in the mouth of his sack. And he said to his brother, 'My money is returned; behold, it is in my sack!' And their hearts leapt and each man turned to his brother in dread, saying, 'What is this that God has done to us?'"[212] We who have lost Rabbi Simon bar Zavid, how many times more so [should we feel stunned and upset].

The Talmud teaches that "The Holy One, Blessed be He, saw that the righteous are few, so He arose and planted some in each generation."[213] How, then, can Rabbi Laya say that the loss of a great rabbi is irreplaceable? The answer comes from a close examination of the comparison he makes to the loss of a precious metal. Although it takes much effort to locate and refine the ore which produces such metals, it is possible to do so. Moreover, the chemical composition of such metals is identical. One ingot of pure gold has the same properties as any other ingot of pure gold. This is not so with great rabbis. Although God never leaves the Jewish people completely bereft of righteous leaders, each such leader has his

---

[211] Ibid. 28:21.

[212] Genesis 42:27-28.

[213] B.T. Yoma 38B.

unique personality and something special which he contributes to the nation.

*This explains Rabbi Levi's comparison of such a loss to the feeling of shock expressed by Joseph's brothers. Instead of rejoicing at the good fortune of finding their money, they were alarmed because they feared that the Egyptians would falsely accuse them of theft. This was true even though it was uncertain whether such an accusation would materialize. In the case of a great rabbi who dies, the members of the community may be upset because they are uncertain as to whether there will be someone of equal caliber to replace him. Rabbi Levi's point is that **no one** can completely replace a Torah scholar who has died because each scholar has his unique strengths which others cannot duplicate. Hence, if Joseph's brothers were upset about the mere **possibility** of calamity, the members of a community which loses a righteous person should feel even greater shock for they have **definitely** suffered a great loss.[214]*

---

[214] See Mareh HaPanim on J.T. Horayoth 3:5 for a similar explanation.

Brachoth 2:8 (continued) (compare Koheleth Rabbah 12:14)

כד דמך רבי לוי בר סיסי, על אבוי דשמואל ואפטר עילוי, "סוֹף
דָּבָר הַכֹּל נִשְׁמָע אֶת הָאֱ-לֹהִים יְרָא [וְאֶת מִצְוֹתָיו שְׁמוֹר כִּי זֶה כָּל
הָאָדָם.]" (קהלת יב:יג). לְמה היה לוי בן סיסי דומה? למלך שהיה לו
כרם והיה בו מאה גפנים והיו עושות כל שנה ושנה מאה חביות של יין.
עמד על חמשים, עמד על ארבעים, עמד על שלשים, עמד על עשרים,
עמד על עשר, עמד על אחד. והיה עושה מאה חביות של יין. והיה אותו
הגפן חביב עליו ככל הכרם כולו. כך היה רבי לוי בר סיסי חביב לפני
הקדוש ברוך הוא ככל אדם. הדא הוא דכתיב, "...כִּי זֶה כָּל הָאָדָם."

When Rabbi Levi bar Sisi died, the father of Samuel entered and eulogized him with the verse, "The end of every matter having been heard, fear God and keep his commandments for this is the whole [purpose] of humanity."[215] What did Levi bar Sisi's life resemble? A king who had a vineyard which had one hundred vines which used to produce one hundred barrels of wine each year. They were reduced to fifty. They were reduced to forty. They were reduced to thirty. They were reduced to twenty. They were reduced to ten. They were reduced to one which used to produce one hundred barrels of wine [each year]. The one vine was as precious to [the king] as the entire vineyard. So Rabbi Levi bar Sisi was as precious to the Holy One, Blessed be He, as all humanity just as it is written, "for this is the whole [purpose] of humanity."[216]

---

215 Ecclesiastes 12:13.
216 Ecclesiastes 12:13.

89

The Mishnah teaches: "Since Rabbi Meir died, there are no more weavers of parables. Since Ben Azzai died, there are no more who learn diligently. Since Ben Zoma died, there are no more sermonizers. Since Rabbi Joshua died, good ceased from the world...."[217]

The editor of the Mishnah expresses the opinion that these rabbis were so great that no later person could surpass certain qualities they possessed. This attitude reflects the general principle that each succeeding generation is on a lower spiritual level than the one that preceded it, with the exception of certain outstanding individuals. Thus, for example, the Talmud reports that when a drought occurred, Rav Judah merely removed one of his shoes and rain immediately fell. By contrast, later generations declared many fasts and cried out profusely to no avail.[218] *Likewise, Rav Zera said in the name of Rava bar Zimona, "If earlier generations were like angels, then we are humans, and if earlier generations were like humans, then we are like donkeys."*[219]

Evidently, Samuel's father thought that the degree of fear of Hashem possessed by Rabbi Levi bar Sisi exceeded that of his contemporaries to such an extent that no one after him could rival it. Thus, the parable talks about a king who starts out owning one hundred vines which gradually decline until he has only one. In former generations, many individuals may

---

[217] Sotah 9:15.
[218] B.T. Ta'anith 24A-B and Brachoth 20A. See also B.T. Brachoth 35B.)
[219] B.T. Shabbath 112B.

have had true fear of Hashem. Gradually their numbers decreased until but one remained. That unique individual was Rabbi Levi bar Sisi who by virtue of his tremendous fear of God merited to learn the secrets of the Torah, consistent with the verse, "The secret of the Lord is with those who fear Him... ."[220] *Samuel's father compared Rabbi Levi bar Sisi to a grapevine because the word for wine in Hebrew (יין), has the same numerical value as the word for secret (סוד).*[221]

---

[220] Psalms 25:14.
[221] For a similar explanation, see Maharzu (Rabbi Ze'ev Wolf Einhorn of Vilna, 19th century) on Koheleth Rabbah 12:14 which parallels this text.

Brachoth 2:8 continued

[When Rav Kahana moved from Babylon to the Land of Israel, he visited the academy of Rabbi Yochanan. Due to his youth, people called him simply "Kahana." He only acquired the title of "Rav" later on.[222] The Babylonian Talmud reports that Rav Kahana died during his visit and Rabbi Yochanan revived him.[223]]

כהנא, הוה עולם סגין כד סליק להכא.
חמתיה חד בר פחין. אמר ליה, "מה קלא בשמיא?"
אמר ליה, "גזר דיניה דההוא גברא מיחתם!" וכן הוות ליה.
ומתפגע ביה, חמתיה חד אחרן. אמר ליה, "מה קלא בשמיא?"
אמר ליה, "גזר דיניה דההוא גברא מיחתם!" וכן הוות ליה.
אמר, "מה סליקית מזכי ואנא איחטי? מה סליקית למיקטלה בני
ארעא דישראל? ניזול וניחות לי מן הן דסליקית."
אתא לגבי רבי יוחנן. אמר ליה, "בר נש דאימיה מבסרא ליה
ואיתתיה דאבוהי מוקרא ליה, להן ייזול ליה?"
אמר ליה, "ייזול להן דמוקרין ליה."
נחת ליה כהנא מן הן דסלק. אתון אמרין ליה לרבי יוחנן, "הא
נחית כהנא לבבל."
אמר, "מה הוה מיזל ליה, דלא מיסב רשותא?"
אמרין ליה, "ההוא מילתא דאמר לך הוא הוה נטילת רשות
דידיה."

---

222 Perush MiBa'al Sefer Chareidim by Rabbi Elazar Azkari of Turkey and the Land of Israel, 1533-1600.
223 B.T. Baba Kama 117A-B.

The entire community went to see Kahana when he ascended here [to the Land of Israel.] A certain rogue saw him and said [mockingly], "What is new in Heaven?"

He answered him, "Your final decree is sealed," and so it was that the rogue died.

Another one saw Kahana and said to him, "What is new in Heaven?"

He answered him, "Your final decree is sealed," and so it was.

Kahana said to himself, "Have I ascended here to acquire merit and yet sinned? Have I ascended to kill the people of the Land of Israel? Let me go and descend from where I have gone up."

He went to Rabbi Yochanan and said, "Regarding a person whose mother disgraces him while his father's second wife honors him, to where should he go?"

Rabbi Yochanan replied, "Let him go to where they honor him."

Kahana descended from where he had gone up [returning to Babylon].

The disciples came and told Rabbi Yochanan, "Behold, Kahana has descended to Babylon."

He responded, "Why did he go without taking permission?"

They said, "That question he posed to you constituted his taking permission."

The sense of Rav Kahana's question about a mother disgracing him was that the Land of Israel is the true "motherland" of every Jew, yet its people repeatedly ridiculed him. By contrast, the people of Babylon, "the second wife," showed him respect.[224]

Rav Kahana phrased his question in an indirect fashion because he feared that if he asked Rabbi Yochanan outright for permission to leave the Land of Israel, the latter would have refused him.[225]

It seems strange that Rav Kahana's only concern about leaving the Land of Israel was that he obtain permission from Rabbi Yochanan. The Rambam rules that, "It is always forbidden to go out from the Land of Israel to a foreign land except to learn Torah, or to marry a woman, or to save [one's property] from heathens and he should [later] return to the Land. Likewise, one may go out to do business. However, to dwell in a foreign land is forbidden unless famine is so severe that a dinar's worth of wheat sells for two dinarim... ."[226] *How is it that Rav Kahana did not worry about this serious prohibition?*

The solution is that one must have peace of mind to learn Torah properly. When a person is under pressure and his mind is filled with anxiety, he cannot succeed in his studies. Thus, for example, the Shulchan Aruch rules that ideally one should temporarily hold off marrying to learn Torah so that the pressures of supporting and caring for a family do not interfere with one's studies. On the other hand, if holding off marriage

---

[224] Ibid. and P'nei Moshe.
[225] P'nei Moshe.
[226] Yad HaChazakah, Hilchoth Melachim 5:9.

94

means that one's desires will hinder his learning, he should marry first.[227] *Hence, one way or another, the key to successful learning is to avoid distractions. The ridicule that Rav Kahana endured obviously caused him great suffering as is clear from the way in which those who taunted him were punished.*[228] *In the passage cited above, the Rambam ruled that one may leave the Land of Israel to learn Torah. Since such severe mocking interfered with his learning, it was permissible for Rav Kahana to leave the Land of Israel to study more comfortably in Babylon. His only reservation was whether Rabbi Yochanan would consent.*

---

[227] Shulchan Aruch, Yoreh Deah 246:2.
[228] Perush MiBa'al Sefer Chareidim explains that Rav Kahana was highly sensitive to being taunted because he was young and hot-blooded at the time.

Brachoth 2:8 continued

רבי זעירא, כד סלק להכא, אזל אקין דם. אזל, בעי מיזבון חדא
ליטרא דקופד מן טבחא. אמר ליה, "בכמה הדין ליטרתא?"
אמר ליה, "בחמשין מניי וחד קורסם."
אמר ליה, "סב לך שיתין," ולא קביל עילוי.
"סב לך ע'." ולא קביל עילוי.
"סב לך פ'."
"סב לך צ'."
עד דמטא מאה ולא קביל עילוי. אמר ליה, "עביד כמנהגך."
ברומשא, נחית לבית וועדא. אמר לון, "רבנן! מה ביש מנהגא
דהכא דלא אכיל בר נש ליטרא דקופד עד דמחו ליה חד קורסם!"
אמרין ליה, "ומה הוא דין?"
אמר לון, "פלן טבחא." שלחון, בעיי מייתיתיה ואשכחון ארוניה
נפקא.
אמרו ליה, "רבי, כל הכין?"
אמר לון, "וייתי עליי דלא כעסית עילוי, מי סברת דמנהגא כן."
רב יסא, כד סליק להכא, אזל ספר. בעי מסחי באהן דימוסן
דטיבריא. פגע ביה חד ליצן ויהב ליה פורקדל חד. אמר ליה, "עד כדון
עונקתיה דההוא גברא רפיא."
והוה ארכונא קאים דאין אחד ליסטים ואזל קם ליה גחיך כל
קבליה.
אמר ליה ארכונא, "מאן הוה עמך?"
תלה עינוי וחמא דההוא גחיך. אמר ליה, "אהן דגחיך, הוא עמי."
נסביה ודניה ואודי ליה על חד קטיל. מי נפקין תרוייהון טעינין
תרתי שרין, מן דעבר רב יסא מסחא. אמר ליה, "ההוא עונקתא דהות
רפיא כבר שנצת."
אמר ליה, "ביש גדא דההוא גברא. ולא כתיב, "וְעַתָּה אַל
תִּתְלוֹצָצוּ פֶּן יֶחְזְקוּ מוֹסְרֵיכֶם..." (ישעיה כח:כב).
רבי פינחס רבי ירמיה בשם רבי שמואל בר רב יצחק: קשה היא

הליצנות שתחילתה ייסורין וסופן כלייה. תחילתה ייסורין, דכתיב
"וְעַתָּה אַל תִּתְלוֹצָצוּ פֶּן יֶחְזְקוּ מוֹסְרֵיכֶם..." (שם שם). וסופן כלייה,
דכתיב "...כִּי כָלָה וְנֶחֱרָצָה שָׁמַעְתִּי מֵאֵת אֲ-דֹנָי ה' צְ-בָאוֹת עַל כָּל
הָאָרֶץ." (שם שם).

When Rav Z'eira ascended here [to the Land of Israel],
he went to have his blood let. He then wanted to buy a pound
of meat from a butcher [since it is healthy to eat meat after a
bloodletting].[229]

He said to the butcher, "How much is this pound of
meat?"

[Seeing that Rav Z'eira was a foreigner, the butcher
decided to play a practical joke and said that it would cost
him,] "Fifty coins and a hammer blow."

[Not realizing that the butcher was joking, Rav Z'eira
answered,] "Take sixty [and forego the hammer blow]."

The butcher would not agree.

"Take seventy."

The butcher would not agree.

"Take eighty."

The butcher would not agree.

"Take ninety".

The butcher would not agree.

Finally, he reached one hundred and the butcher still
would not agree so Rav Z'eira said, "Do as is your custom."

---

[229] Perush MiBa'al Sefer Chareidim.

97

In the evening, Rav Z'eira entered the study hall. He said to those present, "Rabbis, how evil is the custom here that a person cannot eat a pound of meat until they strike him one hammer blow."

They said to him, "Who told you this?"

He replied, "So and so, the butcher."

They sought to summon the butcher to the academy, [but meanwhile he died and] they found that his funeral procession had already started. The rabbis of the academy said to Rav Z'eira, "Master, to this degree you were angry?"

He answered, "May evil come upon me if I was angry at him, for I thought such was the custom."

When Rav Yassa ascended here [to the Land of Israel], he got a haircut whereupon he wanted to bathe in a certain public bathhouse in Tiberias. A certain prankster met up with him and thumped him on the back with a stick saying, "Your neck is still weak [and this will fix it]!"

A Gentile judge was holding court concerning a certain highway robber. The prankster went and stood grinning opposite the highway robber.

The judge said, "Who was with you [when you committed your crimes]?"

The defendant raised his eyes and saw the prankster grinning so he said, "That one who is grinning was with me."

The authorities seized the prankster and tortured him until he confessed to a murder. As the two defendants went out bearing two poles [upon which they were to be hanged], Rav Yassa emerged from the bathhouse. The prankster said, "The neck which was weak has now been hardened!" [I am being punished on your account!]

"It's your own bad luck!" declared Rav Yassa. "Is it not written, 'And now, do not mock lest your torments be increased for utter destruction and ruin I have heard [decreed] from the Lord, God of Multitudes, upon all the earth.'?[230]"

Rabbi Phinehas bar Jeremiah said in the name of Rabbi Samuel bar Rav Isaac: Mocking is a severe matter for its punishment starts with torments and ends up with utter destruction. It begins with torments as it is written, "And now, do not mock lest your torments be increased...," and it concludes with utter destruction as is written, "...for utter destruction and ruin I have heard [decreed] from the Lord, God of Multitudes, upon all the earth."

Rav Z'eira did not curse the butcher who mocked him. In fact, he was not even aware of the mockery. Likewise, Rav Yassa did not curse the prankster. Even so, God punished both severely.

A similar event occurred when the famous scholar Resh Lakish became an outlaw until Rabbi Yochanan convinced him to repent. Resh Lakish then married Rabbi Yochanan's sister. One time, they had a scholarly dispute during which Resh Lakish declared that he had not benefited much from Rabbi Yochanan since he had been a Torah scholar before he strayed from the path of the Torah. When Rabbi Yochanan took offense at this, Resh Lakish became ill and died even though

---

[230] Isaiah 28:22.

Rabbi Yochanan surely did not want such a thing to happen to a person who was the husband of his sister, father of his nephews and nieces, and a brilliant study partner.[231]

This phenomenon occurs because when one displays disrespect for the rabbis, he or she is in for serious trouble even if the object of scorn is highly forgiving or perhaps not even aware of the offense. As Rabbi Eliezer said, "Warm yourself by the fire of the Sages, but be wary of their embers lest you be burned, for their bite is the bite of a fox and their sting the sting of a scorpion... ."[232]

A Torah scholar is not just an ordinary person. He embodies the wisdom and ideals of the Torah. If he becomes an object of scorn, God forbid, people may treat the teachings of the Torah lightly as well. Along these lines, the Shulchan Aruch rules that it is preferable for a scholar not to excommunicate someone who insults him privately even when the offending party has not repented. However, when the insult occurs in public, a scholar may not overlook it. Rather, he should pursue the matter until the offender apologizes.[233] *The above passage shows that even if the scholar ignores the insult, God punishes the offender to uphold the honor of the Torah.*

---

[231] B.T. Baba Metzia 84A according to the interpretation of Maharal ad. loc.

[232] Pirkei Avoth 2:10.

[233] Shulchan Aruch, Yoreh Deah 243:9.

Brachoth 4:1 (Compare B.T. Brachoth 26B and Breishith Rabba 68:9)

ומאיכן למדו ג' תפילות? רבי שמואל בר נחמני אמר: כנגד ג'
פעמים שהיום משתנה על הבריות. בשחר צריך לאדם לומר, "מודה אני
לפניך ה' א-להי וא-להי אבותי שהוצאתני מאפילה לאורה." במנחה
צריך אדם לומר, "מודה אני לפניך ה' א-להי וא-להי אבותי כשם
שזכיתני לראות החמה במזרח, כך זכיתי לראות במערב." בערב צריך
לומר, "יהי רצון מלפניך ה' א-להי וא-להי אבותי כשם שהייתי באפילה
והוצאתני לאורה, כך תוציאני מאפילה לאורה."

רבי יהושע בן לוי אמר: תפילות מאבות למדום. תפילת השחר
מאברהם אבינו: "וַיַּשְׁכֵּם אַבְרָהָם בַּבֹּקֶר אֶל הַמָּקוֹם אֲשֶׁר עָמַד שָׁם אֶת
פְּנֵי ה'." (בראשית יט:כז). ואין "עמידה" אלא תפילה, כמה דתימר, "וַיַּעֲמֹד
פִּינְחָס וַיְפַלֵּל [וַתֵּעָצַר הַמַּגֵּפָה]." (תהלים קו:ל). תפילת המנחה מיצחק
אבינו: "וַיֵּצֵא יִצְחָק לָשׂוּחַ בַּשָּׂדֶה [לִפְנוֹת עָרֶב]..." (בראשית כד:סג). ואין
"שיחה" אלא תפילה, כמה דאת אמר, "תְּפִלָּה לְעָנִי כִי יַעֲטֹף וְלִפְנֵי ה'
יִשְׁפֹּךְ שִׂיחוֹ." (תהלים קב:א). תפילת הערב מיעקב אבינו: "וַיִּפְגַּע בַּמָּקוֹם
וַיָּלֶן שָׁם [כִי בָא הַשֶּׁמֶשׁ]..." (בראשית כח:יא). ואין "פגיעה" אלא תפילה,
כמה דתימר, "[וְאִם נְבִאִים הֵם וְאִם יֵשׁ דְּבַר ה' אִתָּם] יִפְגְּעוּ נָא בַּה'
צְ-בָאוֹת..." (ירמיה כז:יח). ואומר, "[וְאַתָּה אַל תִּתְפַּלֵּל בְּעַד הָעָם הַזֶּה]
וְאַל תִּשָּׂא בַעֲדָם רִנָּה וּתְפִלָּה וְאַל תִּפְגַּע בִּי [כִּי אֵינֶנִּי שֹׁמֵעַ אֹתָךְ]."
(ירמיה ז:טז).

ורבנן אמרי: תפילות מתמידין גמרו. תפלת השחר מתמיד של
שחר, "אֶת הַכֶּבֶשׂ אֶחָד תַּעֲשֶׂה בַבֹּקֶר..." (במדבר כח:ד). תפילת המנחה
מתמיד של בין הערבים, "...וְאֵת הַכֶּבֶשׂ הַשֵּׁנִי תַּעֲשֶׂה בֵּין הָעַרְבָּיִם." (שם
שם). תפילת הערב לא מצאו במה לתלותה, ושנו אותה סתם. הדא היא
דתנינן: **תפילת הערב אין לה קבע ושל מוספין כל היום.** (ברכות ד:א).
אמר רבי תנחומא: עוד היא קבעו אותה כנגד איכול איברים ופדרים
שהיו מתאכלין על גבי המזבח כל הלילה.

From where did the Sages derive the three daily prayers? Rabbi Samuel bar Nachmeni said they correspond to the three times during the day when people notice a change: At dawn a person should say, "I give thanks before You, Lord my God and God of my fathers, that You took me out from thick darkness to light." In the afternoon a person should say, "I give thanks before You, Lord my God and God of my fathers, that just as You found me worthy to see the sun in the east so I merited to see the sun in the west." In the evening one should say, "May it be Your will, Lord my God and God of my fathers, that just as I was in thick darkness and You brought me out to light, so may You cause me again to emerge from thick darkness into light."

Rabbi Yehoshua ben Levi said: The three daily prayers were deduced from the activities of the forefathers. The morning prayer is deduced from our father Abraham, as the verse says, "Abraham arose in the morning [and went] to the place at which he had stood before the Lord."[234] The expression "standing" refers to nothing but prayer, as you will note in the verse, "Phinehas stood and prayed and the plague was stopped."[235] The afternoon prayer is deduced from our father Isaac, as the verse says, "Isaac went out to speak in the field towards evening... ."[236] The expression "speech" refers to nothing but prayer, as you will note in the verse, "The prayer of one oppressed, when he is exhausted and pours forth his

---

234 Genesis 19:27.
235 Psalms 106:30.
236 Genesis 24:63.

speech before the Lord."[237] The evening prayer is deduced from our father Jacob, as the verse says, "He approached the place and lodged there as the sun set... ."[238] The expression "approach" refers to nothing but prayer, as you will note in the verse, "If they are prophets and if the word of the Lord is with them, let them please approach the Lord of Multitudes... "[239] and it also says, "You shall not pray for the sake of this people, do not raise up song and prayer for their sake, and do not approach Me for I shall not listen to you."[240]

The rabbis say that the times for prayer were inferred from the daily sacrifices. They deduced the morning prayer from the daily sacrifice of the morning, as the verse says, "The one lamb you shall prepare in the morning... ."[241] They deduced the afternoon prayer from the daily sacrifice of the afternoon, as the verse says, "...and the second lamb you shall prepare in the afternoon."[242] They found nothing upon which to base the evening prayer so they promulgated it without any analogy. This fits in with the Mishnaic teaching: **The evening prayer has no fixed time limit and the extra holiday prayer may be recited during the entire day.**[243] Rabbi Tanchuma said: They indeed established the evening prayer [based upon the sacrificial service,] corresponding to the consumption of

---

[237] Psalms 102:1.
[238] Genesis 28:11.
[239] Jeremiah 27:18.
[240] Jeremiah 7:16.
[241] Numbers 28:4.
[242] Ibid.
[243] Brachoth 4:1.

limbs and fats, for they were consumed upon the altar throughout the night.

The Babylonian Talmud points out that the different views as to how or why the three daily prayers were established are not completely contradictory to one another. He who holds that Abraham, Isaac and Jacob promulgated them also holds that the Sages supported this usage by reference to the sacrificial service in the Temple.[244]

Rabbi Samuel bar Nachmeni proposes three different prayers corresponding to the three periods of morning, afternoon and night. However, those prayers do not even slightly match the formulation of the prayers established by the Men of the Great Assembly which were in use during his time as well as today. Surely, Rabbi Samuel bar Nachmeni was not suggesting that these brief supplications replace the standard form of prayer.[245] *Rather, Rabbi Samuel bar Nachmeni was alluding to the attitude one should have when reciting the prayers. No matter what situation a person finds himself in, he*

---

[244] B.T. Brachoth 26B.   Contrary to the Jerusalem Talmud, the Babylonian Talmud attributes the view that the Sages established the three daily prayers corresponding to the sacrificial service in the Temple to Rabbi Yehoshua ben Levi. It attributes the position that they were promulgated by Abraham, Isaac and Jacob to Rabbi Yossi bar Chanina. It omits the view that the prayers correspond to the naturally occurring periods of the day.

[245] Rabbi Yisroel Meir Kagan writes in Bi'ur Halachah on Shulchan Aruch, Orach Chaim 1:1 that it is "very appropriate" to recite the supplications Rabbi Samuel bar Nachmeni cites here prior to saying each daily prayer.

must praise and thank God as well as pray to Him for assistance. Thus, whether one faces the bright prospects of the morning or the dismal and dangerous prospects of night, he or she must adopt the same attitude of praise, thankfulness and supplication to the Almighty. This reflects the dictum of the Mishnah that, "A person is obliged to bless God for evil just as he or she blesses Him for good."[246]

The classical commentators point out that Abraham, Isaac and Jacob recited all three daily prayers. How, then, can the Talmud propose that each one established one of the prayer services? What the Talmud means is that Abraham, Isaac and Jacob each had a special approach toward serving Hashem.[247] Abraham adopted the approach of "kindness" חסד, which emphasized serving God with love. Isaac employed "judgment" דין, serving God with awe and fear. Jacob served God through "beauty" תפארת, blending the methods of Abraham and Isaac together harmoniously.[248] Accordingly, each is viewed as having established his own daily prayer service because each approached his prayers with his own unique attitude. This teaches that whatever qualities a person possesses, whether he or she is more inclined to serve Hashem in one fashion or another, one must find a way to express that service through prayer just as the three forefathers of the Jewish people did.

---

[246] Brachoth 9:5.

[247] Maharsha on B.T. Brachoth 26B.

[248] Sefer HaBahir Part I, Section 135 based on Micah 7:20 and Genesis 31:53.

The daily sacrifices to which the Talmud compares the daily prayers are called תמידים, literally "constant" or "continual" sacrifices, the idea being that they were offered on behalf of the Jewish nation every single day without exception in contrast to other sacrifices which were brought on special occasions such as holidays, or for the atonement of certain sins, or as an individual's voluntary offering. This reflects the concept that one must pray to God in a constant fashion, always searching for ways in which to thank and praise Him regardless of the varying circumstances which occur from day to day.

Another point the Talmud may be making is that one should try to engender a sense of self-abnegation when praying. The Mishnah declares that, "We do not stand to pray unless we are in a state of utter submission."[249]

In his most profound prophetic vision, Ezekiel describes the "chariot" or "vehicle" which bears the Divine Presence. The true meaning of this vision is unfathomable to the average human mind. Thus, the Mishnah forbids one to teach its inner meaning publicly.[250] Even privately, one may teach it only to an exceptionally outstanding student and then only by offering a general outline of it, leaving the student to infer the rest from his or her own intelligence.[251] Ezekiel's vision is actually a description of the spiritual structure through which God

[249] Brachoth 5:1.
[250] Chagigah 2:1.
[251] B.T. Chagigah 13A.

created, sustains and guides the world. Hence, it is no wonder that very few can properly grasp it even to a slight degree.

The Midrash declares that, "The Patriarchs are truly the vehicle which bears the Divine Presence,"[252] *meaning that the merit of the Patriarchs was so great that it sustains the spiritual structure through which Hashem supervises all Creation.*[253] *This was possible because the Patriarchs were so devoted in their service of God that they were utterly devoid of any personal motives or desires, their sole ambition being to serve Hashem.*[254] *That the Jewish forefathers established the three daily prayers indicates that we too should try to adopt their attitude of subservience to God's will when we pray.*

The daily sacrifices symbolize the same ideal. The constant sacrifices (תמידים) were completely burned up on the Temple altar in contrast to many other sacrifices parts of which were eaten. This represents the concept of total devotion to Hashem. Just as the daily sacrifices were completely consumed on the altar leaving nothing behind, so should one engaged in prayer attempt to free his or her mind from all worldly thoughts and focus solely on serving Hashem with absolute devotion.

The view of Rabbi Samuel bar Nachmeni also alludes to this concept. Addressing thanks to God at every turn of events, even for something so minor and routine as the unfolding of a day from morning through evening, reflects a spirit of

---

[252] Breishith Rabbah 47:6.
[253] Maharzu on Breishith Rabbah 47:6.
[254] Likutei Amarim Tanya ch. 34.

self-abnegation, a constant and complete realization that one's fate is truly under God's control. This reinforces the point that one who prays must do so in a spirit of utter submission to God.

Brachoth 4:1

רבי יוסי בן חנינא היה מתפלל עם דמדומי חמה כדי שיהא עליו
מורא שמים כל היום. אמר רבי יוסי בן חנינא: ויהא חלקי עם
המתפללים עם דמדומי חמה. מה טעם? "עַל זֹאת יִתְפַּלֵּל כָּל חָסִיד
אֵלֶיךָ לְעֵת מְצֹא..." (תהלים לב:ו). מהו "לְעֵת מְצֹא"? לעת מצויין של
יום.
אחוי דאימיה דרב אדא הוה מצייר גולתיה דרב בצומא רבא.
אמר לו, "כד תיחמי שמשא בריש דיקלי, תיהב ליה גולתי דנצלי
דמנחתא."
ושמשא בריש דיקלי תמן, איממא הוא הכא, דמר רבי יוחנן:
"הָאֹמֵר לַצּוּלָה חֲרָבִי..." (ישעיה מד:כז), זו בבל שהיא זוטו של עולם.
אמר רבי יוחנן: למה נקרא שמה "צוּלָה?" ששם צללו מיתי דור
המבול: "גַּם בָּבֶל לִנְפֹּל חַלְלֵי יִשְׂרָאֵל גַּם לְבָבֶל נָפְלוּ חַלְלֵי כָל הָאָרֶץ."
(ירמיה נא:מט).
כתיב "[וַיְהִי בְּנָסְעָם מִקֶּדֶם] וַיִּמְצְאוּ בִקְעָה בְּאֶרֶץ שִׁנְעָר וַיֵּשְׁבוּ
שָׁם." (בראשית יא:ב). אמר ריש לקיש: למה נקרא שמה "שִׁנְעָר?" ששם
ננערו מיתי דור המבול. דבר אחר: "שִׁנְעָר" שהם מתים בתשנוק, בלא
נר ובלא מרחץ. דבר אחר: "שִׁנְעָר" שהם מנוערים מן המצֹות, בלא
תרומה ובלא מעשר. דבר אחר: "שִׁנְעָר" ששריה מתים נערים. דבר
אחר: "שִׁנְעָר" שהעמידו שונא וער להקדוש ברוך הוא. ואי זה זה?
נבוכדנצר הרשע.

Rabbi Yossi ben Chanina used to pray [the afternoon
prayer] at the time of the reddening of the sun [i.e., close to
sunset[255]] so that the fear of Heaven should be upon him

---

[255] Perush MiBa'al Sefer Chareidim and Rabbi Shlomo Sirilio (Spain and
Jerusalem, 1485-1558). By contrast, P'nei Moshe claims that the morning

throughout the day. [The Torah views the day as beginning in the evening.[256]] Rabbi Yossi ben Chanina would say, "May my lot be with those who pray at the time of the reddening of the sun." What Scriptural basis is there for this? "For this every pious person will pray to you at a favorable time... ."[257] What is a "favorable time?" The time of the dissipation of the day.

The maternal uncle of Rav Adda used to keep Rav's cloak during the Great Fast [Yom Kippur]. Rav said to him, "When you see the sun at the top of the palm trees, give me my cloak so that I may recite the afternoon prayer."

When the sun is at the top of the palm trees there in Babylon, it is still daytime here in the Land of Israel, as Rabbi Yochanan said respecting the verse, "The One who says to the swamp, 'Dry up!'..."[258] that it refers to Babylon which is the bottom of the world.

Said Rabbi Yochanan: Why is it called a swamp (צולה)? Because there the corpses of the Generation of the Flood sank (צללו) as the verse says, "Also at Babylon fell the corpses of Israel just as the corpses of all the world fell at Babylon."[259]

It is written, "It was when they traveled from the East that they found a valley in the Land of Shinar and they settled

---

prayer is under discussion here.

[256] This is based on the order used to describe Creation as, for example, the verse says, "...and it was evening and it was morning, one day." (Genesis 1:5). Perush MiBa'al Sefer Chareidim.

[257] Psalms 32:6.

[258] Isaiah 44:27.

[259] Jeremiah 51:49. Compare this paragraph to Breishith Rabbah 37:4 and B.T. Shabbath 113B.

there."[260] Resh Lakish said: Why was Babylon called Shinar (שנער)? Because there were stirred up (ננערו) the corpses of the Generation of the Flood.

Another interpretation: It is called Shinar (שנער) because they die from being stirred up [i.e., from a chaotic lifestyle] for they are without a lamp and without a bathhouse. [The olive trees of Babylon did not produce oil capable of generating a clear light. Also, bathhouses cannot be dug into the swampy land of Babylon.][261]

Another interpretation: It is called Shinar (שנער) because they are stirred up [removed] from the commandments, not having contributions to the priests nor tithes (תרומה ומעשר) [which commandments apply only in the Land of Israel].

Another interpretation: It is called Shinar (שנער) because its princes die as youths (נערים). [The Torah scholars who reside in Babylon die as youths for, despite their great merit, God confers the blessing of long life only upon those who reside in the Land of Israel as the verse says, "That your days may be increased and the days of your children upon the land which the Lord swore to your fathers to give them... ."[262]][263]

Another interpretation: It is called Shinar (שנער) because it raised up an enemy (שונא) and adversary (ער) against the Holy One, Blessed be He. And who was that? Nebuchadnezzar the Wicked.

260 Genesis 11:2.
261 Rabbi Shlomo Sirilio.
262 Deuteronomy 11:21.
263 Rashi on Breishith Rabbah 37:4.

The Babylonian Talmud states that the rabbis of the Land of Israel sharply criticized those who pray in the late afternoon because by delaying so long, they may miss the proper time for reciting the afternoon prayer.[264] Ironically, the Jerusalem Talmud which was written by the rabbis of the Land of Israel makes no mention of this criticism. To the contrary, it praises one who waits until near sunset to pray.

Perhaps there is no contradiction between these seemingly divergent views, however. The Shulchan Aruch rules that while one may fulfill his obligation by reciting the afternoon prayer from a half hour after midday onward, the **preferred** *time for doing so is from three and a half hours after midday onward.[265] Because it is already more than halfway between noon and sunset at that time, one can fulfill the concept of reciting the afternoon prayer "when the sun reddens." This is nonetheless consistent with the notion that people should not wait until right before sundown to pray because they might accidentally miss the afternoon prayer altogether.[266]*

---

[264] B.T. Brachoth 29B.
[265] Shulchan Aruch, Orach Chaim 233:1. The Rama there explains that for halachic purposes hours are calculated not according to a set measure of time, but proportionately to the day. Thus, for example, if a day starts in the summer at 5:00 a.m. and ends at 8:00 p.m. there are fifteen hours of daylight. Dividing fifteen by twelve yields 1.25 so, for halachic purposes, each hour on that day will actually consist of one hour and fifteen minutes.
[266] Ben Yehoyada on B.T. Brachoth 29B suggests that the criticism of those who delay their prayers only applied to those who are busy working and thus could easily miss the time for reciting the afternoon prayer. Others should indeed wait until late in the day to pray as did the Arizal in

The word Babylon (בבל) in Hebrew means "confusion," as the Torah says concerning the Tower of Babel (Babylon), "Therefore He called its name Babel (בבל), for there the Lord confused the language of all the Earth and from there the Lord scattered them upon the face of the Earth."[267] The passage of the Talmud under review points out that the punishment Hashem chose for Babylon was measure for measure. Because all the corpses of the victims of the Flood descended to Babylon, the people there should have taken note of the kind of retribution that may occur when people rebel against God.[268] Instead of doing so, however, the Babylonians chose to delude themselves into believing that the Flood was some type of natural phenomenon, even theorizing that such disasters might occur on a periodic basis.[269] Thus, they refused to recognize that it was Hashem who brought the Flood. This confusion as to who really runs the world led the people of Babylon to build their Tower. They thought that they might thereby escape future "natural catastrophes." God punished them measure for measure for this mixed up philosophy by mixing up their languages.

The truth is that all sin is caused by confusion for one who clearly recognizes God's sovereignty cannot sin. As Resh Lakish said, "A person does not commit a transgression unless a spirit of foolishness enters him."[270] Accordingly, when the

---

actual practice.
[267] Genesis 11:9.
[268] Compare Breishith Rabbah 26:7.
[269] Me'Am Loez on Genesis 11:1.
[270] B.T. Sotah 3A.

Jewish people sinned, Hashem specifically chose Babylon, the paradigm of sin caused by a confused outlook, as the instrument of Divine retribution to conquer the Land of Israel and exile its people. Along these lines, the Torah warns that if Israel sins, God will punish it with "confusion of the heart" (תמהון לבב).[271] If one transposes the letters of the word "heart" (לבב), they yield "Babylon" (בבל).

In fact, Babylon represents confusion even to the point of insanity. The Book of Daniel reports that the Babylonian King Nebuchadnezzar lost his wits for a lengthy period of time, living like a wild animal in the wilderness.[272] Accordingly, the Talmud defines the word "Shinar" (שנער), a synonym for Babylon, as referring to the insane king, the enemy (שונא) and adversary (ער) of God.

The description of Babylon as swampy and muddy further reinforces this point. God identified Himself to Abraham as "God Almighty" (א-ל שד-י).[273] Rabbi Isaac interprets the word "Almighty" (שד-י) to mean, "I am the One who said to my world and to the heavens, 'Enough!' (די) and to the land, 'Enough!' (די). For had I not said to them, 'Enough!,' (די) even now they would be continuously expanding."[274] The idea is that Hashem created laws of nature which limit and define the behavior of the physical world. Thus, land should remain land and function within the physical

---

271 Deuteronomy 28:28.
272 Daniel 4:28-30.
273 Genesis 17:1.
274 Breishith Rabbah 46:3.

limitations of land. So, too, bodies of water should act only within the laws of nature set for them. The error of the Babylonians, however, was the belief that "Nature" is separate from God; that He did not create, or, at least, does not control, the laws of nature. This confused thinking is symbolized by the swampy, muddy condition of Babylon where earth and water mix.

Torah from Jerusalem

Brachoth 4:1

[Above, the Talmud explained how the morning, afternoon and evening prayers as well as the holiday Mussaf prayers correspond to the Temple service. The Ne'ilah, or concluding prayer, is a fifth prayer recited on certain fast days. Today it is recited only on Yom Kippur. Since this does not correspond to any sacrificial service in the Temple, the Talmud asks what basis the Sages had for instituting it.[275]]

מניין לנעילה? אמר רבי לוי: "[וּבְפָרִשְׂכֶם כַּפֵּיכֶם אַעְלִים עֵינַי מִכֶּם גַּם] כִּי תַרְבּוּ תְפִלָּה [אֵינֶנִּי שֹׁמֵעַ יְדֵיכֶם דָּמִים מָלֵאוּ]." (ישעיה א:טו). מכאן שכל המרבה בתפלה נענה.

מחלפא שיטתיה דרבי לוי. תמן אמר רבי אבא בריה דרב פפי, רבי יהושע דסכנין בשם רבי לוי: "בְּכָל עֶצֶב יִהְיֶה מוֹתָר וּדְבַר שְׂפָתַיִם אַךְ לְמַחְסוֹר." (משלי יד:כג). חנה על ידי שריבתה בתפלה, קצרה בימיו של שמואל, שאמרה, "...וְיָשַׁב שָׁם עַד עוֹלָם." (שמואל א א:כב). והלא אין עולמו של לוי אלא אלא חמשים שנה? דכתיב, "וּמִבֶּן חֲמִשִּׁים שָׁנָה יָשׁוּב מִצְּבָא הָעֲבֹדָה [וְלֹא יַעֲבֹד עוֹד]." (במדבר ח:כה). והוויין ליה חמשין ותרתין? אמר רבי יוסי בר רבי בון: שתים שגמלתו.

וכא אמר הכין? אי אמרה כן ליחיד, הן לציבור.

רבי חייא בשם רבי יוחנן, רבי שמעון בן חלפתא בשם רבי מאיר: "וְהָיָה כִּי הִרְבְּתָה לְהִתְפַּלֵּל לִפְנֵי ה'..." (שמואל א א:יב). מכאן שכל המרבה בתפלה נענה.

From where do we derive the Ne'ilah [concluding] prayer? Rabbi Levi said, [God said to the wicked people of

---

275 P'nei Moshe.

116

Isaiah's generation], "When you stretch forth your hands, I shall hide My eyes from you, even if you are profuse in prayer I shall not listen [for] your hands are full of blood."[276] From here we see that anyone who is profuse in prayer is answered. [God said He would ignore profuse prayers of the wicked, thereby indicating that He *would* listen to those of the righteous, so the Rabbis instituted the additional N'eilah prayer even though it has no counterpart in the Temple service.]

This opposes the philosophical approach employed by Rabbi Levi elsewhere, for Rabbi Abba bar Rav Pappi quoted Rabbi Joshua of Sochnin in the name of Rabbi Levi: "With all toil there will be an advantage, but a word of the lips [will yield] only loss."[277] Hannah, by virtue of extended prayer, shortened the days of Samuel [her son,] for she said, "may he dwell there forever (עַד עוֹלָם)."[278] "Is not the "forever" (עוֹלָם) of a Levite but fifty years as is written, "And from the age of fifty years [the Levite] shall return from the corps of the [Temple] service and he shall no longer serve."[279] [A strict interpretation of this would mean that Samuel should have lived only fifty years.] Yet Samuel lived to fifty-two? Rabbi Yossi bar Rabbi Bon said: The two years during which she weaned him were not included.

Nevertheless, how could Rabbi Levi say both statements? What he said here opposing profuse prayer applies

---

[276] Isaiah 1:15.
[277] Proverbs 14:23.
[278] I Samuel 1:22.
[279] Numbers 8:25.

to a private person, whereas the statement favoring prolonged prayer refers to the community.

Rabbi Chiya quoted Rabbi Yochanan that Rabbi Shimon ben Chalafta said in the name of Rabbi Meir [with respect to Hannah]: "It was when she prayed profusely before the Lord... ."[280] From here we see that whoever is profuse in prayer is answered [even on an individual basis, contrary to the position of Rabbi Levi[281]].

The Babylonian Talmud has a similar discussion of the merits of protracted prayer.[282] There the Gemara praises those who engage in lengthy prayer provided that they do not anticipate positive results, for such anticipation implies that the worshiper is highly deserving. Heaven then scrutinizes the worshiper very closely to see if he or she is truly worthy. The usual result is that the supplicant is found lacking and, accordingly, the request denied or, even worse, punishment follows.[283]

In the passage under consideration, Rabbi Levi points out an important exception to the above-stated rule. When a community prays, it does have a right to anticipate a positive response. There are several reasons for this. First, when individuals pray, they may have difficulty focusing their

---

[280] I Samuel 1:12.
[281] P'nei Moshe.
[282] B.T. Brachoth 32B.
[283] B.T. Brachoth 55A declares that anticipating positive results from prayer is one of three things which cause a person's sins to be remembered in Heaven.

concentration upon their prayers.[284] *Likewise, each individual has certain strengths and weaknesses in observing the Torah. When the community prays, however, its members' efforts combine. Thus, one person who concentrates especially well during a certain part of the service compensates for someone else who does not. In addition, someone who is meticulous in abiding by certain aspects of Torah law helps make up for another who is deficient.*

Secondly, a community represents the entire Jewish people. Hashem promised the ancestors of the Jewish nation that their descendants would carry out a special mission in the history of the world. While such a mission can continue in the absence of a lone individual, it cannot continue if the entire community is destroyed, God forbid. This is why the Mishnah says, "Let all who toil for the community toil altruistically, for the merit of their ancestors aids them and their righteousness lasts forever."[285] *As important as the efforts of Jewish leaders on behalf of the people are, it is the merit of the community itself as the heirs of God's covenant with Abraham, Isaac and Jacob that causes the community to succeed. Hence, the community indeed has a right to expect positive results from its prayers. This explains why certain prayers may only be recited when the community is assembled, and not by lone individuals.*

In light of the above, how can one understand the dispute between Rabbi Levi and Rabbi Meir concerning

---

[284] Compare Maharal in Nethiv Ha'Avodah, chapter 6.
[285] Pirkei Avoth 2:2.

Hannah? Surely Rabbi Meir agrees that an individual has no right to anticipate an answer to his or her prayers.

The answer may be as follows. Scripture states about Hannah that, "She swore an oath and said, 'Lord of Multitudes, if You indeed see the affliction of Your maidservant and remember me and do not forget Your maidservant and grant Your maidservant righteous offspring, I will give him to the Lord all the days of his life... .'"[286] After Samuel was born, Elkanah, Hannah's husband, prepared to take the family to the Tabernacle to offer sacrifices. The text continues, "Hannah did not go up for she said to her husband, '[Wait] until the child is weaned and I will bring him and he shall appear before the Lord and dwell there forever.'"[287] According to Rabbi Levi, this latter verse shows that Hannah anticipated that her earlier prayer would be answered, thereby causing the negative result that Samuel's life was shortened. Rabbi Meir, however, views Hannah's statement as a mere expression of her desire to fulfill the oath she had made during that earlier prayer, not an improper speculation as to its outcome. It is true that her use of the phrase "dwell there forever" (עַד עוֹלָם)[288] foreshadowed a short lifespan for Samuel, but that was only because Hannah was a prophetess whose every remark could foretell a future event. The remark itself did not cause that which it predicted.

---

[286] I Samuel 1:11.
[287] I Samuel 1:22.
[288] Ibid .

120

Brachoth 4:1 (Compare B.T. Brachoth 27B-28A)

ומעשה בתלמיד אחד שבא ושאל את רבי יהושע, "תפלת הערב מהו?"

אמר ליה, "רשות."

בא ושאל את רבן גמליאל, "תפלת הערב מהו?"

אמר ליה, "חובה."

אמר ליה, "והא רבי יהושע אמר לי רשות!"

אמר ליה, "למחר כשאכנס לבית הוועד, עמוד ושאל את ההלכה הזאת."

למחר עמד אותו תלמיד ושאל את רבן גמליאל, "תפלת הערב מהו?"

אמר ליה, "חובה."

אמר ליה, "והא רבי יהושע אמר לי רשות!"

אמר רבן גמליאל לרבי יהושע, "את הוא אומר רשות?"

אמר ליה, "לאו."

אמר ליה, "עמוד על רגליך ויעידו בך!"

והיה רבן גמליאל יושב ודורש ורבי יהושע עומד על רגליו עד שרינגו כל העם ואמרו לרבי חוצפית המתורגמן, "הפטר את העם!"

אמרו לרבי זינון החזן, "אֱמוֹר!" התחיל ואמר, התחילו כל העם ועמדו על רגליהם ואמרו לו, "...כִּי עַל מִי לֹא עָבְרָה רָעָתְךָ תָּמִיד?" (נחום ג׳:יט)

הלכו ומינו את רבי אלעזר בן עזריה בישיבה. בן שש עשרה שנה ונתמלא כל ראשו שיבות.

והיה רבי עקיבא יושב ומצטער ואמר, "לא שהוא בן תורה יותר ממני, אלא שהוא בן גדולים יותר ממני. אשרי אדם שזכו לו אבותיו! אשרי אדם שיש לו יתד במי להיתלות בהו!" וכי מה היתה יתידתו של רבי אלעזר בן עזריה? שהיה דור עשירי לעזרא.

וכמה ספסלין היו שם? רבי יעקב בר סיסי אמר: שמונים ספסלין היו שם של תלמידי חכמים חוץ מן העומדים לאחורי הגדר. רבי יוסי בר

רבי אבון אמר: שלש מאות היו שם חוץ מן העומדים לאחורי הגדר, כיי
דתנינן תמן: ...ביום שהושיבו את רבי אלעזר בן עזריה בישיבה... .
(זבחים א:ג)

**תמן תנינן: זה מדרש דרש רבי אלעזר בן עזריה לפני חכמים
בכרם ביבנה...** . (כתובות ד:ו). וכי כרם היה שם? אלא אלו תלמידי
חכמים שהיו עשוין שורות שורות כרם.

מיד הלך לו רבן גמליאל אצל כל אחד ואחד לפייסו בביתו. אזל
גבי רבי יהושע. אשכחיה יתיב עביד מחטין. אמר ליה, "אילין את חיי?"
אמר ליה, "ועד כדון את בעי מודעי? אוי לו לדור שאתה
פרנסו!"

אמר ליה, "נעניתי לך."

ושלחון גבי רבי אלעזר בן עזריה חד קצר, ואית דמרין רבי
עקיבא הוה. אמר ליה, "מי שהוא מזה בן מזה יזה. מי שאינו לא מזה
ולא בן מזה יימר למזה בן מזה מימך מי מערה ואפרך אפר מקלה?"
אמר ליה, "נתרציתם? אני ואתם נשכים לפתחו של רבן
גמליאל."

אף על פי כן, לא הורידוהו מגדולתו, אלא מינו אותו אב בית
דין.

There was an incident involving a certain student who
came and asked Rabbi Joshua, "What is the law regarding the
evening prayer? [Is it obligatory or merely optional?]"

He replied, "It is optional."

The student came and asked Rabban Gamliel, "What is
the law regarding the evening prayer?"

He replied, "It is obligatory."

The student said, "But Rabbi Joshua told me it is
optional!"

"Tomorrow when I enter the academy of the Sanhedrin, rise and ask about this law."

The next day at the academy, the same student stood and asked Rabban Gamliel, "What is the law regarding the evening prayer?"

He replied, "It is obligatory."

The student said, "But Rabbi Joshua told me it is optional!"

Rabban Gamliel said to Rabbi Joshua, "Are you the one who said it is optional?"

Rabbi Joshua replied, "No."

"Stand on your feet and let them testify against you!"[289]

Rabban Gamliel proceeded to sit and lecture while Rabbi Joshua stood on his feet until all the listeners complained and told Rabbi Chutzpith the translator, "Dismiss the people!"[290]

---

[289] The Talmud does not identify "them," i.e., those were supposed to testify against Rabbi Joshua. Tosafoth in B.T. Bekoroth 36A sub verba "Amod Al Raglecha" (עמוד על רגלך) deletes the phrase "let them testify against you" (ויעידו בך) because the idea of having anyone testify against Rabbi Joshua does not apply. According to those scholars who include this phrase in the text, perhaps it refers to Rabbi Joshua's feet. Let them "testify" or "prove it," meaning to let Rabbi Joshua remain standing until his feet become weary and he admits to what he said.

[290] It was customary for a translator to repeat the words of the readings from the Torah and Propets in the vernacular. (Yad HaChazakah, Hilchoth Tefillah 12:10.) In this instance, however, the rabbis of the Sanhedrin obviously knew the translation of any material Rabban Gamliel might quote. Accordingly, the translator's function was to repeat what he said in a loud, clear voice so that all present could hear. (Rashi on B.T. Brachoth 27B sub verba "HaTurgeman" (התורגמן)).

123

The rabbis then told Rabbi Zinon, the manager, "Tell [Rabban Gamliel that we wish to replace him]." He began to tell Rabban Gamliel. All the people then stood on their feet and started to tell him, "...for upon whom has your evil not constantly passed?"[291] [Rabban Gamliel had offended Rabbi Joshua on several prior occasions.[292]] They proceeded to appoint Rabbi Elazar ben Azariah head of the academy. He was only sixteen years old, but his head became full with gray hair [miraculously so that everyone might respect him despite his youth.]

Rabbi Akiva was upset [that he had not been appointed head of the academy on this occasion]. He said, "It is not because he is more knowledgeable in Torah than I am, but because he is the son of great scholars. Happy is the man whose ancestors caused him merit! Happy is the man who has a peg from which to be suspended!" And who was the "peg" for Rabbi Elazar ben Azariah? He was a tenth generation descendant of Ezra.

How many benches were added in the academy [to accommodate the additional scholars who came to study after Rabbi Elazar ben Azariah was appointed]? Rabbi Yaakov bar Sissi said, "There were eighty benches of scholars there, not including those who stood behind the wall." Rabbi Yossi bar Rabbi Abon said, "Three hundred were there, not including those who stood behind the wall."

---

[291] Nahum 3:19. The reference is to the King of Assyria.
[292] B.T. Brachoth 27B enumerates the other incidents.

This accords with that which we learn in the Mishnah in Zevachim [that a halachah which was in dispute was clarified] **"...on the day that they installed Rabbi Elazar ben Azariah in the academy...**"[293] [implying that no law was left in doubt because so many scholars flocked to the academy.[294]] We learn elsewhere in the Mishnah: **"This is the exposition which Rabbi Elazar ben Azariah delivered before the sages in the vineyard of Yavneh... ."**[295] Was there a vineyard there? Rather, this refers to the scholars who sat in rows upon rows like a vineyard.

Immediately, Rabban Gamliel went to each and every rabbinical colleague to placate him at his home. He went to Rabbi Joshua and found him sitting making needles. He said, "From these you earn your livelihood?"

Rabbi Joshua answered, "And until now you did not know [how difficult it is for the rabbis to support themselves]? Woe to the generation which has you as its leader!"

"I apologize." [Rabbi Joshua immediately accepted Rabban Gamliel's apology and the two were reconciled.]

They sent a launderer to Rabbi Elazar ben Azariah, and some say it was Rabbi Akiva whom they sent. He said to Rabbi Elazar ben Azariah, "A priest who sprinkles purifying water, the son of a priest who sprinkles purifying water, should perform the sprinkling. Should one who is not a priest who sprinkles purifying water nor the son of a priest who sprinkles

---

293 Zevachim 1:3.
294 P'nei Moshe.
295 Ketuboth 4:6.

purifying water say to one who is, 'Your water is cave water and your ashes are ashes from an ordinary blaze!'?" [The reference is to the red heifer sacrifice, the ashes of which were mixed with spring water and sprinkled upon people to purify them from certain types of ritual defilement. The ceremony can only be performed by a member of the hereditary priesthood. Rabbi Akiva suggested that just as it would be inappropriate for someone who is not a member of the hereditary priesthood to criticize the validity of a priest's performance of the ceremony, so Rabban Gamliel, whose ancestors had presided over the Sanhedrin for generations, should now serve as its head.[296]]

Rabbi Elazar ben Azariah replied, "You have reconciled? Let us hasten to the entrance of Rabban Gamliel's home to reinstate him!"

Even so, they did not lower Rabbi Elazar ben Azariah entirely from his position. Rather they appointed him vice-president of the Sanhedrin.

How could Rabbi Joshua deny that he had said that the evening prayer is optional? Surely he did not mean to lie, God forbid. Tosafoth explains that the term "optional," as used here, does not mean that there is not obligation whatsoever to recite the evening prayer. Rather, it is optional in the sense that if one is faced with the choice of performing another mitzvah or reciting the evening prayer, one should perform the other mitzvah. Likewise, if one forgot to say the evening

---

[296] P'nei Moshe.

prayer and went to bed, he need not get up to say it. However, to omit recitation of the evening prayer for no particular reason is not permitted.[297] *This means that Rabbi Joshua could legitimately offer two different responses to the question without being inconsistent because in one sense the prayer is optional while in another sense it is obligatory.*[298]

As another solution to the above question, Etz Yosef suggests that Rabbi Joshua merely denied contradicting Rabban Gamliel out of respect for the latter.[299] *Such action would be comparable to that of the angel who read Sarah's thoughts that she could not bear children because "my husband is old."*[300] *When the angel repeated this to Abraham, he quoted Sarah as saying, "because I am old"*[301] *to preserve family harmony.*[302]

One way or another, Rabban Gamliel must have understood Rabbi Joshua's good intentions. Why, then, did he mistreat Rabbi Joshua in the first place? The Babylonian Talmud recounts how Rabban Gamliel refused admission to the yeshiva to any scholar who was in any way insincere ("his inside is not like his outside"). That is one reason why so many additional students came to the study hall after the appointment of Rabbi Elazar ben Azariah when standards were

---

[297] Tosafoth on B.T. Brachoth 26A sub verba "Ta'ah VeLo" (טעה ולא) and on Chagigah 9A sub verba "Oh Tefillah" (או תפילה).

[298] Ben Yehoyada on B.T. Brachoth 27B.

[299] Etz Yosef on B.T. Brachoth 27B in Ein Yaakov.

[300] Genesis 18:12.

[301] Genesis 18:13.

[302] Rashi on Genesis 18:13.

relaxed.[303] *Because he detested any form of hypocrisy, Rabban Gamliel felt his actions were justified even though he knew Rabbi Joshua had acted properly in responding as he did.*

It is fashionable in certain circles to suggest that the Jewish religion is "undemocratic" or "anti-democratic." It is true that the Torah provides for religious decisions to be made only by qualified scholars, not by a plebiscite. However, as the instant passage demonstrates, this does not mean that the Torah approves tyranny.

The Rambam rules that a son is entitled to inherit his father's position as king only if he possesses fear of Heaven and is otherwise qualified.[304] *A Jewish king is also subject to numerous restrictions. Thus, for example, the Rambam writes that "The king is forbidden to drink in the manner that leads to drunkenness...rather he should occupy himself with Torah and the needs of Israel day and night... ."*[305] *In addition, "One who sets aside the king's command because he is occupied with a Mitzvah, even a minor Mitzvah, is exempt [from punishment by the king]."*[306]

Along these lines, one finds the Talmud describing the functioning of town meetings and elected town councils.[307] *Likewise, prior to appointing Bezalel to design the Tabernacle and its utensils, God instructed Moses to make sure that the people approved this selection, thereby demonstrating that*

---

[303] B.T. Brachoth 28A.
[304] Yad HaChazakah, Hilchoth Melachim 1:7.
[305] Yad HaChazakah, Hilchoth Melachim 3:5.
[306] Yad HaChazakah, Hilchoth Melachim 3:9.
[307] B.T. Megillah 26A-27A.

Jewish leaders must be subject to popular approval.[308] *Rabbi Don Isaac Abravanel goes so far as to suggest that the Torah does not require the Jewish people to appoint a king at all. Provisions for the same were only set forth in the event the Jewish people insist they want a king. Ideally, a Jewish society should function along purely Torah-directed democratic lines.*[309]

However, if one's pays close attention to Rabban Gamliel's behavior, one sees that the passage under consideration goes much further than condemning tyranny. Rabban Gamliel had close political connections with the Roman rulers of the Land of Israel.[310] *He could easily have turned to them for help to put down the "rebellion" during which he was deposed. In the version of this story found in the Babylonian Talmud, Rabbi Akiva indeed expresses concern that the servants of Rabban Gamliel might try to harass the other rabbis.*[311] *However, nothing of the kind occurred. To the contrary, the Babylonian Talmud reports that Rabban Gamliel continued to attend the sessions of the Sanhedrin.*[312] *Even more startling, he apologized to Rabbi Joshua for his behavior!*

The Mishnah identifies the ability to admit the truth as one of the signs which identifies a true sage.[313] *Moreover, this*

---

[308] B.T. Brachoth 55A.
[309] Don Isaac Abravanel on Deuteronomy 17:14.
[310] Ediyuoth 7:7.
[311] B.T. Brachoth 28A.
[312] B.T. Brachoth 28A.
[313] Pirkei Avoth 5:7.

is a sign of true leadership. Judah condemned his daughter-in-law, Tamar, to death when he thought she had become pregnant illicitly. When she confronted him with evidence that he himself had caused the pregnancy, the Torah says, "Judah recognized [the evidence] and said, 'She is more righteous than I am... .'"[314] It was just this willingness to confess wrongdoing and set things right that earned Judah the distinction of being the forebear of all later Jewish kings.[315] One sees this trait in Judah's descendant, King David, who admitted wrongdoing in the case of Bathsheva and repented.[316]

Rabban Gamliel himself was a scion of the royal House of David.[317] When one considers how many rulers throughout history have ruthlessly clung to power using any means at their disposal including brutal violence, the contrast is striking. Even in today's democratic societies when politicians resign in the face of scandal, it is rare to find one who actually admits wrongdoing. By extreme contrast, Rabban Gamliel never lost sight of the fact that his function was solely to serve God and the Jewish people.

One might wonder why Rabban Gamliel and Rabbi Joshua, according to one opinion, sent a launderer with a message for Rabbi Elazar ben Aazariah at a time when the

---

[314] Genesis 38:26.
[315] Rashi on B.T. Sotah 7B sub verba "Lahem L'vadam Nitna" (להם לבדם נתנה). (Rashi may have had a different text of the Tosefta on Brachoth than the one extant today.)
[316] II Samuel 12:13.
[317] Breishith Rabbah 98:8 states that Hillel the Elder was a descendant of King David. Rabban Gamliel was Hillel's great great grandson.

relationship among the rabbis was so strained. One would think that this would compound the tension by implying an insult to the Sanhedrin. The answer may be that many sages were not "professional rabbis." Rather, they engaged in various trades to support themselves. Thus, in this very passage one finds that Rabbi Joshua was a needlemaker. Perhaps the launderer referred to here was a younger student who practiced a trade as well as studying. It may have been customary to use such younger students as messengers for the more senior rabbis.

On a deeper level, according to Jewish tradition, great wisemen have often communicated with each other by means of hints. For example, the Torah says that when Jacob saw the wagons Joseph sent from Egypt, his spirit was revived.[318] Jacob's sons had already informed him that Joseph was still alive. Why was it that Jacob's spirit was not revived before seeing the wagons? Rashi explains that when Joseph left his father many years before, the two had been studying the laws of the calf whose neck is broken (עגלה ערופה).[319] The Hebrew word for "wagons" is "agaloth" (עגלות), similar to the word for "calf" (עגלה). By referring to the section of the Torah they were studying before Joseph's disappearance, Joseph hinted that just as he had been a conscientious Jew when studying the laws of the Torah under the tutelage of his illustrious father, so

---

[318] Genesis 45:27.

[319] This is a ceremony performed when a corpse is found near a city. See Deuteronomy 21:1-9.

he had remained righteous and faithful to the Torah in Egypt. Jacob understood this hint and it revived his spirit.[320]

The Mishnah quotes Rabban Gamliel's son as saying that, although it is permitted to give laundry to a non-Jewish launderer immediately before the Sabbath, Rabban Gamliel had the strict custom to turn in white garments three days in advance to avoid the appearance that he had ordered the non-Jew to work on the Sabbath.[321] *Sending a launderer to Rabbi Elazar ben Azariah might have hinted at Rabban Gamliel's willingness to go beyond the letter of the law and that his actions were based on his sincere opposition to any type of hypocrisy as noted above. For this reason, he deserved reinstatement.*

---

[320] Rashi on Genesis 45:27.
[321] Shabbath 1:9 as understood by Tosafoth on B.T. Avodah Zarah 21B sub verba "Mai Ta'ama" (טעמא מאי).

Brachoth 4:3 (Compare B.T. Brachoth 28B-29A and B.T. Rosh HaShanah 32A)

מתניתין: רבן גמליאל אומר: בכל יום אדם מתפלל שמונה
עשרה. ורבי יהושע אומר: מעין שמונה עשרה. רבי עקיבא אומר: אם
שגורה תפלתו בפיו, יתפלל שמונה עשרה, ואם לאו, מעין שמונה
עשרה.

גמרא: ולמה שמונה עשרה? אמר רבי יהושע בן לוי: כנגד
שמונה עשרה מזמורים שכתוב מראשו של תילים עד "יַעַנְךָ ה' בְּיוֹם צָרָה
[יְשַׂגֶּבְךָ שֵׁם אֱ-לֹהֵי יַעֲקֹב]." (תהלים כ:ב). אם יאמר לך אדם, "תשע
עשרה הן," אֱמוֹר לוֹ, "לָמָּה רָגְשׁוּ גוֹיִם [וּלְאֻמִּים יֶהְגּוּ רִיק]" (תהלים ב:א)
לית הוא מינהון."

מכאן אמרו: המתפלל ולא נענה צריך תענית.

אמר רבי מנא: רמז לתלמידי חכמים, שאדם צריך לומר לרבו,
"תשמע תפילתך."

אמר רבי סימון: כנגד י"ח חוליות שבשדרה, שבשעה שאדם
עומד ומתפלל צריך לשוח בכולן. מה טעם? "כָּל עַצְמוֹתַי תֹּאמַרְנָה ה'
מִי כָמוֹךָ ... ." (תהלים לה:י).

אמר רבי לוי: כנגד י"ח אזכרות שכתוב ב"[מִזְמוֹר לְדָוִד] הָבוּ
לה' בְּנֵי אֵלִים [הָבוּ לה' כָּבוֹד וָעֹז.]" (תהלים כט:א).

אמר רבי הונה: אם יאמר לך אדם, "תשע עשרה אינון," [בגרסת
דפוס ויניציה "שבע עשרה אינון"] אֱמוֹר לוֹ, "של מינים כבר קבעו
חכמים ביבנה."

התיב רבי אליעזר בר רבי יוסי קומי רבי יוסי: והא כתיב, "...אֵ-ל
הַכָּבוֹד הִרְעִים..." (תהלים כט:ג)! אמר ליה: והתני: "כולל של מינים ושל
פושעים ב'מכניע זדים,' ושל זקנים ושל גרים ב'מבטח לצדיקים,' ושל
דוד ב'בונה ירושלים.'" אית לך מספקא לכל חדא וחדא מנהו אדכרה.

רבי חנינא בשם רבי פנחס: כנגד י"ח פעמים שאבות כתובים
בתורה; אברהם יצחק יעקב. אם יאמר לך אדם, "י"ט הם," אֱמוֹר לוֹ,
"וְהִנֵּה ה' נִצָּב עָלָיו [וַיֹּאמַר אֲנִי ה' אֱ-לֹהֵי אַבְרָהָם אָבִיךָ וֵא-לֹהֵי יִצְחָק

הָאָרֶץ אֲשֶׁר אַתָּה שֹׁכֵב עָלֶיהָ לְךָ אֶתְּנֶנָּה וּלְזַרְעֶךָ]" (בראשית כח:יג) לֵית
הוּא מִינַהוֹן. אִם יֹאמֶר לָךָ אָדָם, "י" ז הם," אֱמוֹר לוֹ, "[הַמַּלְאָךְ הַגֹּאֵל אֹתִי
מִכָּל רָע יְבָרֵךְ אֶת הַנְּעָרִים] וְיִקָּרֵא בָהֶם שְׁמִי וְשֵׁם אֲבֹתַי אַבְרָהָם וְיִצְחָק
[וְיִדְגּוּ לָרֹב בְּקֶרֶב הָאָרֶץ]" (בראשית מח:טז) מִינַהוֹן.

רבי שמואל בר נחמני בשם רבי יוחנן: כנגד י"ח ציווייין שכתוב
בפרשת משכן שני. אמר רבי חייא בר ווא: ובלבד מן, "...אֶתּוֹ אֵת
אָהֳלִיאָב בֶּן אֲחִיסָמָךְ לְמַטֵּה דָן..." (שמות לא:ו) עד סופיה דסיפרא.

שבע של שבת מניין? אמר רבי יצחק: כנגד ז' קולות שכתוב
ב,"[מִזְמוֹר לְדָוִד] הָבוּ לה' בְּנֵי אֵלִים..." (תהלים כט:א).

אמר רבי יודן אנתוריא: כנגד שבע אזכרות שכתוב ב"מִזְמוֹר
שִׁיר לְיוֹם הַשַּׁבָּת." (תהלים צב:א).

תשע של ראש השנה מניין? אמר רבי אבא קרטוגנא: כנגד
תשע אזכרות שכתוב בפרשת חנה, וכתיב בסופה "...ה' יָדִין אַפְסֵי אָרֶץ..."
(שמואל א ב:י).

כ"ד של תעניות מניין? רבי חלבו ורבי שמעון בר רב נחמן,
תרווייהון אמרין: כנגד כ"ד פעמים שכתוב בפרשה של שלמה "רינה"
ו"תפילה" ו"תחינה."

**Mishnah: Rabban Gamliel says, "Each day a person
should pray the eighteen benedictions [of the silent prayer
(עמידה) ordained by the ancient rabbis]," whereas Rabbi
Joshua says, "A prayer similar to the eighteen benedictions
[in abbreviated form is also permissible]." Rabbi Akiva
says, "If one can pray fluently, one should recite the
eighteen benedictions, and if not, a prayer similar to the
eighteen benedictions."[322]**

---

[322] Shulchan Aruch 110:1 rules according to Rabbi Akiva.

Gemara: Why did the sages choose eighteen? Rabbi Joshua ben Levi says: Corresponding to the eighteen chapters from the beginning of the Book of Psalms until "May the Lord answer you in the day of trouble; may the Name of the God of Jacob uplift you."[323] If someone will point out to you that there are nineteen chapters before that verse, tell him that the chapter commencing, "Why have nations become agitated and peoples uttered folly?"[324] is not included. [The first two chapters of the Book of Psalms should really be counted as only one.]

Based on this, people say that one who prays but is not answered should fast. [The verse, "May God answer you in the day of trouble...,"[325] written after the first eighteen chapters of the Psalms implies that if one is not answered after reciting the eighteen benedictions of the silent prayer, one should "trouble" oneself by fasting.[326]]

Rabbi Manna says: This verse hints at scholars, teaching that a man should say to his rabbi, "May your prayer be heard."

Rabbi Simon says: The eighteen benedictions correspond to the eighteen vertebrae which are in the spine for at the time when one stands and prays, one should bend all of them. What is the Scriptural basis for this? "All my bones say, 'Lord who is like You?'... ."[327]

Rabbi Levi says: They correspond to the eighteen references to the Tetragrammaton written in the chapter, "A

---

[323] Psalms 20:2.
[324] Psalms 2:1.
[325] Psalms 20:2.
[326] Perush M'Ba'al Sefer Chareidim.
[327] Psalms 35:10.

Psalm of David: Render [praise] unto the Lord, sons of the mighty; render unto the Lord honor and strength."[328]

Rabbi Huna said: If someone will say to you that there are only seventeen benedictions in the daily prayer, tell him that the one for heretics was already established [by the Sanhedrin] at Yavneh.

Rabbi Eliezer bar Rabbi Yossi raised an objection before Rabbi Yossi: But it is written, "...the God of glory thundered... ."[329] [This phrase does not employ the Tetragrammaton, but refers to God (א-ל), so the silent prayer should have nineteen benedictions, not eighteen.] He answered: Have we not learned: One includes the heretics and sinners in the one benediction which refers to "He who subjugates the wicked," and one includes elders and converts in the benediction which refers to "the Refuge of the righteous," and one includes that of David in the benediction which refers to "Who builds Jerusalem."[330] Thus you have enough references to the Tetragrammaton for each of them.[331]

Rabbi Chanina said in the name of Rabbi Phinehas: The benedictions of the silent prayer correspond to the eighteen times the forefathers Abraham, Isaac and Jacob are written together in the Torah. If someone will say to you that there are nineteen such references, tell him that "Behold the Lord stood by him and said, "I am the Lord, God of Abraham your father

---

[328] Psalms 29:1.
[329] Psalms 29:3.
[330] Tosefta Brachoth 3:25.
[331] See commentary below for a full explanation of this passage.

and God of Isaac. The land upon which you lie I shall give to you and your seed,'"[332] is not included [for although it was addressed to Jacob, it does not mention his name.[333]] If someone will say to you that there are but seventeen such references, tell him that the verse, "The angel which redeemed me from all evil shall bless the youths and my name shall be called upon them and the names of my fathers, Abraham and Isaac, and they shall flourish greatly in the midst of the earth,"[334] is included among them. [Since Jacob refers to his name as being called upon Ephraim and Menashe, it is as though it were explicitly stated in the verse.[335]]

Rabbi Samuel bar Nachmeni said in the name of Rabbi Yochanan: They correspond to the eighteen commands written in the second passage of the Torah which deals with the Tabernacle. Rabbi Chiya bar Vava said: One should only count from, "...with him Oholiab son of Ahisamach of the tribe of Dan..."[336] until the end of the book of Exodus.

From where do the seven benedictions of the Sabbath prayer derive? Rabbi Isaac said: They correspond to the seven "voices" written in "A Psalm of David: Render [praise] unto the Lord, sons of the mighty; render unto the Lord honor and

---

[332] Genesis 28:13.
[333] P'nei Moshe.
[334] Genesis 48:16.
[335] P'nei Moshe.
[336] Exodus 31:6.

strength."[337]   [E.g., "The voice of the Lord is upon the water... ."[338]]

Rabbi Yudan of Antoria said: They correspond to the seven references to the Tetragrammaton written in "A chapter of song for the Sabbath day."[339]

From where do the nine benedictions of the Rosh HaShanah prayer derive? Rabbi Abba of Carthage said: They correspond to the nine references to the Tetragrammaton written in the section of the Prophets dealing with Hannah at the end of which is written, "...the Lord judges the ends of the earth..."[340] [alluding to Rosh HaShanah which is a day of judgment].[341]

From where do the twenty-four benedictions of fast day prayers derive?[342] Rabbi Chelbo and Rabbi Simon bar Rabbi Nachman both said: They correspond to the twenty-four times the expressions "song," "prayer," and "supplication" are written in the section of the Prophets dealing with King Solomon.

The Babylonian Talmud asks what the "prayer similar to the eighteen benedictions" mentioned in the Mishnah is?

---

[337] Psalms 29:1.
[338] Psalms 29:3.
[339] Psalms 92:1.
[340] I Samuel 2:10.
[341] Pesikta Rabbathai 46:1 states that God "remembered" Hannah on Rosh HaShanah by granting her prayer that she become pregnant.
[342] When the rabbis decreed certain special fasts in Talmudic times, they added on to the eighteen standard benedictions. See Ta'anith 2:2.

Samuel explains that it means reciting the first three benedictions in their entirety, then reciting a formula which incorporates all thirteen middle benedictions in abbreviated form, and finishing by reciting the last three benedictions in their entirety.[343]

Rabbi Yochanan and Resh Lakish taught that "Whoever makes an unnecessary blessing transgresses, 'You shall not take the name of the Lord your God in vain...   .'"[344] *Accordingly, the editors of the Talmud thought it important to explain why the ancient rabbis ordained eighteen separate blessings instead of simply combining the middle ones as the Mishnah suggests might be possible. Likewise, on the Sabbath or Rosh HaShanah, the middle blessing could be incorporated into the benediction "May You be pleased" (רצה) just as is done for the blessing for the New Month (ראש חדש) and intermediate festival days. Thus, the sages offered several explanations as to why separate blessings were necessary.*[345]

Rabbi Aryeh Leib Gordon cites many classic Jewish texts which ascribe additional symbolism to having eighteen benedictions in the silent prayer aside from what is set forth in this passage.[346] *Thus, the Babylonian Talmud offers a lengthy explanation for the benedictions which blends Scriptural*

---

[343]   B.T. Brachoth 29A.   Rav offers a different explanation, but the halachah accords with Samuel.

[344]   Exodus 20:7; B.T. Brachoth 33A.

[345]   P'nei Yehoshua on B.T. Brachoth 29A makes this last point.

[346]   Rabbi Aryeh Leib Gordon in Tikun Tefillah found in Otzar HaTefilloth, Volume I, pages 306-312.

proofs with an elucidation of their logical progression.[347] *For instance, the phrase "Render [praise] unto the Lord, sons of the mighty"*[348] *provides a Scriptural basis for the first benediction which mentions Abraham, Isaac and Jacob because "sons of the mighty" refers to the Patriarchs. The positioning of the eighth blessing which refers to healing is symbolically appropriate because baby boys are circumcised when they are eight days old and require healing.*

The Midrash also offers an extensive homily linking various historical events to each of the eighteen blessings. For example, when Abraham was saved during his war with the four kings,[349] *the ministering angels uttered the first one: "Blessed are You Lord Who shields Abraham." When Isaac was spared from being sacrificed by his father,*[350] *he said, "Blessed are You Lord Who revives the dead."*[351]

To properly understand the passage of the Jerusalem Talmud under review, one must know a little about the history of the silent prayer (עמידה). The Gemara explains that the one hundred twenty Men of the Great Assembly, among whom were several prophets, formulated the eighteen benedictions of the silent prayer.[352] *The blessing which contains a petition to*

---

[347] B.T. Megillah 17B-18A.
[348] Psalms 29:1. This is a literal translation of בני אלים which can also be rendered simply "mighty men" or "noble men."
[349] Genesis 14:1-16.
[350] Genesis 22:1-19.
[351] Pirkei D'Rabbi Eliezer, chapter 27.
[352] B.T. Megillah 17B-18A. The precise order of the blessings became forgotten over time and was re-established by Rabbi Shimon HaPakuli

eliminate heretics and evildoers is also of ancient origin, but was not part of the standard form of prayer. Instead, it was used only at times when heretics persecuted loyal Jews just as nowadays the blessing "Who answers at the time of trouble" (הָעוֹנֶה בְּעֵת צָרָה) is added only on fast days. Due to the infrequency of its use, the Talmud records how, at one point, Rabban Gamliel had to inquire as to whom among the sages knew or could figure out the correct formulation of this blessing. Apparently, the benediction still did not become a standard part of the silent prayer because the following year Rabban Gamliel could not remember its formulation, something he certainly would have been able to do if he had been reciting it in the interim.[353]

When the sages finally established the blessing concerning heretics as a standard part of the Amidah to be recited as an additional blessing together with all the others, the rabbis living in Babylonia retained all eighteen original benedictions so that the number became nineteen. They found support for this innovation in a number of ways.[354] *By contrast, the rabbis living in the Land of Israel reformulated the silent prayer in order to maintain the number of blessings at eighteen because that number alludes to so many important concepts. Accordingly, they combined the blessing which refers to King David and the Messiah (אֶת צֶמַח דָּוִד) with the one*

---

around 100 C.E.
[353] B.T. Brachoth 28B-29A. Rabbi Aryeh Leib Gordon in Tikun Tefillah found in Otzar HaTefilloth, Volume I, pages 306-312 offers other evidence of the ancient origin of this blessing.
[354] B.T. Brachoth 28B.

Torah from Jerusalem

which refers to building Jerusalem (בונה ירושלים) resulting in a blessing which concluded "God of David and Builder of Jerusalem" (א-לוהי דוד ובונה ירושלים). Together with the blessing concerning heretics, the total number remained eighteen.[355]

This makes the text under consideration clear. Rabbi Huna says that if anyone will object that there are only seventeen blessings in the silent prayer because two blessings have been combined into one and the one for heretics is not really counted, the answer is that the one for heretics does indeed count now that it has been incorporated into the standard form of prayer. Rabbi Eliezer bar Rabbi Yossi then objected that the phrase "...the God of glory thundered... ."[356] justifies the addition of a nineteenth benediction and supports the usage of the Babylonian rabbis whose formulation of the silent prayer had nineteen blessings. The Talmud responds that a Tosefta authorizes the combination of similar concepts in the same benediction, including combining the blessing which refers to King David (את צמח דוד) with the one which refers to building Jerusalem (בונה ירושלים). It is not necessary to justify an additional nineteenth blessing because the number can remain eighteen. This Tosefta represents the view of the rabbis of the Land of Israel who kept the number of blessings in the silent prayer at eighteen. Of course, the normative

---

355 Rabbi Aryeh Leib Gordon in Tikun Tefillah found in Otzar HaTefilloth, Volume I, pages 306-312.
356 Psalms 29:3.

halachah practiced by all Jews today follows the view of the Babylonian school.

Of all the allusions cited by the passage under consideration, perhaps the most easily understandable one is that which refers to the ancient forefathers. According to the view that it was they who ordained the three daily prayers, it makes sense for the eighteen benedictions to correspond to eighteen references to them in the Tanach. Surely the merit of the illustrious forebears of the Jewish nation helps make prayer efficacious. Still, why was eighteen considered such an important number? What do the other allusions mean?

The Midrash explains that Hashem offered the Torah to other nations. However, each one wanted to know what the Torah required. When God told them, the people of each nation pointed to some aspect of the Torah which they felt incapable of observing. For example, when God told the descendants of Esau that the Torah says, "You shall not murder,"[357] they objected that Isaac blessed their ancestor Esau telling him, "By your sword shall you live... ."[358] Similarly, Hashem explained to the descendants of Ishmael that the Torah commands, "You shall not steal."[359] They responded that God had told Abraham that Ishmael would be "...a wild man, his hand against all and the hand of all against him... ."[360] A similar dialog took place with all the other

---

[357] Exodus 20:13.
[358] Genesis 27:40.
[359] Exodus 20:13.
[360] Genesis 16:12.

nations of the world. Each refused to accept the Torah, for to do otherwise would have meant acting contrary to their national consciousness.[361] *Not so Israel! The Torah says, "And he [Moses] took the Book of the Covenant and read it in the hearing of the people, and they said, 'All that the Lord has said we will do and we will understand.'"*[362] *The people were so strong in their faith and so willing to serve Hashem that they undertook to obey all the laws of the Torah first and hold off inquiring into their details until later.*

The Midrash teaches that the Psalm which commences "A Psalm of David: Render [praise] unto the Lord, sons of the mighty; render unto the Lord honor and strength"[363] *describes the Giving of the Torah.*[364] *Thus, the Psalm uses the term "the voice of the Lord" seven times, referring to the "voice" which gave the Torah. By ordaining a prayer formulation which alludes to this Psalm, the rabbis meant to call to the mind of the worshiper the Giving of the Torah. That way, when one prays, he will strive to engender in himself the strong and enduring faith that filled the hearts of those Jews who received the Torah. Lest one think it impossible to attain this lofty goal, one should bear in mind the Midrashic teaching that the souls of all Jews who would ever live were present at the Giving of the Torah. One need only reach deep within himself or herself to unlock the source of such faith.*[365]

---

361 Sifrei on Deuteronomy 33:2.
362 Exodus 24:7.
363 Psalms 29:1.
364 Yalkut Shimoni on Psalms 29.
365 Tanchuma 3 on Deuteronomy (referring to Deuteronomy 29:14).

Furthermore, just as receiving the Torah required three days of preparation,[366] so prayer requires proper preparation. The Mishnah goes so far as to say that pious people of old used to spend an hour preparing for each prayer.[367] Preparation for prayer also takes place today because we recite blessings and Psalms before reciting the silent prayer.

That the eighteen benedictions correspond to eighteen commands for building the Tabernacle also reflects this idea. One cannot offer a sacrifice in just any old way. Rather, one must offer sacrifices in a Tabernacle, the structure and dimensions of which are precisely prepared in advance. So too, proper prayer requires preparation so that the worshiper will approach the service with the proper frame of mind.

As noted earlier, one's attitude at the time of prayer should be one of submission to Hashem's will and faith in Him. Just as the Jews accepted the Torah on faith without knowing the details of their undertaking, much less understanding why God commanded them to obey any of the laws of the Torah, so the supplicant today must place full trust in Hashem. The fact that one should bow his or her body during prayer using the eighteen vertebrae of the back echoes this idea of submission. Moreover, as pointed out above, the Patriarchs epitomized the concept of utter submission to God's will. Accordingly, the eighteen blessings also correspond to the eighteen times that all three are mentioned together in the Torah.

---

[366] Exodus 19:10-11.
[367] B.T. Brachoth 5:1.

The Mishnah teaches that eighteen is the ideal age for marriage.[368] *Thus, the number eighteen may allude to the concept that one's commitment to God during prayer should rise to the level of his or her commitment to a spouse in marriage. Similarly, when one wraps the Tefillin straps around his middle finger before commencing the morning prayers, he repeats the verses, "You are betrothed to me forever; you are betrothed to me in righteousness and justice, in kindness and in mercy. You are betrothed to me in faith and you shall know the Lord."*[369] *When a person marries, he or she has no idea exactly how things will work out. The prospective bride and groom only know that they admire many positive traits in one another. Based on that, each partner to a marriage has faith that the marriage will succeed. The Jewish people exercised the same faith at the Giving of the Torah and it is this type of faith one must try to have during prayer.*

One can also learn from the passage under consideration that everyone can accomplish something with prayer. One should not worry that he or she does not have a lofty spiritual level. The Torah was given publicly in the presence of all Jews great and small, young and old. All the other nations of the world heard about it as well.[370] *Prayer, too, can be meaningful and effective for every human being whether highly intelligent or of modest ability, whether exceedingly pious or not.*

---

[368] Pirkei Avoth 5:21.
[369] Hosea 2:21-22.
[370] Yalkut Shimoni on Psalms 29.

The number eighteen itself alludes to this concept. The word Chai (חי) in Hebrew means "life" and has a numerical value of eighteen. The Talmud teaches that Chai (חי) refers to the righteous who are considered "alive" even after death.[371] *If one who is dead and departed from the world can still be considered alive, then one should surely not think that Hashem will not recognize or accept one's prayers merely because he or she occupies a low spiritual status. The rabbis incorporated all kinds of secret meanings into the prayer formula so that anyone who recites it resembles a completely righteous person whose prayers can be heard.*

---

[371] B.T. Brachoth 18A-B.

Brachoth 4:4

רבי יסא, רבי חלבו, רבי ברכיה, רבי חלבו מטי בה בשם רבי
אבדומה דמן חיפא: צריך אדם להסב פניו לכותל להתפלל. מה טעם?
"וַיַּסֵּב אֶת פָּנָיו אֶל הַקִּיר [וַיִּתְפַּלֵּל אֶל ה']..." (מלכים ב כ:ב). באיזה קיר
נשא עיניו? רבי יהושע בן לוי אמר: בקיר של רחב נשא עיניו. "...כִּי
בֵיתָהּ בְּקִיר הַחוֹמָה..." (יהושע ב:טו). אמר לפניו, "רבונו של עולם, רחב
הזונה, שתי נפשות הצילה לך. ראה כמה נפשות הצלת להו!" הדא היא
דכתיב, "וַיָּבֹאוּ הַנְּעָרִים [הַמְרַגְּלִים וַיֹּצִיאוּ אֶת רָחָב וְאֶת אָבִיהָ וְאֶת אִמָּהּ
וְאֶת אַחֶיהָ וְאֶת כָּל אֲשֶׁר לָהּ וְאֵת כָּל מִשְׁפְּחוֹתֶיהָ הוֹצִיאוּ...]" (יהושע
ו:כג).

תני רבי שמעון בן יוחי: אפילו היתה במשפחתה מאתים אנשים
והלכו ודבקו במאתים משפחות, כולהם ניצולו בזכותה. אבותי שקירבו
לך כל הגרים האילו, על אחת כמה וכמה.

רבי חיננא בר פפא אמר: בקירות בית המקדש נשא עיניו.
"[וַיֹּאמֶר אֵלַי בֶּן אָדָם אֶת מְקוֹם כִּסְאִי וְאֶת מְקוֹם כַּפּוֹת רַגְלַי אֲשֶׁר אֶשְׁכָּן
שָׁם בְּתוֹךְ בְּנֵי יִשְׂרָאֵל לְעוֹלָם וְלֹא יְטַמְּאוּ עוֹד בֵּית יִשְׂרָאֵל שֵׁם קָדְשִׁי הֵמָּה
וּמַלְכֵיהֶם בִּזְנוּתָם וּבְפִגְרֵי מַלְכֵיהֶם בָּמוֹתָם.] בְּתִתָּם סִפָּם אֶת סִפִּי וּמְזוּזָתָם
אֵצֶל מְזוּזָתִי וְהַקִּיר בֵּינִי וּבֵינֵיהֶם [וְטִמְּאוּ אֶת שֵׁם קָדְשִׁי בְּתוֹעֲבוֹתָם אֲשֶׁר
עָשׂוּ וָאֲכַל אֹתָם בְּאַפִּי]" (יחזקאל מג:ז-ח). בני אדם גדולים היו ולא היו
יכולין לעלות ולהתפלל בבית המקדש בכל שעה, והיו מתפללין בתוך
בתיהם. והקדוש ברוך הוא מעלה עליהם כאילו מתפללין בבית המקדש.
אבותי שעשו לך את כל השבח הזה, על אחת כמה וכמה.

רבי שמואל בר נחמן אמר: בקירה של שונמית נשא עיניו
שנאמר, "וַתֹּאמֶר אֶל אִישָׁהּ הִנֵּה נָא יָדַעְתִּי כִּי אִישׁ אֱ-לֹהִים קָדוֹשׁ הוּא
עֹבֵר עָלֵינוּ תָּמִיד.] נַעֲשֶׂה נָּא עֲלִיַּת קִיר קְטַנָּה [וְנָשִׂים לוֹ שָׁם מִטָּה וְשֻׁלְחָן
וְכִסֵּא וּמְנוֹרָה וְהָיָה בְּבֹאוֹ אֵלֵינוּ יָסוּר שָׁמָּה.]" (מלכים ב ד:ט-י). אמר
לפניו, "רבונו של עולם, השונמית קיר אחת עשתה לאלישע והחיית את
בנה. אבותי שעשו לך את כל השבח הזה, על אחת כמה וכמה תתן לי
נפשי!"

148

ורבנן אמרי: בקירות לבו נשא עיניו. "מֵעַי מֵעַי אֹוחִילָה [אוֹחִילָה
קרי] קִירוֹת לִבִּי הֹמֶה לִי...." (ירמיה ד:יט). אמר לפניו, "רבונו של עולם,
חיזרתי על רמ"ח איברים שנתת בי ולא מצאתי שהכעסתיך באחת מהן.
על אחת כמה וכמה תינתן לי נפשי!"

Rabbi Yassa, Rabbi Chelbo, Rabbi Berachia and Rabbi
Chelbo of Tova[372] stated in the name of Rabbi Avdumeh from
Haifa: A person should turn his face to the wall to pray. What
is the Scriptural basis for this? "[King Hezekiah] turned his
face to the wall and prayed to the Lord... ."[373] To which wall
did he lift his eyes? Rabbi Joshua Ben Levi said: To the wall
of Rahav he lifted his eyes "...because her house was in the
wall of the city... ."[374] King Hezekiah said, "Master of the
Universe, because Rahav the harlot saved two lives for You,
see how many lives you saved for her." Thus it is written, "The
young men who were spies came and took out Rahav and her
father and her mother and her siblings and all that was hers and
all her families they took out... ."[375] Rabbi Shimon bar Yochai
taught: Even if she had two hundred people in her family who
went and married into two hundred other families, all were
saved in her merit. King Hezekiah continued, "My ancestors
who brought near to You all these converts, how much more so
should You save my life!" [The reference is to King Solomon

---

372 This is the correct version of the text according to Perush MiBa'al
Sefer Chareidim.
373 II Kings 20:2.
374 Joshua 2:15.
375 Joshua 6:23.

149

who converted one hundred fifty thousand non-Jewish workers when he built the First Temple.[376]

Rabbi Chinana bar Papa said: To the walls of the Temple he lifted his eyes as Scripture says, "And He said to me, 'Son of man [you have seen] the place of My throne and the place of the soles of My feet where I shall dwell in the midst of the Children of Israel forever and the Children of Israel shall no longer defile My holy name, they or their kings with their debauchery and with the corpses of their kings at their death by placing their threshold near My threshold and their doorpost near My doorpost with but a wall between Me and between them and they defile My holy name with their abominations which they have done and I have consumed them in My wrath."[377] These were great men who could not always ascend to pray in the Temple so they would pray in their homes and the Holy One, Blessed be He, considered it as though they prayed in the Temple. Because my ancestors made all this honor for You, how much more so should You heed my prayers. [Although the verse refers to wicked people, God did credit them for initially trying to draw close to Him by placing their palaces near the Temple. If He viewed even wicked people so favorably, how much more so should He favor King Hezekiah whose righteous ancestor King Solomon built the Temple.[378]]

---

[376] P'nei Moshe citing I Kings 5:29 and B.T. Yevamoth 79A.
[377] Ezekiel 43:7-8. Rashi explains that the kings built their palaces close to the Temple.
[378] Korban Ha'Eidah (Rabbi David Fraenkel of Berlin) on J.T. Sanhedrin 10:2.

Rabbi Samuel bar Nachman said: To the wall of the Shunamite woman he lifted his eyes as the verse says, "She said to her husband, 'Behold, now I know that he [Elisha] is a holy man of God who continually visits to us. Let us now make a small attic in the wall and place for him there a bed and a table and a chair and a lamp; and it will be when he comes to us, he may turn in there.'"[379] King Hezekiah said, "Master of the Universe, the Shunamite woman made but one wall for Elisha and You miraculously resuscitated her son [when he died]. Because my ancestors made all this honor for You, how much more so should You spare my life."

The rabbis say: To the walls of his heart he lifted his eyes as the verse says, "My innards! My innards! I tremble! The walls of my heart reverberate within me... ."[380] King Hezekiah said, "Master of the Universe, I have analyzed the two hundred forty-eight limbs You fixed in me and do not find that I have vexed You with any of them, so how much more so should You spare my life." [Had I served You properly only with the majority of my limbs, it would have been fitting for You to save my life. This is even more the case when I have served You perfectly with all my limbs.[381]]

The halachah is that one should try to pray next to a wall without any other objects in front of him so as to avoid

---

[379] II Kings 4:9-10.
[380] Jeremiah 4:19.
[381] Korban Ha'Eidah on J.T. Sanhedrin 10:2.

distractions.[382] *However, if that is merely the standard form of prayer, then King Hezekiah did nothing unique and there would be no particular reason for the verse to mention this point. Moreover, there would be no special reason for God to respond favorably. This may explain why the sages of the Talmud offer homiletic interpretations of King Hezekiah's "turning his face to the wall."*[383]

The Talmud teaches that Hashem does not deny reward to anyone who performs a good deed, however slight that deed may be.[384] *For instance, Rav taught that because King Balak of Midian offered forty-two sacrifices to God, he merited to have Ruth and King Solomon descend from him, although his evil motive in performing those sacrifices was the destruction of Israel.*[385] *Similarly, Esau despised his birthright and was only too willing to forfeit his spiritual heritage in exchange for material gain. Nonetheless, the Midrash declares that as a reward for shedding three tears when he discovered that Isaac transferred his blessings to Jacob, Esau was given Mount Seir which always receives plentiful rainfall.*[386]

---

[382] B.T. Brachoth 5B and Shulchan Aruch, Orach Chaim 90:21.
[383] P'nei Moshe, however, states that the sages based their explanations on the fact that the Tanach uses the phrase "turned his face to *the* wall" rather than "to *a* wall," thereby indicating that some particular wall is meant.
[384] B.T. Pesachim 118A and Baba Kama 38B.
[385] B.T. Sotah 47A.
[386] Tanna D'Bei Eliyahu Rabba 14:5 and Zuta 2:3 referring to Genesis 27:38.

On the other hand, one finds God punishing great and righteous people for shortcomings that might seem trivial, perhaps not even noticeable, in ordinary people. For example, Hashem commanded Moses to speak to a rock to bring forth water for the thirsty Jews in the desert. God had told Moses to strike a rock for the same purpose on a previous occasion so when speaking to it did not produce the desired result, Moses struck the rock. God then punished Moses by denying him the right to enter the Land of Israel because God judges the righteous down to a hairsbreadth.[387]

Rabbi Eliyahu Dessler teaches that everyone has a "point of free will" (נקודת בחירה) which depends upon his or her individual circumstances. Accordingly, a person who grew up in a strictly observant home may have no desire to eat non-kosher food and will not receive much reward for not doing so, whereas someone raised in a non-observant home may acquire great merit for observing the kosher dietary laws. Similarly, one with great intellectual aptitude who easily completes a course of Torah study may not receive as much reward as one who overcomes his lack of interest or ability and accomplishes the same thing. Hashem has a sliding scale, so to speak, applying stricter standards to those who are capable of higher spiritual attainment.[388]

In light of the above, it is difficult to understand King Hezekiah's argument in the Talmudic passage under review.

---

[387] Numbers 20:7-12 and see B.T. Yevamoth 121B.
[388] Michtav MiEliyahu, Section II, Avodath HaAdam, Kuntres B'chirah, Part I, Chapter 2.

Rahav was a harlot who lived in the unsavory surroundings of corrupt, decadent Jericho. When confronted by the spies Joshua sent, she states quite frankly that she knows the Jews will win the war and wants to guarantee her safety and that of her family in exchange for the help she offers.[389] *Perhaps her simple acknowledgment of God's existence and dominion represent greater achievements than those of King Solomon because Rahav had so much to overcome to gain that recognition.*

If so, how can King Hezekiah make the argument that because his ancestor King Solomon converted thousands of Gentiles or built a beautiful Temple, he should have even more merit? Hashem does not view these matters in terms of the simple mathematics that Rahav only saved two people whereas King Solomon converted one hundred fifty thousand. Rather, God judges King Solomon's merit in the specific context of King Solomon's particular circumstances. This means that one cannot necessarily compare King Solomon who possessed tremendous wealth, wisdom and other resources to Rahav or to the wicked kings who located their palaces near the Temple or to the Shunamite woman.

Perhaps the validity of King Hezekiah's reasoning lies in the following. The building of the Temple is not a commandment that is within any single individual's ability to perform or fail to perform. The Temple is the focus of Jewish communal worship and, as such, the commandment to build it is addressed to the entire Jewish nation. Thus, if King

---

[389] Joshua 2:9-13.

Solomon did not build it, perforce someone else would. Likewise, that one hundred fifty thousand workers should convert cannot rightly be attributed to the efforts of King Solomon. Jewish law does not recognize forced conversions so while King Solomon may have influenced the workers, they had complete free will and could have refused to convert.

Accordingly, King Hezekiah is not pointing out that King Solomon earned great merit because he built the Temple, for that would have been accomplished one way or another regardless of whether King Solomon chose to do it. Nor is King Hezekiah suggesting that King Solomon was fully responsible for the mass conversion of those who labored at building the Temple. Rather, the fact that God selected King Solomon as the conduit through whom the Temple was built and through whom so many Gentiles converted proves in and of itself that King Solomon possessed tremendous merit and had attained a lofty spiritual level.[390] King Hezekiah's plea is not that Hashem should compare what others accomplished to what King Solomon accomplished per se. Rather, God Himself has shown His high esteem for King Solomon by having him accomplish all that he did. Consequently, God should save King Hezekiah's life for the sake of King Solomon whom He so highly favored.

---

[390] As the Babylonian Talmud says, "Good things are brought about through those who are innocent and bad things are brought about through those who are guilty." (B.T. Shabbath 32A) That King Solomon could accomplish what he did shows that he must have been great.

155

Brachoth 5:1 (Compare B.T. Brachoth 31A)

תני: לא יעמוד אדם ויתפלל לא מתוך שיחה ולא מתוך שחוק
ולא מתוך קלות ראש ולא מתוך דברים בטלין, אלא מתוך דבר של
תורה. וכן, אל יפטר אדם מתוך חבירו לא מתוך שיחה ולא מתוך שחוק
ולא מתוך קלות ראש ולא מתוך דברים בטלים, אלא מתוך דבר של
תורה, שכן מצינו בנביאים הראשונים שהיו חותמין את דבריהן בדברי
שבח ובדברי נחמות.

אמר רבי אלעזר: חוץ מירמיהו שחתם בדברי תוכחות. אמר לו
רבי יוחנן: עוד הוא בדברי נחמות חתם ואמר, "[וַיִּכְתֹּב יִרְמְיָהוּ אֶת כָּל
הָרָעָה אֲשֶׁר תָּבוֹא אֶל בָּבֶל אֶל סֵפֶר אֶחָד אֵת כָּל הַדְּבָרִים הָאֵלֶּה הַכְּתֻבִים
אֶל בָּבֶל. וַיֹּאמֶר יִרְמְיָהוּ אֶל שְׂרָיָה כְּבֹאֲךָ בָבֶל וְרָאִיתָ וְקָרָאתָ אֵת כָּל
הַדְּבָרִים הָאֵלֶּה. וְאָמַרְתָּ ה' אַתָּה דִבַּרְתָּ אֶל הַמָּקוֹם הַזֶּה לְהַכְרִיתוֹ לְבִלְתִּי
הֱיוֹת בּוֹ יוֹשֵׁב לְמֵאָדָם וְעַד בְּהֵמָה כִּי שִׁמְמוֹת עוֹלָם תִּהְיֶה. וְהָיָה כְּכַלֹּתְךָ
לִקְרֹא אֶת הַסֵּפֶר הַזֶּה תִּקְשֹׁר עָלָיו אֶבֶן וְהִשְׁלַכְתּוֹ אֶל תּוֹךְ פְּרָת. וְאָמַרְתָּ]
כָּכָה תִּשְׁקַע בָּבֶל [וְלֹא תָקוּם מִפְּנֵי הָרָעָה אֲשֶׁר אָנֹכִי מֵבִיא עָלֶיהָ וְיָעֵפוּ
עַד הֵנָּה דִּבְרֵי יִרְמְיָהוּ]." (ירמיה נא:ס-סד). לפי שהיה ירמיה חוזר
ומתנבא על בית המקדש, יכול בחורבן בית המקדש חתם. תלמוד לומר,
"...עַד הֵנָּה דִּבְרֵי יִרְמְיָהוּ." (שם סד). במפולת של מחריביו חתם, לא חתם
בדברי תוכחות.

והכתיב, "[וְיָצְאוּ וְרָאוּ בְּפִגְרֵי הָאֲנָשִׁים הַפֹּשְׁעִים בִּי כִּי תוֹלַעְתָּם
לֹא תָמוּת וְאִשָּׁם לֹא תִכְבֶּה] וְהָיוּ דֵרָאוֹן לְכָל בָּשָׂר." (ישעיה סו:כד)?
בעובדי כוכבים ומזלות היא עסקינן.

והכתיב, "כִּי אִם מָאֹס מְאַסְתָּנוּ [קָצַפְתָּ עָלֵינוּ עַד מְאֹד]." (איכה
ה:כב)? "הֲשִׁיבֵנוּ [ה' אֵלֶיךָ וְנָשׁוּבָה [וְנָשׁוּבָה קרי] חַדֵּשׁ יָמֵינוּ כְּקֶדֶם]" (שם
כא) תחת "כִּי אִם מָאֹס מְאַסְתָּנוּ... ".

אף אליהו לא נפטר מאלישע אלא מתוך דבר של תורה. "וַיְהִי
הֵמָּה הֹלְכִים הָלוֹךְ וְדַבֵּר [וְהִנֵּה רֶכֶב אֵשׁ וְסוּסֵי אֵשׁ וַיַּפְרִדוּ בֵּין שְׁנֵיהֶם וַיַּעַל
אֵלִיָּהוּ בַּסְעָרָה הַשָּׁמָיִם]." (מלכים ב ב:יא). במה היו עוסקין? רבי אחווא
בר רבי זעירא אמר: בקריית שמע היו עוסקין, היך מה דאמר, "וְדִבַּרְתָּ

בָּם... ." (דברים ו:ז). רבי יודה בן פזי אמר: בבריאת עולם היו עוסקין,
היך מה דאמר, "בִּדְבַר ה' שָׁמַיִם נַעֲשׂוּ... ." (תהלים לג:ו). רבי יודן בריה
דרבי אייבו אמר: בנחמות ירושלים היו עוסקין, כמה דאמר, "דַּבְּרוּ עַל
לֵב יְרוּשָׁלַם [וְקִרְאוּ אֵלֶיהָ כִּי מָלְאָה צְבָאָהּ כִּי נִרְצָה עֲוֹנָהּ כִּי לָקְחָה מִיַּד
ה' כִּפְלַיִם בְּכָל חַטֹּאתֶיהָ.]" (ישעיה מ:ב). ורבנן אמרין: במרכבה היו
עוסקין, היך מה דאת אמר, "וְהִנֵּה רֶכֶב אֵשׁ וְסוּסֵי אֵשׁ [וַיַּפְרִדוּ בֵּין שְׁנֵיהֶם
וַיַּעַל אֵלִיָּהוּ בַּסְעָרָה הַשָּׁמָיִם.]" (מלכים ב ב:יא).

We learn: A person should not get up and pray directly
from conversing, nor directly from laughing, nor directly from
frivolity, nor directly from idle talk, but rather from a word of
Torah. Likewise, a person should not depart from his friend
directly from conversing, nor directly from laughing, nor
directly from frivolity, nor directly from idle talk, but rather
from a word of Torah, for so we find that the early prophets
used to conclude their pronouncements with words of praise
and consolation.

Rabbi Elazar said: Except for Jeremiah who concluded
with words of reproof.

Rabbi Yochanan responded to him: Even he concluded
with words of consolation and said, "Jeremiah wrote all the evil
which would come upon Babylonia in one scroll...And he said
to Seriah...When you finish reading this scroll, tie a stone to it
and cast it into the Euphrates and say 'Thus shall Babylonia
sink and not rise in the face of the evil which I bring upon it
and [its people] shall become worn out.' Until here are the

words of Jeremiah."[391] Because Jeremiah repeatedly prophesied about the Temple, perhaps he concluded with the destruction of the Temple [which, in fact, is the topic of the last chapter of the Book of Jeremiah]. That is why the text reads "Until here are the words of Jeremiah."[392] He concluded with the downfall of those who destroyed the Temple and did not conclude with words of reproof. [The last chapter of the Book of Jeremiah with its prophecies about the destruction of the Temple is written out of order, such prophecies having actually been uttered prior to the ones in the second to last chapter which describe the downfall of Babylonia. The Hebrew Bible does not necessarily record matters in their chronological order (אין מוקדם ומאוחר בתורה).[393]]

But is it not written [at the end of the Book of Isaiah], "They shall go forth and see the corpses of those men who sin against me, for their worm [which rots them] shall not die and their fire [which burns them] shall not be extinguished and they shall be contemptible before all flesh."?[394] Answer: The verse refers to heathens.

But is it not written [at the end of the Book of Lamentations], "For though You have rightfully despised us, You have raged against us excessively."?[395] Answer: The verse, "Cause us to return, Lord, to You and we shall return;

---

391 Jeremiah 51:60-64.
392 Jeremiah 51:64.
393 Perush MiBa'al Sefer Chareidim.
394 Isaiah 66:24.
395 Lamentations 5:22.

158

renew our days as [they were] before"[396] should be repeated after that verse.

Likewise Elijah did not depart from Elisha except with of a word of Torah, as Scripture states, "They were walking and speaking (ודבר) when behold, a chariot of fire and horses of fire separated between the two of them and Elijah ascended in a whirlwind to the Heavens."[397] With what topic of study were they occupied? Rabbi Achva bar Rabbi Z'eira said: They were occupied with the recital of Shema just as it says [in the text of the Shema], "...you shall speak (ודברת) in them... ."[398] [This is implied by the reference in both verses to "speaking," the Hebrew root of which is דבר.] Rabbi Judah ben Pazi said: They were occupied with the Creation of the Universe just as it says, "By the word (דבר) of the Lord the Heavens were made... ."[399] Rabbi Yudan the son of Rabbi Aibbo said: They were occupied with the consolation of Jerusalem just as it says, "Speak (דברו) upon the heart of Jerusalem and call to her, for her legions shall fill her, because her sin is forgiven, because she took double [punishment] from the hand of the Lord for all her sins."[400] The scholars say: They were occupied with the Workings of the Chariot[401] just as it says [in the verse

---

[396] Lamentations 5:21.
[397] II Kings 2·11.
[398] Deuteronomy 6:7.
[399] Psalms 33:6.
[400] Isaiah 40:2.
[401] The mystical secrets of the Torah hinted at in the beginning of the Book of Ezekiel.

describing Elijah's departure itself], "...behold, a chariot of fire and horses of fire ... ."[402]

The verse "Cause us to return, Lord, to You and we shall return; renew our days as [they were] before"[403] appears as the second to last verse in the Book of Lamentations but is traditionally repeated again at the end of the book in accordance with this passage of the Talmud. However, this practice does not really answer the Talmud's initial question. If Jeremiah actually wrote the verses in the order that he did, then he meant to conclude the Book of Lamentations with the verse "For though You have rightfully despised us, You have raged against us excessively"[404] contrary to the premise that one should always conclude on a positive note. The custom of repeating the second to last verse may express the optimism of the Jewish people, but that does not change the fact that Jeremiah did not write it that way.

*The point of the Talmud is that although they have suffered so much throughout history, the Jews as a people have not abandoned Judaism, but have remained loyal to God and His Torah. Accordingly, they merit redemption. This means that the last two verses of the Book of Lamentations should be read **together** as one unit: "Cause us to return Lord to You and we shall return; renew our days as [they were] before*

---

[402] II Kings 2:11.
[403] Lamentations 5:21.
[404] Lamentations 5:22.

because though You have rightfully despised us, You have raged against us excessively." Since the last verse is really a subordinate clause which explains the first verse, it is proper to view the first verse as coming at the end. This means that rather than being merely a custom to repeat the verse, there is a quasi-grammatical basis for doing so and it is as though Jeremiah in fact wrote it that way.[405]

Chidushei Gaonim[406] points out that before Elijah ascended to Heaven, Scripture says, "It was as they were passing that Elijah said to Elisha, 'Say what I should do for you before I am taken from you!' Elisha said, 'May I please have double your spirit [of prophecy].' He [Elijah] said, 'You have asked a difficult thing. If you see me taken from you, it shall be so for you, and if not, it shall not be.'"[407] Thus, the Talmud does not need to speculate as to what Elijah and Elisha were discussing. The Tanach explicitly states what the topic was! Accordingly, Chidushei Gaonim explains that what bothered the sages of the Talmud was that something more than what is recorded in the Book of Kings must have happened to warrant the miraculous transformation of Elijah into an angel just at that time. Therefore, each sage suggested that some special topic was under discussion, the study of which had the power to effectuate this miracle.

---

[405] Perush MiBa'al Sefer Chareidim.
[406] Found at the end of the selections of Tractate Brachoth of the Jerusalem Talmud in the Romm Vilna edition of Ein Yaakov.
[407] II Kings 2:9-10.

The Talmud's analysis based on parallel uses of words with the Hebrew root דבר, *meaning "speak," seems strange because the Hebrew Bible contains hundreds of words with that root. The rabbis of the Talmud must have found something besides the mere use of a word with the root* דבר *in the verses they were scrutinizing which justified making those associations.*

*Perhaps the view that the two prophets were studying the Creation of the Universe when Elijah departed finds support from the fact that the verse "By the word (*דבר*) of the Lord the Heavens were made..."[408] refers to the Heavens just as the verse which describes Elijah's departure says, "...Elijah ascended in a whirlwind to the Heavens."[409]*

*It is customary to recite the Shema (*שמע*) just before one dies.[410] Accordingly, it makes sense to say that this might have been the topic of discussion just before Elijah ascended to Heaven.*

Finally, Malachi prophesied, "Behold, I will send you Elijah the Prophet before the coming of the great and awesome day of the Lord."[411] At the time of Elijah's departure, it was fitting for him to discuss with Elisha how he will eventually return to announce the advent of the Messiah. Hence,

---

[408] Psalms 33:6.

[409] II Kings 2:11.

[410] Sefer Ta'amei HaMinhagim p. 426 in the note continuing from the previous page on section 1006 citing the work "Ma'avar Yavok." (מעבר יבוק).

[411] Malachi 3:23.

according to one opinion, the topic of conversation was the ultimate redemption of Jerusalem.

Brachoth 5:1 (continued)

רבי חזקיה, רבי יעקב בר אחא, רבי יסא בשם רבי יוחנן: לעולם
לא יהא הפסוק הזה זז מתוך פיך: "ה' צְ-בָאוֹת עִמָּנוּ מִשְׂגָּב לָנוּ אֱ-לֹהֵי
יַעֲקֹב סֶלָה." (תהלים מו:ח). רבי יוסי בי רבי אבון, רבי אבהו בשם רבי
יוחנן וחברייא: "ה' צְ-בָאוֹת אַשְׁרֵי אָדָם בֹּטֵחַ בָּךְ." (תהלים פד:יג). רבי
חזקיה בשם רבי אבהו: יהי רצון לפניך ה' א-להינו וא-להי אבותינו
שתצילנו משעות החצופות הקשות הרעות היוצאות המתרגשות לבוא
לעולם.

Rabbi Hezekiah quoted Rabbi Jacob bar Acha who quoted Rabbi Yassa in the name of Rabbi Yochanan: Never let this verse be removed from your mouth, "The Lord of Multitudes is with us, a Stronghold for us is the God of Jacob forever."[412] Rabbi Yossi of the academy of Rabbi Abon quoted Rabbi Abahu in the name of Rabbi Yochanan and the colleagues: "Lord of Multitudes, happy is the man who trusts in You."[413] Rabbi Hezekiah said in the name of Rabbi Abahu: "May it be pleasing before You, Lord our God and God of our fathers, to save us from distressing times, difficult and evil, which issue and rage forth upon the world."

This passage in the Talmud forms the basis for the custom of reciting the verses "The Lord of Multitudes is with us, a Stronghold for us is the God of Jacob forever"[414] and

---

[412] Psalms 46:8 and 12.
[413] Psalms 84:13.
[414] Psalms 46:8 and 12.

"Lord of Multitudes, happy is the man who trusts in You"[415] *during the morning prayer service. However, instead of reciting the brief prayer cited in the name of Rabbi Abahu afterwards, the verse "Lord save [us]; may the King answer us in the day of our calling"*[416] *follows. Apparently this is because there is a tradition that each of the three Patriarchs, Abraham, Isaac and Jacob, recited one of these verses.*[417] *Moreover, this latter verse expresses much the same idea as the prayer formulated by Rabbi Abahu. Also, Rabbi Akiva says that one who recites these three verses will not be harmed throughout the day.*[418]

Recitation of these three verses is so important that they are repeated three times after the section of the morning prayer services dealing with the incense offering, again during Hodu (הודו) and yet again during Uva LeTzion (ובא ציון).

The Talmud teaches that the person who offered the incense in the Temple was blessed with wealth. To make sure that every priest had an opportunity to receive that blessing, no priest was permitted to perform the service twice.[419] *During times when the Temple does not stand, the recitation of the prayer service replaces the sacrificial service, as the Prophet Hosea said, "...our lips compensate for bullocks."*[420] *The*

---

[415] Psalms 84:13.

[416] Psalms 20:10.

[417] Rabbi Chaim Yosef David Azulai (Chida) in Yosef Tehilloth on Psalms 46:8 citing Rabbi Moshe Cordervero and the Arizal.

[418] Cited in Etz Yosef in Siddur Otzar HaTefilloth, Vol. I, p. 178.

[419] B.T. Yoma 26A.

[420] Hosea 14:3 with Rashi's commentary.

recitation of verses from Psalms which emphasize how Hashem controls the affairs of the world and the importance of trusting Him is especially appropriate in the context of a service the blessing for which is abundance, because in the midst of abundance people may feel self-satisfied and forget God.

These three verses together contain eighty letters. They are repeated a total of five times during the morning service yielding four hundred letters altogether. The words "Ra Ayin" (רע עין) meaning "evil eye" in Hebrew have a numerical value of four hundred. Rabbeinu Bachya explains that this is why the Egyptian slavery lasted four hundred years and Esau approached Jacob with four hundred men. The number four hundred reflects the spiritual evil at the root of the Egyptian slavery and Esau's opposition to Jacob.[421] Hence, recitation of these verses counteracts the forces associated with the evil eye.

Rabbi Dov Ber of Mezeritch explains the concept of the evil eye as follows: Everything in the universe emanates from Hashem even though that emanation is not readily apparent to human beings. God causes unseen spiritual forces to constantly maintain the existence of every aspect of the universe. When a person takes special notice of a physical object, he or she thereby implies that such object is separate from God. This can interfere with the connection between the

---

[421] Rabbeinu Bachya on Genesis 15:13. On a related note, the number eighty refers to strength (גבורה) as the verse says: "The days of our years total seventy years, if with strength, eighty years... ." (Psalms 90:10) The five-fold repetition alludes to the "five strengths" (ה' גבורות) or aspects of judgment which the recitation of these verses mitigates.

*physical object being observed and its spiritual source, thereby
harming the object. This is true even when the observer's
intentions are completely friendly.*[422]

*These verses stress trust in God and His Providence, the
belief that everything in the universe does indeed emanate from
Him. By reciting them, the worshiper counteracts the
pernicious influence of the "evil eye."*

*Rabbi Aryeh Leib Gordon points out that it is no
coincidence that Rabbi Yochanan was the one to stress the
importance of reciting these verses. Trusting in Hashem for
sustenance was a focal point of Rabbi Yochanan's life.*[423]

*The Talmud reports that when Rabbi Yochanan and his
colleague, Ilfa, found themselves without sufficient means to
support themselves, they decided to cease their scholarly
pursuits to go into business. Rabbi Yochanan overheard two
ministering angels criticizing him and his colleague for
abandoning full time Torah study to occupy themselves with
temporal matters. Rabbi Yochanan inferred that this was a
message from Heaven that if he returned to his studies, he
would succeed in such a way that his financial needs would be
met. Indeed, upon returning, the other scholars of the academy
appointed him their dean and provided him with ample*

---

[422] Maggid Devarav LeYaakov, chapter 73. The opposite is also true. A
truly righteous person sees the inner spiritual connection between every
object in the universe and its spiritual source. This is what gives great
rabbinical leaders (צדיקים) the power to properly advise their followers.
[423] Rabbi Aryeh Leib Gordon, Iyun Tefillah in Siddur Otzar HaTefilloth,
Vol. I, p.156-158.

support.[424] *Thus, Rabbi Yochanan saw in his own life a clear example of Divine Providence consistent with the verse "The Lord of Multitudes is with us, a Stronghold for us is the God of Jacob forever."*[425]

On another occasion, Rabbi Yochanan traveled from Tiberias to Sepphoris in the company of Rabbi Chiya bar Abba. As they passed various fields, vineyards and orchards, Rabbi Yochanan pointed out the ones he had once owned but had sold to enable himself to study Torah full time. Rabbi Chiya bar Abba became upset and began to cry because Rabbi Yochanan had nothing left in his old age. Rabbi Yochanan, however, comforted him by pointing out that while God created the universe in six days, Moses had to remain on Mount Sinai for the longer period of forty days to receive the Torah, suggesting that the study of Torah is greater than the work of Creation. Thus, Rabbi Yochanan concluded that the Torah knowledge he had acquired was worth the sacrifice.[426] *This attitude finds expression in the verse "Lord of Multitudes, happy is the man who trusts in You."*[427]

---

[424] B.T. Ta'anith 21A with Rashi sub verba Malach Rabbi Yochanan (מלך רבי יוחנן).
[425] Psalms 46:8 and 12.
[426] Shir HaShirim Rabbah on Song of Songs 8:7.
[427] Psalms 84:13.

Brachoth 5:1 (continued)

אמר רבי יוחנן: המתפלל בתוך ביתו כאילו מקיפו חומה של
ברזל. מחלפה שיטתיה דרבי יוחנן תמן! אמר רבי אבא אמר רבי חייא
בשם רבי יוחנן: צריך לאדם להתפלל במקום שהוא מיוחד לתפילה. וכה
אמר אכן! כאן ביחיד וכאן בציבור.

רבי פנחס בשם רבי הושעיא: המתפלל בבית הכנסת כאילו
מקריב מנחה טהורה. מה טעם? "...כַּאֲשֶׁר יָבִיאוּ בְנֵי יִשְׂרָאֵל אֶת הַמִּנְחָה
בִּכְלִי טָהוֹר בֵּית ה'." (ישעיה סו:כ).

רבי אבהו בשם רבי אבהו: "דִּרְשׁוּ ה' בְּהִמָּצְאוֹ..." (ישעיה נה:ו).
איכן הוא מצוי? בבתי כנסיות ובבתי מדרשות. "...קְרָאֻהוּ בִּהְיוֹתוֹ
קָרוֹב." (שם שם). איכן הוא קרוב? [בבתי כנסיות ובבתי מדרשות.]
אמר רבי יצחק בי רבי אלעזר: ולא עוד, אלא שא-להיהן עומד על גבן.
מאי טעמא? "...אֱ-לֹהִים נִצָּב בַּעֲדַת אֵ-ל בְּקֶרֶב אֱ-לֹהִים יִשְׁפֹּט." (תהלים
פב:א).

רב חסדא אמר: זה שנכנס לבית הכנסת צריך להכנס לפנים
משני דלתות. מה טעם? "אַשְׁרֵי אָדָם שֹׁמֵעַ לִי לִשְׁקֹד עַל דַּלְתֹתַי יוֹם יוֹם
[לִשְׁמֹר מְזוּזֹת פְּתָחָי]." (משלי ח:לד). "דַלְתֹתַי" ולא "דַלְתִּי," "מְזוּזֹת"
ולא "מְזוּזַת." אם עשה כן, מה כתיב תמן? "כִּי מֹצְאִי מָצָאי [מָצָא קְרֵי]
חַיִּים [וַיָּפֶק רָצוֹן מֵה']." (משלי ח:לה).

רב חונא אמר: זה שהוא הולך לבית הכנסת צריך להקל את
רגליו. מה טעם? "וְנֵדְעָה נִרְדְּפָה לָדַעַת אֶת ח'..." (הושע ו:ג). וכשהוא
יוצא, צריך להלך קימעא. מה טעם? "כִּי עַתָּה צְעָדַי תִּסְפּוֹר [לֹא תִשְׁמוֹר
עַל חַטָּאתִי]" (איוב יד:טז).

אמר רבי יוחנן: ברית כרותה היא: היגע תלמודו בבית חכנסת,
לא במהרה הוא משכח.

אמר רבי יוחנן ענתנייתא: ברית כרותה היא: היגע בתלמודו
בצנעה, לא במהרה הוא משכח. מה טעם? "...וְאֶת צְנוּעִים חָכְמָה."
(משלי יא:ב).

אמר רבי יוחנן: ברית כרותה היא: הלמד אגדה מתוך הספר, לא

בִּמְהֵרָה הוּא מַשְׁכַּח.

אָמַר רְבִּי תַנְחוּם: הַסּוֹבֵר תַלְמוּדוֹ, לֹא בִּמְהֵרָה הוּא מַשְׁכַּח. מַה

טַעַם? "...פֶּן תִּשְׁכַּח אֶת הַדְּבָרִים אֲשֶׁר רָאוּ עֵינֶיךָ... ." (דברים ד:ט).

Rabbi Yochanan said: When one prays in his home, it is as though an iron wall surrounds him [to protect him, for surely his prayers are heard[428]]. This is contrary to Rabbi Yochanan's position elsewhere, as Rabbi Abba quoted Rabbi Chiya in the name of Rabbi Yochanan: "A person should pray in a place which is specially designated for prayer [i.e., a synagogue]," whereas here he says otherwise. There is no contradiction because the first statement refers to praying in private while the second refers to praying in public. [When a person prays at a time during which no communal prayers are being recited, it is best to do so in the privacy of one's home so as to concentrate properly. However, whenever the community is praying, one should join them.[429]]

Rabbi Phinehas said in the name of Rabbi Hoshaya: One who prays in the synagogue is as though he offers a pure meal offering [in the Temple]. What is the Scriptural source for this? "...just as the Children of Israel bring the meal offering in

---

[428] P'nei Moshe.
[429] P'nei Moshe. The Shulchan Aruch, however, rules that even if one missed praying together with the community and must pray privately, it is preferable to do so in the synagogue. (Orach Chaim 90:9) This is apparently based on B.T. Brachoth 6A where Abba Benjamin says, "A person's prayer is not heard except in the synagogue."

a pure vessel [to the] House of the Lord."[430] [The verse suggests a connection between a pure vessel in which one brings a meal offering and the House of the Lord which is a vessel or conduit for prayer.[431] Moreover, the meal offering was the poor person's offering, being the least expensive sacrifice one could bring to the Temple. This reflects the idea that one's prayers need not be elaborate and that one need not concentrate upon all their arcane meanings. Rather, God favors sincere devotion from the heart.[432]]

Rabbi Abahu said in the name of Rabbi Abahu:[433] "Seek out the Lord when he is accessible... ."[434] Where is He accessible? In the synagogues and study halls. "...call Him when He is near."[435] When is He near? In the synagogues and study halls.[436] Rabbi Isaac of the academy of Rabbi Elazar said: Not only is He always close, but their God stands on their backs! What is the Scriptural source for this? "God stands

---

[430] Isaiah 66:20.
[431] Etz Yosef.
[432] Rabbi Yaakov Ibn Chaviv in HaKothev.
[433] Some texts read "Rabbi Jeremiah said in the name of Rabbi Abahu," however it is possible that there was more than one Talmudic scholar named Rabbi Abahu so that one might quote the other. See Tosafoth on B.T. Baba Bathra 77A sub verba Mi Kan Tanna (מי כאן תנא) which states that there were two scholars named Rabbi Isaac bar Avdimi.
[434] Isaiah 55:6.
[435] Isaiah 55:6.
[436] P'nei Moshe. This last phrase is omitted in the main text of the printed edition but is cited from the Rome manuscript.

among the congregation of God; in the midst of judges, He renders judgment."[437]

Rabbi Chisda said: One who enters the synagogue should go in a distance of more than the length of two doorways. [If one enters and remains right at the doorway, it appears as though he or she is anxious to leave.[438]] What is the Scriptural source for this? "Happy is the person who listens to Me, to attend My doors daily, to guard the doorways of my entrances."[439] The verse says "My doors," not "My door" and "doorways," not "doorway." If one does so, what is written there? "For one who finds me finds life and acquires favor from the Lord."[440]

Rabbi Chuna[441] said: One who goes to the synagogue should lighten his or her feet [i.e., move quickly]. What is the Scriptural source for this? "Then we shall understand how to chase after knowing the Lord... ."[442] And when one exits, one should walk slowly. What is the Scriptural source for this? "For now You count my steps, You do not observe my sins."[443] [When a person walks slowly from the synagogue taking many

---

[437] Psalms 82:1.
[438] Rashi on B.T. Brachoth 8A, sub verba "Shiur Shel Shnei Pethahim" (שיעור של שני פתחים).
[439] Proverbs 8:34.
[440] Proverbs 8:35.
[441] Rabbi Chuna (חונא) is probably the same as Rabbi Huna (הונא) found in the Babylonian Talmud, the difference in spelling merely reflecting how the pronunciation of Aramaic often differed between Babylonia and the Land of Israel.
[442] Hosea 6:3.
[443] Job 14:16.

steps, God notes this mark of respect and overlooks that person's sins.]

Rabbi Yochanan said: There is a firmly established guarantee that one who struggles over his studies in the synagogue will not readily forget them.

Rabbi Yochanan of Anthanyatha said: There is a firmly established guarantee that one who struggles over his studies privately will not readily forget them. What is the Scriptural source for this? "...and with the modest is wisdom."[444] [Although one will benefit from studying in the holy surroundings of the synagogue, he should not show off, but do so modestly.]

Rabbi Yochanan said: There is a firmly established guarantee that one who studies Aggadah from a written text will not readily forget it.

Rabbi Tanchum said: One who delves deeply into his learning will not readily forget it. What is the Scriptural source for this? "...lest you forget the words which your eyes saw... ."[445] [Although the verse refers to the Giving of the Torah, since no one could have literally seen the words spoken then, the phrase must mean to delve into the Torah.[446]]

The Talmud records that Rabbi Yochanan and Rabbi Shimon bar Lakish used to study a book of Aggadoth on the Sabbath. The Talmud questions how they could do this when

---

444 Proverbs 11:2.
445 Deuteronomy 4:9.
446 P'nei Moshe.

173

there is a prohibition against writing down the Oral Torah. The Talmud answers that if the sages did not write down the Oral Torah, it would be forgotten altogether due to intense persecution.[447] *If, ideally, one should not commit the Oral Torah to writing, how can Rabbi Yochanan praise the study of Aggadah from a written text?*

Perhaps Rabbi Yochanan is not suggesting that the Aggadoth themselves be written out or studied from a written text. Rather, he means that one should learn the Aggadah while reading the Written Torah since most Aggadah is based on verses of the Written Torah or interprets such verses. Just as people often use key words to aid memory, one will remember more when studying Aggadic material while one studies the Scriptural verses to which it pertains.

The commentators explain that the preference for learning in the synagogue is only in a locality where no study hall (בית מדרש) exists.[448] *Why should studying Torah in a study hall or synagogue make such a difference? Cannot a person study just as well somewhere else?*

The holy surroundings of the synagogue or study hall influence a person's attitude towards what he is learning. There is an important difference between one who learns in the comfort of his home surrounded by the mundane environs of his everyday life and leaving those environs behind to enter a holy place. However subtly, the milieu of the study hall or

---

[447] B.T. Gittin 60A with Rashi ad loc..
[448] Shulchan Aruch, Yoreh Deah 246:22 with commentary of Turei Zahav and Sifthei Kohen.

174

synagogue engenders a special reverence towards the Torah, leading the student to view it not merely as another branch of knowledge to be mastered but as the holy word of God. This special attitude contributes greatly to the motivational factor needed to succeed in Torah learning.

While it is true that the desire to learn and a reverent attitude are important to success in Torah study, there is an additional factor which is required. To truly excel in Torah learning requires Divine assistance. This is why Rabbi Yochanan of Anthanyatha adds that part of the recipe for success lies in studying discreetly, with a humble attitude. Only when one learns Torah as a method of serving God rather than as a means for flaunting his intellectual skills can he expect Divine assistance in his endeavor.

This explains why Rabbi Tanchum cited Scriptural proof to show that one who delves deeply into his learning will not readily forget it. Common sense dictates that when one spends more time on a topic, one will remember it better. However, Rabbi Tanchum's point is that it is not necessarily reviewing many times in and of itself which aids memory, but rather the **attitude** *towards learning that such reviewing engenders. When a person takes a subject seriously, he wants to delve deeply into it and fully understand it. When one shows such devotion to Torah, Heaven helps him retain what he has learned.*

Brachoth 5:1

רבי יוחנן הוה יתיב, קרי קומי כנישתא דבבל בציפורין. עבר
ארכונא ולא קם ליה מקומוי. אתון, בעיין מימחוניה.
אמר לון, "ארפוניה! בנימוסיא דברייה הוא עסיק."
רבי חנינא ורבי יהושע בן לוי עלון קומי אַנְטִיפּוֹתָא דקיסרין.
חמתון וקם מן קומיהון.
אמרין ליה, "מן קומוי אילין יהודאי את קאים?!?"
אמר לון, "אפיהון דמלאכין חמית!"
רבי יונה ורבי יוסי עלון קומי אָרְסָקִינָס בְּאַנְטוֹכְיָא. חמתון וקם
מן קומיהון.
אמרין ליה, "מן קומי אילין יהודאי את קאים לך?!?"
אמר לון, "אפיהון דהני אנא חזי בקרבא ונצחי!"
רבי אבון על קומי מלכותא. כי נפיק, הפך קדל. אתון, בעיין
מיקטלוניה וחמין תרין זיקוקין דנור נפקין מקדליה ושבקוה, לקיים מה
שנאמר, "וְרָאוּ כָּל עַמֵּי הָאָרֶץ כִּי שֵׁם ה' נִקְרָא עָלֶיךָ וְיָרְאוּ מִמֶּךָּ." (דברים
כח:י).
תני רבי שמעון בן יוחי: "וְרָאוּ כָּל עַמֵּי הָאָרֶץ כִּי שֵׁם ה' נִקְרָא
עָלֶיךָ... ." "כָּל," אפילו רוחות, אפילו שידים.
רבי יניי ורבי יונתן הוו מטיילין באסלטין. חמתון חד ושאל בהון.
אמר להון, "שלמכון רבייא."
אמרין, "אפילו תואר חברות אין עלינו לרעה."

Rabbi Yochanan was reciting the Shema (שמע) in front
of the Babylonian synagogue in Sepphoris. When a Roman
official passed, he did not rise before him [because he did not
wish to interrupt his recitation]. The official's servants sought
to beat Rabbi Yochanan. The official said, "Leave him alone.
He is occupied with his duties towards his Creator."

Rabbi Chanina and Rabbi Joshua ben Levi entered the presence of the ruler of Caesaria.[449] Upon observing them, he rose before them. His underlings said, "From before these Jews you arise?!?" He said to them, "Faces of angels have I seen!"

Rabbi Jonah and Rabbi Yossi entered the presence of Ursicinus in Antioch. Upon observing them, he rose before them. His underlings said, "From before these Jews you arise?!?" He said to them, "I see a vision of their faces during battle and win!"

Rabbi Abon entered the royal presence. When he emerged he turned his back towards the king [rather than backing away while facing the king as was customary[450]]. The king's servants approached and wanted to kill him, but they saw two fiery sparks emerging from the back of his neck and left him alone, thus fulfilling that which is written, "All the peoples of the earth shall see that the Name of the Lord is called upon you and they shall fear you."[451]

---

[449] P'nei Moshe cites the Midrash Rabbah that this ruler was Antipater and the term for ruler which the Talmud uses (אנטיפותא) resembles Antipater. However, this cannot be the Antipater who ruled the Land of Israel during the time of Julius Caesar and was the father of King Herod because that Antipater's reign took place more than two hundred years before Rabbi Chanina and Rabbi Joshua ben Levi lived. The prefix "ante" in Latin means "before" and "pater" means "father" so the name Antipater itself means "before the father," probably indicating an official, the word "father" here denoting the king. Thus, perhaps the word "Antipater" served both as the title of an official and a proper name just as the word "duke" in English is a title of nobility but can also be a proper name, "Duke."

[450] P'nei Moshe.

[451] Deuteronomy 28:10.

Rabbi Shimon bar Yochai taught: "All the peoples of the earth shall see that the Name of the Lord is called upon you and they shall fear you."[452] The word "all" means to include even spirits and even demons.

Rabbi Yanai and Rabbi Jonathan were walking through a village square. A demon[453] saw them and greeted them, saying, "May you have great peace!" The rabbis said to themselves, "Even though he acts towards us as a colleague [by addressing us in this manner and not calling us "rabbis"], he still cannot harm us."

Although many Romans persecuted Jews with intense hatred, a particular Roman official may have logically concluded that Rabbi Yochanan did not ignore him out of disrespect but only because he was immersed in prayer. Likewise the noble bearing of the rabbis may have impressed a Roman official so that he rose before them.[454] Hence, had the Talmud related only the first two incidents, one might think that these events were mere natural occurrences.

---

452 Deuteronomy 28:10.

453 This appears to be the view of P'nei Moshe and is consistent with the flow of the text. Perush MeBa'al Sefer Chareidim, however, says that they met a government official. Perhaps he understands the text that way because demons do not frequent inhabited places such as village squares. (See B.T. Pesachim 112A.) In addition, the term "demon" was sometimes used in the Talmud to refer to the anti-Semitic Romans because the editors feared retaliation if they criticized the Romans directly.

454 Compare Brachoth 32B-33A which tells of a certain pious person who did not interrupt his prayers to greet a Roman official and convinced him to leave him in peace.

The Talmud, however, makes the point that the aberration of a Roman anti-Semite honoring rabbis results from the rabbis identifying themselves with God's will. Thus, while a Roman king may have forgiven Rabbi Abon's indiscretion of turning his back on him by reasoning that the rabbi was unfamiliar with the custom or forgot about it, as was undoubtedly the case,[455] the Talmud states that two fiery sparks repelled the king's servants. God Himself, not the natural benevolence of earthly rulers, protects His faithful servants.

Rabbi Eliezer the Great taught that the verse "All the peoples of the earth shall see that the Name of the Lord is called upon you and they shall fear you"[456] refers to the head Tefillin.[457] Hence, the two fiery sparks may represent the two straps of the head Tefillin which extend from the knot at the back of the head. Elsewhere, the Talmud states that Hashem, so to speak, wears Tefillin which contain Scriptural verses praising Israel corresponding to the parchments of the Tefillin Jews wear which contain verses praising God.[458] Thus, the donning of Tefillin symbolizes the unique relationship between God and the Jewish people; the absolute identity of the Jew with God. It is this intense, devoted relationship which brings about supernatural protection.

---

[455] Perush MiBa'al Sefer Chareidim.
[456] Deuteronomy 28:10.
[457] B.T. Brachoth 6A.
[458] B.T. Brachoth 6A.

When Moses asked God to "...show me please Your glory,"[459] *God responded that "...no human shall see Me and live...you shall see My back but My face shall not be seen."*[460] *The Talmud explains that Hashem showed Moses the knot of His head Tefillin.*[461] *One could hardly expect bigoted pagans to recognize or respect the greatness of the rabbis. Still, even they could occasionally catch enough of a glimpse of the truth to be impressed. Perhaps the sparks the king's servants saw were a sudden intense recognition that Jews are God's servants whom they dare not harm.*

---

[459] Exodus 33:18.
[460] Exodus 33:20 and 23.
[461] B.T. Brachoth 7A.

Brachoth 5:1 (continued)

ריש לקיש מנהגו באוריתא סגין. הוה נפיק ליה לבר מתחומא
דשבתא והוא לא ידע, לקיים מה שנאמר, "...בְּאַהֲבָתָהּ תִּשְׁגֶּה תָמִיד."
(משלי ה:יט).

רבי יודן בי רבי ישמעאל מנהגיה באוריתא סגין. הוות גולתיה
שרעה מיניה וחכינה מזדהרא לה.
אמרין ליה תלמידוי, "רבי, הא גולתך שריעה."
אמר לון, "ולית ההיא רשיעתא זהירא לה?"

Resh Lakish[462] became so involved in his Torah studies
that he walked out of the Sabbath boundary[463] without
realizing it, thereby fulfilling that which is written, "...for the
love of it you shall constantly err."[464]

Rabbi Yudan of the academy of Rabbi Ishmael became
so involved in his Torah studies that his cloak slipped off
[without his realizing it] and a serpent guarded it. His disciples
said to him, "Master, your cloak has slipped off!" He answered
them, "Isn't that evil one guarding it?"

*The stories in this section of the Talmud reflect the
verses, "The feet of His pious ones He guards... "*[465] *and "One*

---

[462] A popular acronym for Rabbi Shimon ben Lakish.
[463] In general, it is forbidden to walk more than 2,000 cubits away from
an inhabited area on the Sabbath.
[464] Proverbs 5:19.
[465] I Samuel 2:9.

who observes a commandment shall not know evil... ."[466]
However, if God protects the righteous from evil, one has to
wonder how Resh Lakish wandered out of the Sabbath
boundary. The verse "No sin shall befall the righteous and the
wicked are full of evil"[467] implies that a righteous person will
not commit a sin even accidentally.

Tosafoth explains that Heaven only protects the
righteous from eating non-kosher food because that is a great
disgrace, but the righteous may accidentally commit other sins
such as desecrating the Sabbath.[468] Thus, according to one
opinion, when Rabbi Yishmael ben Elisha was reading near an
oil lamp, he forgot that it was the Sabbath and adjusted the
wick.[469]

In the passage under review, however, it is possible that
Resh Lakish did not commit a sin at all. When a person
transgresses the Sabbath because that person did not
remember that it was the Sabbath or because he did not know
that what he was doing constituted a transgression, he is liable
as an accidental sinner (שוגג). However, when a person is so
preoccupied that he does not realize what he is doing at all
(מתעסק), he is not even considered an accidental sinner.[470]
This was the case with Resh Lakish. He became so engrossed
in his studies that he did not realize where he was going or

---

[466] Ecclesiastes 8:5.
[467] Proverbs 12:21.
[468] Tosafoth sub verba "Rabbi Nathan" (רבי נתן) in B.T. Shabbath 12B.
[469] B.T. Shabbath 12B.
[470] B.T. Shabbath 157B.

what he was doing at all. Accordingly, his walking outside the Sabbath boundary did not count even as an accidental sin.

Brachoth 5:1 (continued) (Compare B.T. Brachoth 33A)

אמרין עליו על רבי חנינא בן דוסא שהיה עומד ומתפלל ובא
חברבר והכישו ולא הפסיק את תפילתו, והלכו ומצאו אותו חברבר מת,
מוטל על פי חורו. אמרו, "אי לו לאדם שנשכו חברבר ואי לו לחברבר
שנשך את רבי חנינא בן דוסא."
מה עיסקיה דהדין חברבריא? כד הוות נכית לבר נשא, אין בר
נשא קדים למיא, חברברא מיית, ואין חברברא קדים למיא, בר נשא
מיית.
אמרו לו תלמידיו, "רבי, לא הרגשת?"
אמר להן, "יבא עלי, ממה שהיה לבי מתכוין בתפילה אם
הרגשתי!"
אמר רבי יצחק בר אלעזר: ברא לו הקדוש ברוך הוא מעיין תחת
כפות רגליו לקיים מה שנאמר, "רְצוֹן יְרֵאָיו יַעֲשֶׂה וְאֶת שַׁוְעָתָם יִשְׁמַע
וְיוֹשִׁיעֵם." (תהלים קמה:יט).

They said about Rabbi Chanina ben Dosa that he was
standing and praying when a venomous lizard bit him. He did
not interrupt his prayer. Others went and found the lizard dead
and stretched out at the mouth of its den, so people said, "Woe
to the person whom the venomous lizard bites and woe to the
venomous lizard that bites Rabbi Chanina ben Dosa!"

What is the nature of this venomous lizard? When it
bites a person, if the person reaches water first, the lizard dies,
but if the lizard reaches water first, the person dies.

His students said to Rabbi Chanina ben Dosa, "Master,
did you not feel anything?"

He answered them, "I swear that I was so focused on
prayer that I did not feel it!"

Rabbi Isaac bar Elazar said: The Holy One, Blessed be He, created a spring beneath the soles of his feet to fulfill that which it says, "He does the will of those who fear him; He hears their cries and saves them."[471]

The Babylonian Talmud has a somewhat different version of how this incident took place. One detail it adds is that Rabbi Chanina ben Dosa placed the lizard over his shoulder, carried it to town and said, "See my children, it is not the venomous lizard which kills, but sin which kills."[472] The commentators state that the species of venomous lizard the Talmud describes is a cross-breed of a lizard and a snake.[473]

When Hashem first created man and woman, their evil inclination (יצר הרע) and good inclination (יצר טוב) were in perfect equilibrium such that, left on their own, they would never have sinned. The snake, a wholly external force, enticed them to disobey God. After that first sin, the evil inclination became dominant as the verse says, "...for the inclination of the heart of man is evil from his youth... ."[474]

---

[471] Psalms 145:19.

[472] B.T. Brachoth 33A.

[473] Rashi on B.T. Brachoth 33A and P'nei Moshe on the text here. The names used for the lizard also imply that it is a hybrid. In the Babylonian Talmud it is called Arod (ערוד), the letters of which may be rearranged to read "Du-Ra" (דו רע), meaning "two evils." (Compare Ben Yehodyada on B.T. Brachoth 33A). In the Jerusalem Talmud it is called Chabarbar (חברבר) meaning "combination" or "hybrid" from the root word "Chaver" (חבר).

[474] Genesis 8:21. Derech HaShem, Rabbi Moshe Chaim Luzzatto 1:3:1-8. Compare B.T. Sanhedrin 38B that God reduced Adam's size after

185

Even today, however, the evil inclination has two main aspects, one internal and the other external. There are internal instincts such as selfishness, greed, hatred and conceit which drive people away from Hashem and His Torah. There are also external forces such as societal or peer pressure and other elements of one's environment which may lead a person astray. The hybrid lizard which the Talmud describes represents the combination of internal and external forces which lead people astray; the quintessential evil inclination.

*Even so, people retain the free will to resist the evil inclination. That is why Rabbi Chanina ben Dosa points out that its is not the lizard (the evil inclination) which kills, but rather sin (the **decision** to listen to the evil inclination) which kills.*

Perhaps this explains why the Talmud says that if the venomous lizard reaches water first, its victim dies but if the victim reaches water first, the lizard dies. Torah study is often compared to water. Just as water always flows to the lowest places, so Torah knowledge resides only with those who are sincerely humble.[475] The Talmud says that, "The Holy One, Blessed be He, created the evil inclination and created the Torah as a remedy."[476] Intense Torah study is a remedy for those enticed by the evil inclination. Hence, one who is bitten by the venomous lizard (evil inclination) but reaches water (Torah study) first will defeat the evil inclination.

---

the latter sinned.
[475] B.T. Ta'anith 7A.
[476] B.T. Baba Bathra 16B and see also B.T. Kiddushin 30B.

This explains why the evil inclination fights so strongly to prevent people from learning Torah. As Rabbi Meir said, "If you wish to slacken from Torah study, there are many excuses for slackening."[477] *Once a person finds an excuse for neglecting Torah study, he opens the door to finding other excuses so that, eventually, he stops learning altogether. Accordingly, if the venomous lizard (evil inclination) reaches water (Torah study) first, that is, convinces a person to slacken his studies, the person will die; he will be trapped in a downward spiral of sin.*

---

[477] Pirkei Avoth 4:10.

Brachoth 5:2 (compare J.T. Ta'anith 1:1)

מִשְׁנָה: מַזְכִּירִין "גְּבוּרוֹת גְּשָׁמִים" בִּתְחִיַּית הַמֵּתִים...
גמרא: כְּשֵׁם שֶׁתְּחִיַּית הַמֵּתִים חַיִּים לָעוֹלָם, כָּךְ יְרִידַת גְּשָׁמִים
חַיִּים לָעוֹלָם. רבי חייא בר אבא שמע לה מן הדא: "יְחַיֵּנוּ מִיֹּמָיִם בַּיּוֹם
הַשְּׁלִישִׁי יְקִמֵנוּ וְנִחְיֶה לְפָנָיו. וְנֵדְעָה נִרְדְּפָה לָדַעַת אֶת ה' כְּשַׁחַר נָכוֹן
מֹצָאוֹ [וְיָבוֹא כַגֶּשֶׁם לָנוּ כְּמַלְקוֹשׁ יוֹרֶה אָרֶץ.]" (הושע ו:ב-ג).

Mishnah: We mention the "force of the rain" (גבורות גשמים) in the blessing for the revival of the dead (תחית מתים)[478]... .

Gemara: Just as the revival of the dead bestows life to all the world, so rainfall bestows life to all the world. Rabbi Chiya bar Abba derived this principle from the following verses, "He shall enliven us after two days; upon the third day He shall raise us up and we shall live before Him. Then we shall understand how to chase after knowing the Lord as surely as the dawn goes forth; it shall come like the rain for us, as the Spring rain quenches the land."[479]

The view expressed in this passage that "the revival of the dead bestows life to all the world" accords with that of Rav Yosef in the Babylonian Talmud where he says that the future

---

[478] The second blessing of the silent prayer.
[479] Hosea 6:2-3. Rashi explains that the "two days" refer to the two times the Temple was destroyed. Thus, the prophet declares that God will rejuvenate the Jewish people after each destruction and that the third Temple will never be destroyed.

resurrection of the dead applies to both wicked and righteous people. By contrast, Rabbi Abahu says that a day during which rain falls is greater than the future resurrection because rain falls for all alike whereas only the righteous will be resurrected.[480] Interestingly, this dispute has continued down through the ages. Thus, for example, the Rambam declares that the resurrection will take place only for the righteous.[481] By contrast, Rabbi Saadia Gaon suggests that two resurrections will take place. One for the righteous followed later on by another general resurrection.[482]

Both views, however, appear to contradict the verse in the Book of Daniel which says, "Many of those who sleep in the dust of the earth shall awaken, these to eternal life and these to disgrace, to eternal humiliation."[483] This verse states that even the wicked will be revived, contrary to Rabbi Abahu. On the other hand, the wicked will be punished, contrary to Rav Yosef who views the revival as a beneficial event similar to rain.

Rabbi Abahu, who says that only the righteous are revived, must read the end of the verse as being unrelated to its beginning, as follows: "Many of those who sleep in the dust of the earth shall awaken, these [who are righteous] to eternal

---

[480] B.T. Ta'anith 7A.
[481] Commentary to Sanhedrin Mishnah 10:1.
[482] Sefer Emunoth Ve'Deoth, Treatise VII, Chapter VII ("The Book of Beliefs and Opinions," translated by Rabbi Samuel Rosenblatt (Yale University Press: New Haven, 1948), p. 277, et. seq.), and see Rabbi Abraham Ibn Ezra's commentary on Daniel 12:2.
[483] Daniel 12:2.

*life and these [who are wicked shall not arise, but be doomed]
to disgrace, to eternal humiliation. "*

*Rav Yosef, however, apparently reads the verse as
originally translated above, implying that both righteous and
wicked shall participate in the resurrection. This is
problematic because he regards the resurrection of the dead as
a very positive thing. Just as rain benefits both the righteous
and the wicked, so will the resurrection. The explanation must
be as follows: The Mishnah in Sanhedrin states that, "All
Israel has a portion in the World to Come...," yet then goes on
to list several categories of people who have no share in the
World to Come, the idea being that people who disobey the
Torah in less serious ways still have some share in the future
reward whereas those whose wickedness falls within certain
extreme categories do not.[484] Hence, when Rav Yosef talks
about the resurrection applying even to the wicked, he means
less serious sinners whereas certain heretics, those who lead
the public astray from the teachings of the Torah, and others
described in the Mishnah in Sanhedrin will not participate in
the resurrection. Rav Yosef must understand the verse in
Daniel as applying to the latter group.*

---

[484] Mishnah Sanhedrin 10:1. See also B.T. Rosh HaShanah 17A which
limits eternal damnation to only a few severe categories of sinners.

Brachoth 5:2 (continued) (compare B.T. Ta'anith 3A-3B)

כתיב, "וַיֹּאמֶר אֵלִיָּהוּ הַתִּשְׁבִּי מִתּשָׁבֵי גִלְעָד אֶל אַחְאָב חַי ה׳
אֱ-לֹהֵי יִשְׂרָאֵל אֲשֶׁר עָמַדְתִּי לְפָנָיו אִם יִהְיֶה הַשָּׁנִים הָאֵלֶּה טַל וּמָטָר כִּי
אִם לְפִי דְבָרִי." (מלכים א יז:א). רבי ברכיה אמר רבי יסה ורבנן. חד
אמר: בין על הטל ובין על המטר נשמע לו. וחרנא אמר: על המטר
נשמע לו ועל הטל לא נשמע לו.

מאן דמר על המטר נשמע לו ועל הטל לא נשמע לו מן הדא:
"[וַיְהִי יָמִים רַבִּים וּדְבַר ה׳ הָיָה אֶל אֵלִיָּהוּ בַּשָּׁנָה הַשְּׁלִישִׁית לֵאמֹר] לֵךְ
הֵרָאֵה אֶל אַחְאָב וְאֶתְּנָה מָטָר [עַל פְּנֵי הָאֲדָמָה.]" (מלכים א יח:א).

ומאן דמר בין על הטל בין על המטר נשמע לו, איכן הותר נדרו
של טל? אמר רבי תנחומא אָדְרָעָיָה: סברין מימר, נדר שהותר מכללו
הותר כולו.

אית דבעי מימר בבנה של צָרְפִית: "וַיִּקְרָא אֶל ה׳ וַיֹּאמַר ה׳
אֱ-לֹהָי [הֲגַם עַל הָאַלְמָנָה אֲשֶׁר אֲנִי מִתְגּוֹרֵר עִמָּהּ הֲרֵעוֹתָ לְהָמִית אֶת
בְּנָהּ.]" (מלכים א יז:כ). אמר רבי יודה בן פָּזִי: לאחד שגנב נרתיקו של
רופא עם כשהוא יוצא נפצע בנו. חזר אצלו. אמר לו, "אדוני הרופא,
רפא את בני."

אמר לו, "לך והחזר את הנרתק שכל מיני רפואות נתונין בו ואני
מרפא את בנך."

כך אמר לו הקדוש ברוך הוא לאליהו: "לך והתר נדרו של טל,
שאין המתים חיים אלא בטללים, ואני מחיה את בנה של צרפית."

ומניין שאין המתים חיים אלא בטללים? "יִחְיוּ מֵתֶיךָ נְבֵלָתִי
יְקוּמוּן הָקִיצוּ וְרַנְּנוּ שֹׁכְנֵי עָפָר כִּי טַל אוֹרֹת טַלֶּךָ וָאָרֶץ רְפָאִים תַּפִּיל."
(ישעיה כוּוֹט). אמר רבי תנחום אָדְרָעָיָה: וארעא תפקידיה וְנַעֲלִיט.

רבי יעקב דכפר חנן בשם ריש לקיש: בשעה שעשה אברהם
זקינך רצוני, נשבעתי לו שאיני זז טל מבניו לעולם. מה טעם? "...לְךָ טַל
יַלְדֻתֶיךָ." (תהלים קי:ג). וכתיב בתריה, "נִשְׁבַּע ה׳ וְלֹא יִנָּחֵם..." (תהלים
קיד).

אמר רבי יודא בן פזי: בדייתיקי נתתיו לאברהם, במתנה נתתיו

לו. "וְיִתֶּן לְךָ הָאֱ-לֹהִים מִטַּל הַשָּׁמַיִם [וּמִשְׁמַנֵּי הָאָרֶץ וְרֹב דָּגָן וְתִירֹשׁ.]"
(בראשית כז:כח).

אמר רבי שמואל בר נחמני: בשעה שישראל באין לידי עבירה
ומעשים רעים, הגשמים נעצרים. הן מביאין להן זקן אחד כגון רבי יוסי
הגלילי והוא מפגיע בעדם והגשמים יורדים, אבל הטל אינו יורד בזכות
ברייה. מה טעם? "[וְהָיָה שְׁאֵרִית יַעֲקֹב בְּקֶרֶב עַמִּים רַבִּים] כְּטַל מֵאֵת ה'
כִּרְבִיבִים עֲלֵי עֵשֶׂב אֲשֶׁר לֹא יְקַוֶּה לְאִישׁ וְלֹא יְיַחֵל לִבְנֵי אָדָם." (מיכה
ה:ו).

It is written, "Elijah the Tishbite from the inhabitants of Gilead said to Ahab, 'By the life of the Lord, God of Israel, before Whom I have stood, if [during] these years there will be dew and rain except by my word.'"[485] Rabbi Berachyah, in the name of Rabbi Yassa, had a dispute with the other scholars of the academy. One side said: Both as to dew and as to rain his prayer was heard. The other side said: As to the rain, his prayer was heard, but as to the dew his prayer was not heard.

The one who says that as to the rain his prayer was heard, but as to the dew his prayer was not heard derives his view from the following: "After many days, the word of the Lord was to Elijah in the third year, saying, 'Go and appear to Ahab and I will give rain upon the face of the land.'"[486] [Since only rain is mentioned, but not dew, it appears that God only stopped the rain.]

According to the one who says both as to dew and as to rain his prayer was heard, how was Elijah's vow concerning

---

[485] I Kings 17:1.
[486] I Kings 18:1.

dew released? Rabbi Tanchum of Idra said that the students of the academy figured that a vow which is partly released is wholly released. [Since the verse says that God released Elijah from his vow with respect to rain, his vow with respect to dew was also released even though dew is not explicitly mentioned.][487]

There are those who wanted to say that the vow as to dew was released at the time of the episode involving the son of the lady of Zarphath as the verse says, "He called to the Lord and said, 'Lord, my God, also upon the widow with whom I visit have You done evil to kill her son?'"[488] Rabbi Judah ben Pazzi said that this may be compared to one who stole the medical kit of a doctor. After a while, the thief's son was injured. He returned and said, "Honored physician, heal my son." He responded to him, "Go and return the kit which has stored in it all types of remedies and I will heal your son." So the Holy One, Blessed be He, said to Elijah, "Go release your vow concerning dew, for the dead do not live except by means of dew, and I will revive the son of the lady of Zarphath."

From where do we know that the dead are not revived except by means of dew? Scripture says, "May Your dead live! May my deceased rise! Awaken and sing inhabitants of the dust for a dew of sprouting is your dew, but the wicked

---

[487] B.T. Ta'anith 3A-3B suggests a third approach: Ordinary dew did not stop during the period covered by Elijah's oath. However, "dew of blessing," dew that falls at just the right time and in just the right manner to benefit crops, did stop.
[488] I Kings 17:20.

shall fall to the ground."[489] Rabbi Tanchum of Idra explained the last part of the verse (וארץ רפאים תפיל) to mean "the land shall eject those with whom it is entrusted."

Rabbi Jacob from the village of Chanan said in the name of Resh Lakish that God told Elijah, "At the time that Abraham your ancestor performed My will, I swore to him that I would never remove dew from his descendants. What is the Scriptural basis for this? "...from your dawning, from the dew of your youth," after which is written, "The Lord swore and will not retract... ."[490]

Rabbi Judah ben Pazzi said that God said, "As a deeded gift I gave it to Abraham, as a present I gave it to him," as the verse says, "May God give you from the dew of the heavens and from the fat of the earth and abundant grain and wine."[491]

Rabbi Samuel bar Nachmeni said: At a time when Israel comes within the grip of sin and evil deeds, the rains are stopped. They bring for themselves an elder such as Rabbi Yossi HaGalili who entreats on their behalf and the rains fall, but the dew does not descend in the merit of any creature. What is the Scriptural basis for this? "The remnant of Jacob shall be many in the midst of the nations as dew from the Lord, as mists upon the grass which do not hope for man and do not await people."[492]

---

489 Isaiah 26:19.
490 Psalms 110:3-4.
491 Genesis 27:28.
492 Micah 5:6.

The Babylonian Talmud proclaims that three keys are in the hands of Hashem Himself and not controlled by any intermediary: the keys to childbirth, rain and resurrection of the dead.[493] *Similarly, the Talmud states that life, children and livelihood (which corresponds to rain because rain causes the earth to yield food)*[494] *are not dependent upon merit but upon luck* (מזל).[495] *This means that God preordains how long one will live, whether one will be rich or poor and whether one will have children, all as part of His overall master plan for humanity.*

These three things also correspond to the three ways in which humankind was cursed when Adam and Eve ate from the Tree of Knowledge. At that time, God told Eve that she would suffer during childbirth.[496] *He informed Adam that he would have to suffer to earn his livelihood.*[497] *God also drove Adam and Eve out of the Garden of Eden so that they could not eat from the Tree of Life and live forever.*[498]

Human beings often lash out at those who offend them, seeking vengeance. By contrast, when Hashem punishes those who disobey His will, He does so for their own benefit. When

---

[493] B.T. Ta'anith 2A.
[494] So says Rabbi Yochanan in B.T. Ta'anith 2A-B. Others reckon the key to earning a livelihood as a fourth key which is exclusively in the hands of the Almighty. (Tanchuma Parshath VaYera 35 and Tur Shulchan Aruch, Orach Chaim 114)
[495] B.T. Mo'ed Katan 28A.
[496] Genesis 3:16.
[497] Genesis 3:17.
[498] Genesis 3:22-23.

God punished humankind after Adam and Eve sinned, He did so with "curses" that have the potential to help people overcome the evil inclination and earn a share in the World to Come. The dangers of childbirth, the difficulties of earning a living and the ominous specter of eventual death challenge humanity to have faith in God. When things are easy, people have an unfortunate tendency to slacken from their religiosity as the verse says, "Jeshurun grew fat and kicked; grew fat, thickened, covered [with fat] and abandoned God who made him, he spurned the Rock of his salvation."[499] *The very problems which people must address during their lifetimes goad them to turn to God.*

This concept is especially true with respect to death. Sadly, it is sometimes only in the face of death that people come to ponder the true meaning of life. This, in turn, leads them to Hashem and Torah. As the Mishnah says, "Repent one day before your death."[500] *The fact that no one knows when he or she will die forces people to constantly strive to improve themselves. Also, because life is finite, people have a motive to make the most out of it, to devote themselves wholeheartedly to learning Torah and performing Mitzvoth for, as Hillel said, "If not now, when?"*[501] *If people lived forever, they would not be motivated to repent or try to improve themselves spiritually because they would always rationalize that they could do so later. So it is the very "curse" of death that gives people the*

---

[499] Deuteronomy 32:15. Jeshurun denotes the People of Israel.
[500] Pirkei Avoth 2:10.
[501] Pirkei Avoth 1:14.

opportunity to overcome their evil impulses and draw close to God.

It appears that Elijah accomplished the unusual feat of totally overcoming the evil inclination. An individual on his spiritual level did not need the prospect of death to drive him to reject the evil inclination. That is why Hashem gave him control of the keys to childbirth, rain and resurrection of the dead. Thus, as the passage under review points out, Elijah controlled the rain and also revived a dead child. He also did not die as people normally do, but was carried away in a whirlwind at the end of his life.[502]

That no future reward would be possible without the challenges of death, childbirth and earning a livelihood is hinted at by the Talmud's statement that without dew there can be no resurrection. The word "dew" (טל) in Hebrew has the same letters as "curse" (לט), alluding to the "curses" God gave to Adam and Eve. It is these very "curses" which offer humanity the chance to earn eternal reward.

---

[502] Although this passage of the Talmud does not mention childbirth, Elijah was especially zealous about the mitzvah of circumcision and visits the circumcision of every Jewish baby. See Shulchan Aruch, Yoreh Deah 265:11. See also Shir HaShirim Rabbah 1:9 which says that the future resurrection will be accomplished through Elijah.

Brachoth 5:3 (compare B.T. Brachoth 33B-34A)

משנה: האומר, "על קן צפור יגיעו רחמיך," ו"על טוב יזכר
שמך," "מודים מודים," משתקין אותו...

גמרא: רבי פינחס בשם רבי סימון: כקורא תיגר על מדותיו של
הקדוש ברוך הוא. על קן ציפור הגיעו רחמיך ועל אותו האיש לא הגיעו
רחמיך?

רבי יוסי בשם רבי סימון: כנותן קיצבה למדותיו של הקדוש
ברוך הוא. עד קן ציפור הגיעו רחמיך.

אית תניי תני, "על," "ואית תניי תני, "עד." מאן דמר "על" מסייע
לרבי פינחס ומן דמר "עד" מסייע לרבי יוסי.

אמר רבי יוסי בי רבי בון: לא עבדין טבות שעושין למדותיו של
הקדוש ברוך הוא רחמים. ואילין דמתרגמין, "[וְעַתָּה לְכָה וְאֶשְׁלָחֲךָ אֶל
פַּרְעֹה וְהוֹצֵא אֶת] עַמִּי בְנֵי יִשְׂרָאֵל [מִמִּצְרָיִם.] (שמות ג:י): "כמה דאנא
רחמן בשמים, כך תהוון רחמנין בארעא. 'תורתא או רחילה יתה וית ברה
לא תיכסון תרויהון ביומא חד,'" לא עבדין טבאות, שהן עושין מדותיו
של הקדוש ברוך הוא רחמים.

**Mishnah: If one says [during prayer], "Your mercies
extend to a bird's nest"** [The sense of such a prayer being
that just as God shows mercy to birds by requiring Jews to
shoo away the mother bird from her nest before taking the
eggs or young, so should He show mercy to the
petitioner.]**...we silence him** [because it is wrong to state
that God's commandments have known reasons. **Rather,**

they are decrees which must be obeyed even if not understood.[503]

Gemara: Rabbi Phinehas said in the name of Rabbi Simon: [We silence one who prays thus because it is] as though he complains about the attributes of the Holy One, Blessed be He. [It is as though he says,] "Your mercies extend to a bird's nest, but Your mercies do not extend to me?"

Rabbi Yossi said in the name of Rabbi Simon: [We silence one who prays thus because it is] as though he sets a limit upon the attributes of the Holy One, Blessed be He. [It is as though he says,] "Your mercies extend only as far as a bird's nest."

There are sages who read the text of the Mishnah as "to a bird's nest" (על) and there are sages who read the text of the Mishnah as "until a bird's nest" (עד). Those who reads "to a bird's nest" support the view of Rabbi Phinehas while those who read "until a bird's nest" support the view of Rabbi Yossi.

Rabbi Yossi of the academy of Rabbi Bon said: They do not act properly who explain the attributes of the Holy One, Blessed be He, as mercy. [There was a custom in ancient times whereby a translator would translate each verse of the Torah after it was read in the synagogue. Such translations often included a brief explanation of the verse.[504]] Those who interpret such verses as "And now, go, I will send you to Pharaoh and you shall take out my people the Children of Israel from Egypt"[505] to mean, "Just as I am merciful in Heaven, so

---

[503] P'nei Moshe and see Rashi on B.T. Brachoth 33B.
[504] See, for example, Megillah 4:4.
[505] Exodus 3:10 and see also 7:4 for a similar expression.

you be merciful on earth. 'A female ox or ewe, it and its
offspring you shall not slaughter together on the same day'[506]"
do not act properly for they explain the attributes of the Holy
One, Blessed be He as mercy. [Attempting to explain God's
taking the Jews out of Egypt or the commandment not to
slaughter a mother animal and its offspring on the same day as
flowing from a character trait of mercy is wrong because God
has no character traits and the reasons for His actions are
unknown.]

*The Rambam states in his famous "Guide for the
Perplexed" (מורה נבוכים) that there is a difference of opinion
as to whether the commandments of the Torah have reasons or
not.[507] He himself holds the opinion that all commandments do
have an underlying rationale and that the reason for
commandments such as sending away the mother bird before
seizing her young or not slaughtering a calf and its mother on
the same day are designed to inculcate in Jews the
characteristic of mercy.[508] The Rambam contends that the
contrary view expressed by the Mishnah and Gemara that such
commandments are decrees without an underlying rationale
merely represents a different point of view.[509] Many scholars
have wondered at how the Rambam could contradict a*

---

[506] Leviticus 22:28.
[507] Guide for the Perplexed (מורה נבוכים) III:26.
[508] The Ramban (Rabbi Moshe Ben Nachman of Spain, 1194-1270) on
Deuteronomy 22:6 endorses and elaborates upon this view.
[509] Guide for the Perplexed (מורה נבוכים) III:48.

Mishnah which none of the Tannaim opposed (סתם משנה) and which is repeated in Tractate Megillah, again uncontested.[510] In addition, the Rambam himself rules as a matter of practical halachah in the Yad HaChazakah that one who prays in the fashion described in this passage must be silenced.[511]

The answer may be that the Rambam distinguished between halachic application and theoretical interpretation. For purposes of practical day to day halachic procedure, the Rambam rules according to the plain, uncontradicted view of the Mishnah. However, he felt himself free to offer an opposing theoretical view if there was a sufficient basis in traditional Jewish thinking for doing so. Authority for the Rambam's view is indeed found in the Midrash which states, "Why is a child circumcised after eight days? Because the Holy One, Blessed be He, bestowed His mercy upon him to wait until he has strength. Just as the mercy of the Holy One, Blessed be He, is upon humanity, so is His mercy upon animals. From where do we see this? It says, '...and from the eighth day onward it shall be accepted as a sacrifice...'[512] [meaning that God wished Jews to show pity on the mother animal and did not want the baby animal to be whisked off immediately for slaughter[513]]. Not only that, but the Holy One, Blessed be He, said, 'An ox or sheep, it and its offspring you shall not slaughter together on the same day.'[514] And just as

---

[510] Megillah 4:9.
[511] Yad HaChazakah, Hilchoth Tefillah 9:7.
[512] Leviticus 22:27.
[513] Maharzu ad loc.
[514] Leviticus 22:28.

the Holy One, Blessed be He, bestowed His mercy upon animals, so He was filled with mercy upon birds. From where do we see this? It says, 'When a bird's nest shall happen before you in the way, in any tree or on the ground [with] fledglings or eggs and the mother hovers upon the fledglings or upon the eggs, you shall not take the mother with the offspring. You shall surely send away the mother, and the offspring you may take for yourself... .'[515] [516] *Thus, the Rambam had a traditional source upon which to base his point of view and, so, had a right to express it on a theoretical level. For purposes of making a halachic ruling, however, he had to follow the authoritative dictates of the Mishnah and Gemara.*[517]

---

[515] Deuteronomy 22:6-7.

[516] Devarim Rabbah 6:1.

[517] See Rabbi Yom Tov Lipman Heller in his Tosafoth Yom Tov commentary to Brachoth 5:3 where he suggests a similar distinction.

Brachoth 5:5 (compare B.T. Brachoth 34B)

משנה: המתפלל וטעה, סימן רע לו. ואם שליח ציבור הוא,
סימן רע לשולחיו, ששלוחו של אדם כמותו. אמרו עליו על רבי
חנינא בן דוסא שהיה מתפלל על החולים ואומר, "זה חי וזה מת."
אמרו לו, "מנין אתה יודע?" אמר להם, "אם שגורה תפילתי בפי, יודע
אני שאני מקובל, ואם לאו, יודע אני שהוא מטורף."
גמרא: רבי אחא בר יעקב אמר: ובלבד באבות. מעשה ברבן
גמליאל שחלה בנו ושלח שני תלמידי חכמים אצל רבי חנינא בן דוסא
בעירו. אמר לון, "המתינו לי עד שאעלה לעלייה." ועלה לעלייה וירד.
אמר להו, "בטוח אני שנינוח בנו של רבן גמליאל מחליו," וסיימו.
באותה שעה תבע מהן מזון.

Mishnah: If a worshiper makes a mistake when
reciting his prayers, it is an evil omen for him and if he is
the cantor, it is an evil sign for those whom he represents
because one's agent is the same as himself. They said about
Rabbi Chanina ben Dosa that when he used to pray for the
sick, he would say, "This one shall live and this one shall
die." They said to him, "How do you know?" He said to
them, "If my prayer is fluent in my mouth, I know that my
petition has been accepted, but if not, I know that it was
rejected."

Gemara: Rabbi Acha bar Yaakov said: [An error in
reciting one's prayers is an evil omen] only when [the first
blessing of the silent prayer which mentions the] Patriarchs is
involved.

There was an incident involving Rabban Gamliel whose
son became ill. He sent two disciples to Rabbi Chanina ben

Dosa's hometown. The latter said to them, "Wait for me while I go up to the attic." He went up to the attic and came back down. He said to them, "I am certain that the son of Rabban Gamliel has recovered from his sickness." They took note of that moment and later discovered that at that same time, Rabban Gamliel's son asked for food [having indeed recovered].

*One could understand if the Talmud stated that God gives a sign at the **end** of a prayer that it was not accepted, but how does it make sense for God to send a sign to the worshiper at the **beginning** of his or her prayers that they will not be accepted? Of course God already knows in advance what the worshiper will request, but if the merit of prayer helps a situation, how can God issue a decision beforehand?*

Rabbi Elimelech of Lizensk explains that God created all possible outcomes of a situation in potential before He created the world. Thus, when God responds to a prayer, He does not "change His mind." Rather, he merely brings to fruition that which already existed in potential when He created the world. If a person can utter his or her prayers fluently, it means that a positive outcome potentially exists. If, however, he or she has trouble praying, it means that no such outcome is possible.[518]

---

[518] No'am Elimelech, Parshath VaYechi by Rabbi Elimelech of Lizensk (1717-1787).

Brachoth 6:1 (Compare B.T. 35A-B)

כתיב, "...לַה׳ הָאָרֶץ וּמְלוֹאָהּ תֵּבֵל וְיֹשְׁבֵי בָהּ." (תהלים כד:א).
הנהנה כלום מן העולם מעל עד שיתירו לו המצות.
אמר רבי אבוה: כתיב, "[לֹא תִזְרַע כַּרְמְךָ כִּלְאָיִם] פֶּן תִּקְדַּשׁ
הַמְלֵאָה הַזֶּרַע אֲשֶׁר תִּזְרָע וּתְבוּאַת הַכָּרֶם." (דברים כב:ט). העולם כולו
ומלואו עשוי ככרם. ומהו פדיונו? ברכה.

It is written, "To the Lord [belong] the earth and its
contents, the world and those who inhabit it."[519]   One who
benefits from the world in any manner commits a desecration
unless the commandments authorize him to do so. [This means
that one may not eat until he or she observes the commandment
of first reciting a blessing.[520]]

Rabbi Abuha says: "Do not plant your vineyard with a
mixture [of seeds] lest the growth of the seed which you plant
and the produce of the vineyard become abominable."[521]   The
world and its contents are like a vineyard [whose owner must
take the fruits it yields during the fourth year after it was
planted to Jerusalem or redeem them for money which he or
she then takes to Jerusalem and uses to purchase food].   And
how is it redeemed?   By a blessing.

[*Rabbi Abuha bases his exposition on the similarity
between the phrases "and its contents"* (וּמְלוֹאָהּ) *and "the*

---

[519] Psalms 24:1.
[520] Etz Yosef.
[521] Deuteronomy 22:9.

growth" (המלאה).[522]   *However, the verse pertaining to a vineyard actually discusses the prohibition against planting seeds of other plants together with grape seeds (כלאי הכרם), not the law of redeeming grapes from vines which are four years old (כרם רבעי). What is the connection between the prohibition of planting seeds of other plants together with grape seeds (כלאי הכרם) and the idea that one must not benefit from the world without first reciting a blessing?*

The Ramban writes that the reason for the prohibition against planting seeds of different species together as well as similar prohibitions against interbreeding different animal species is that creating such mixtures demonstrates a belief that God's creation is defective and in need of improvement.[523]

The Ramban's explanation sounds strange. If one were to take this view to its logical conclusion, then the Torah should have forbidden the cultivation and processing of food altogether since all such activities suggest that the world is not perfect in its natural state.

Moreover, the Midrash specifically rejects the Ramban's position. A Roman officer once challenged Rabbi Akiva by saying, "Why do you circumcise yourselves? Surely you cannot mean to improve upon that which God has created?"

Rabbi Akiva presented the Roman with stalks of wheat and fine cakes. "Aren't these cakes better than mere stalks of

---

[522] Etz Yosef. P'nei Moshe, however, says that the homiletic is simply based on the extra letter ה, meaning "the," in the phrase "produce of the vineyard" (תבואת הכרם) which could have been written "produce of a vineyard" (תבואת כרם).
[523] Ramban on Leviticus 19:19.

wheat?" he retorted. "God created many things in nature which humans can improve."[524] *Accordingly, it does not appear that Hashem expects or desires people to refrain from improving upon creation. To the contrary, the mitzvah of circumcision implies that God **wants** people to improve the world.*

*Perhaps the Ramban means as follows. God's **original** creation was perfect and not in need of any improvement. Only when Adam and Eve sinned in the Garden of Eden did things change. As a result of that sin, God told Adam that he would henceforth have to work for a living. Thus, all the work and preparation required to produce food was introduced into the world. Nonetheless, the Torah seeks to remind us that things were not always this way and, indeed, ideally should not be so. Therefore, while the Torah does not prohibit all efforts by humankind to improve the state of the world, it does prohibit planting certain mixtures of seeds as a reminder that God's original handiwork was perfect and not subject to improvement. Only because of human sin are such "improvements" necessary.*

Now one can understand the connection between a verse which discusses the prohibition against planting mixtures of seeds and the obligation to recite a blessing before eating. The act of sinning is a denial of God. This was especially so with respect to Adam and Eve who had direct contact with God, who had only one commandment to observe (not to eat from the

---

[524] Midrash Tanchuma, Parshath Thazria, 5 and Breishith Rabbah 11:6.

207

*Tree of Knowledge) and who lived under ideal circumstances
in the Garden of Eden where all their needs were met.*

*The essence of the recitation of a blessing is
acknowledgment of God. Accordingly, the recitation of a
blessing rectifies the sin of Adam and Eve. By acknowledging
God, one who recites a blessing helps restore the world to its
original state of perfection, a state which humans would not
need to improve had Adam and Eve not sinned. However, if
one fails to say a blessing, he or she fails to help restore
perfection to the world just as one who plants forbidden
mixtures denies the original perfection of the universe.*

Brachoth 6:1 (continued)

רבי יחזקיה, רבי ירמיה, רבי אבון בשם רבי שמעון בן לקיש:
"אָמַרְתְּ לַה' אֲ-דֹנָי אָתָּה טוֹבָתִי בַּל עָלֶיךָ." (תהלים טז:ב). אם אכלת
וברכת, כביכול, כאלו משלך אכלת. דבר אחר: "טוֹבָתִי בַּל עָלֶיךָ,"
מבלה אני טובתי בגופך. דבר אחר: "טוֹבָתִי בַּל עָלֶיךָ," יבללו כל
הטובות ויבואו עליך.

אמר רבי אחא: מהו "בַּל עָלֶיךָ?" שאיני מביא טובה על העולם
מבלעדיך, כמה דאת אמר, "[וַיֹּאמֶר פַּרְעֹה אֶל יוֹסֵף אֲנִי פַרְעֹה] וּבִלְעָדֶיךָ
לֹא יָרִים אִישׁ אֶת יָדוֹ [וְאֶת רַגְלוֹ בְּכָל אֶרֶץ מִצְרָיִם]" (בראשית מא:מד).
תני רבי חייא: "וּבַשָּׁנָה הָרְבִיעִת יִהְיֶה כָּל פִּרְיוֹ] קֹדֶשׁ הִלּוּלִים
[לַה']." (ויקרא יט:כד). מלמד שהוא טעון ברכה לפניו ולאחריו. מיכן
היה רבי עקיבא אומר: לא יטעום אדם כלום עד שיברך.

Rabbi Yechezekiah, Rabbi Jeremiah and Rabbi Abon
said in the name of Rabbi Shimon ben Lakish: "[If] you said to
the Lord, 'You are the Lord,' [then further] recognition of Me
is not required of you."[525] If you ate and blessed God, then, so
to speak, it is as though you ate from what belongs to you.
[The phrase "You are the Lord" implies recognizing God by
uttering a benediction.[526]] Another interpretation: "recognition
of Me is not required of you" (טובתי בל עליך) means "I will
exhaust my good upon your body" (מבלה אני טובתי בגופך) [If
you recite a blessing when you eat, I will fulfill my blessings in
you.] Another interpretation: "recognition of Me is not

---

[525] Psalms 16:2.
[526] Perush MiBa'al Sefer Chareidim.

required of you" means "all good things will be blended together (יבללו) and come upon you."

Rabbi Acha said: What does the expression "is not required of you" (בל עליך) mean? I will not bring good to the world without you, just as Scripture states [that when Pharaoh appointed Joseph as his viceroy, he told him], "...without you (ובלעדיך) no man shall lift his hand or his foot in all the Land of Egypt."[527] [In other words, the phrase טובתי בל עליך should be read טובתי בלעדיך.]

Rabbi Chiya taught: "In the fourth year all its fruit shall be sanctified in praises unto the Lord."[528] [The plural form "praises"] teaches that a blessing is required before and after eating.[529] Based on this, Rabbi Akiva used to say, "A person should not partake of anything before reciting a blessing."

*The expression "I will **exhaust** my good upon your body" (מבלה אני טובתי בגופך) implies a perfect type of blessing which lacks nothing. Sometimes physical blessings can be spiritual curses. For example, one who is very wealthy may turn from Hashem in the false belief that he is secure in his wealth and does not "need" God's help. The expression "I will exhaust my good upon your **body**" implies that God will give material blessings in such a way that the recipient will realize that they are only for his or her **body**, but that spiritual*

---

527 Genesis 41:44.
528 Leviticus 19:24.
529 P'nei Moshe.

perfection remains a goal for which one must continue to strive.

Along similar lines, there can be too much of certain types of physical blessings. For instance, the Talmud points out that a moderate amount of rain is beneficial, but too much rain causes flooding and destruction. "I will exhaust my good upon your body" implies that God will give His blessings in the right amount, the amount that will benefit "your body," but no more.[530]

The expression "all good things will be blended together (יבללו) and come upon you" also bears these implications. Hashem will blend physical and spiritual blessings in such a way that the physical blessings do not cause one to ignore the spiritual, and these blessings will come in the right measure. In addition, not all blessings are readily compatible with one another. For example, it is a blessing to have a carefree life and also a blessing to have children, but it is difficult to raise children and yet remain carefree. The idea that "all good things will be blended together (יבללו) and come upon you" suggests that God will bestow blessings in a manner in which they can all be realized.[531]

---

[530] Compare Sefer Benayahu.
[531] Ibid.

Brachoth 7:2 (Compare J.T. Nazir 5:3, Breishith Rabbah 91:3 and Koheleth Rabbah 7:12)

[A Nazirite is a person who, for a period of time, vows to refrain from: (a) cutting his or her hair; (b) consumption of grapes or grape products; and (c) contamination with the dead. After the term of the vow ends, the Nazirite cuts his or her hair and brings three sacrifices to the Temple. As with any oath, an expert rabbi may cancel a Nazirite's vow if certain halachic requirements are met.]

תני: *שלש מאות נזירין עלו בימי רבי שמעון בן שטח. מאה וחמשים מצא להן פתח ומאה וחמשים לא מצא להן פתח.*
אתא גבי ינאי מלכא. אמר ליה, "אית הכא תלת מאה נזירין בעיין תשע מאה קרבנין, אלא יהב את פלגא מן דידך ואנא פלגא מן דידי."

שלח ליה ארבע מאה וחמשין. אזל לישנא בישא ומר ליה, "לא יהב מן דידיה כלום."

שמע ינאי מלכא וכעס. דחל שמעון בן שטח וערק. בתר יומין, סלקון בני נש רברבין מן מלכותא דפרס גבי ינאי מלכא. מן דיתבין אכלין, אמרין ליה, "נהירין אנן דהוה אית הכא חד גבר סב והוה אמר קומין מילין דחכמה."

תני לון עובדא. אמרין ליה, "שלח ואייתיתיה."

שלח ויהב ליה מילא ואתא ויתיב ליה בין מלכא למלכתא. אמר ליה, "למה אפליית בי?"

אמר ליה, "לא אפליית בך. את מממונך ואנא מן אורייתי, דכתיב, 'כִּי בְּצֵל הַחָכְמָה בְּצֵל הַכָּסֶף... .'" (קהלת ז:יב).

אמר ליה, "ולמה ערקת?"

אמר ליה, "שמעית דמרי כעס עלי ובעית מקיימה הדין קרייא, 'לֵךְ עַמִּי בֹּא בַחֲדָרֶיךָ וּסְגֹר דְּלָתְיךָ [דְּלָתְךָ קרי] בַּעֲדֶךָ] חֲבִי כִמְעַט רֶגַע

212

עַד יַעֲבוֹר [יַעֲבָר קרי] זָעַם." (ישעיה כו:כ).
וִקְרָא עָלָי, "...וְיִתְרוֹן דַּעַת הַחָכְמָה תְּחַיֶּה בְּעָלֶיהָ." (קהלת ז:יב).
אָמַר לֵיהּ, "וּלְמָה יָתְבַת בֵּין מַלְכָּא לְמַלְכְתָא?"
אָמַר לֵיהּ, "בְּסִיפְרֵי דְּבֶן סִירָא כְּתִיב, "סַלְסְלֶיהָ וּתְרוֹמְמֶךָּ וּבֵין
נְגִידִים תּוֹשִׁיבֶךָ."

Three hundred Nazirites ascended to Jerusalem in the days of Rabbi Shimon ben Shetach. For one hundred fifty he found a halachic opening [with which to annul their Nazirite vows] and for one hundred fifty he found no opening.

He came to King Yannai and said to him, "There are three hundred Nazirites who require nine hundred sacrifices. If you supply half from your resources, I will supply half from mine."

King Yannai sent him four hundred fifty sacrificial animals. A certain slanderer told the king, "Rabbi Shimon ben Shetach did not supply any of his own." King Yannai believed the report and grew angry.

Fearing the king, Rabbi Shimon ben Shetach fled.

After many days, several great nobles from the Persian kingdom ascended to visit King Yannai. As they sat and feasted with him, they said, "We recall that there was a certain elderly man here who used to speak words of wisdom before us." The king recounted what had happened to which they responded, "Send forth and bring him."

King Yannai sent forth and gave Rabbi Shimon ben Shetach a guarantee of safe passage. The latter came and sat between the king and queen.

Said the king, "Why did you mock me?"

"I did not mock you. You contributed from your money and I from my Torah wisdom [by finding a way in which to cancel the vows of half the Nazirites, thus eliminating the need to bring half of the sacrifices], as it is written, 'For [just as a person takes refuge] in the shadow of wisdom [so may one find refuge] in the shadow of money...'.[532]"

"Why did you flee?" asked King Yannai.

"I heard that my master was angry at me and took heed of the verse, "Go My people, come into your rooms and close your doors behind you; hide for a bit of a moment until anger passes."[533]

King Yannai applied to Rabbi Shimon ben Shetach the verse, "...and abundant knowledge of wisdom gives life to its masters."[534]

"Why did you sit between the king and queen?" continued King Yannai.

"In the book of Ben Sira it is written, 'Explore it [the Torah] and it shall uplift you; it shall cause you to sit among rulers.'[535]"

One striking problem raised by this passage is why Rabbi Shimon ben Shetach did not simply come straight out and tell King Yannai what he was doing in the first place. Why

---

532 Ecclesiastes 7:12.
533 Isaiah 26:20.
534 Ecclesiastes 7:12.
535 A similar expression is found in Proverbs 4:8. B.T. Brachoth 48A reports Rabbi Shimon ben Shetach as quoting the latter verse.

not explain that he intended to "contribute" his half of the sacrifices for the Nazirites by releasing them from their vows and so avoid a confrontation with the king? The version of this story which appears in the Midrash has King Yannai pose this very question to Rabbi Shimon ben Shetach. The latter's response is that if he had fully explained the situation, the king would have refused to contribute to the cause.[536] *Rather than resolve the question, the Midrash makes it more pointed. Since the Torah forbids deception even for noble purposes,*[537] *how could Rabbi Shimon ben Shetach trick King Yannai into contributing to the Nazirites?*

Perhaps Rabbi Shimon ben Shetach knew that King Yannai would, upon reflection, really want to participate in this mitzvah. However, the king was unusually short-tempered. The Talmud reports that King Yannai once became so enraged when the rabbis questioned his priestly lineage that he executed many of them and forced Rabbi Shimon ben Shetach to flee the realm.[538] *Accordingly, Rabbi Shimon ben Shetach feared that if he told King Yannai in a straightforward manner what was really going on, the king would angrily refuse to participate, an action he would later regret. The fact that the two of them later reconciled supports this proposition.*

One can understand that Rabbi Shimon ben Shetach might press King Yannai to contribute towards other religious

---

[536] Breishith Rabbah 91:3.
[537] Shulchan Aruch, Yoreh Deah 228:6, et. seq.
[538] B.T. Kiddushin 66A. B.T. Sanhedrin 19A-B gives a different version of events and states that the angel Gabriel killed the rabbis. Both passages, however, support the view that King Yannai had a short temper.

needs such as, for example, if people did not have money to purchase wine for Kiddush or Matzoth for Passover, but why worry about the sacrifices for the Nazirites? The Torah does not command anyone to assume the duties of a Nazirite. If certain individuals wished to adopt this practice, they should have made certain beforehand that they would have the required sacrifices. Surely they had no right to make such a vow and then expect others to provide for them.

The explanation for Rabbi Shimon ben Shetach's behavior may that although the vow to become a Nazirite is voluntary, there are certain circumstances where it is highly appropriate. For example, Rabbi Judah the Prince states that if one sees a suspected adulteress (סוטה) receiving Divine punishment by means of the testing water (מי סוטה), he should vow to become a Nazirite because consumption of alcohol can lead to licentiousness and a Nazirite is temporarily forbidden to consume grape products.[539] Similarly, Rabbi Simeon the Righteous praised a young man who vowed to become a Nazirite after he found himself taking pride in his beautiful hair because a Nazirite must shave off his hair at the expiration of the term of the vow.[540]

Perhaps the Nazirites Rabbi Shimon Ben Shetach sought to help had experiences which inspired them to make their vows. In fact, it appears that certain forms of disobedience to the Torah were widespread in his time. For instance, the Talmud states that R. Shimon Ben Shetach took the unusual

---

[539] B.T. Sotah 2A.
[540] B.T. Nazir 4B.

step of executing eighty women in a single day in order to stem the witchcraft prevalent in that era.[541] *Such witchcraft included forbidden sexual practices and idolatry.*[542] *Accordingly, the three hundred people whom Rabbi Shimon ben Shetach wanted to help may have felt constrained to become Nazirites even though not strictly required to do so. Wishing to encourage this commendable practice, R. Shimon ben Shetach arranged for the sacrifices or the release of the vows after the Nazirites accomplished their purpose by fulfilling the other requirements of their vows.*

---

[541] Sanhedrin 6:4 and Me'am Lo'ez on Exodus 8:14 (Exodus Vol.1, page 107.)
[542] Rambam, Moreh Nevuchim Part III, Chapter 37.

Torah from Jerusalem

Brachoth 7:3 Compare B.T. Yoma 69B

כתיב, "וַיְבָרֶךְ עֶזְרָא אֶת ה' הָאֱ-לֹהִים הַגָּדוֹל... ." (נחמיה ח:ו).
במה הוא גידלו? גדלו בשם המפורש. רב מתנה אמר: גדלו בברכה.
רבי סימון בשם רבי יהושע בן לוי: למה נקרו אנשי כנסת
הגדולה? שהחזירו הגדולה ליושנה. אמר רבי פנחס: משה התקין
מטבעה של תפילה, "...הָאֱ-ל הַגָּדֹל הַגִּבֹּר וְהַנּוֹרָא... ." (דברים י:יז) ירמיה
אמר, "...הָאֱ-ל הַגָּדוֹל הַגִּבּוֹר...," (ירמיה לב:יח), ולא אמר "הַנּוֹרָא." למה
אמר "הַגִּבּוֹר?" לזה נאה לקרות גבור שהוא רואה חורבן ביתו ושותק.
ולמה לא אמר "נוֹרָא?" אלא שאין נורא אלא בית המקדש שנאמר,
"נוֹרָא אֱ-לֹהִים מִמִּקְדָּשֶׁיךָ... ." (תהלים סח:לו). דניאל אמר, "...הָאֱ-ל
הַגָּדוֹל וְהַנּוֹרָא...," (דניאל ט:ד), ולא אמר "הַגִּבּוֹר." בניו מסורין בקולרין!
היכן היא גבורתו? ולמה אמר "הַנּוֹרָא?" לזה נאה לקרות נורא
בנוראות שעשה לנו בכבשן האש. וכיון שעמדו אנשי כנסת הגדולה,
החזירו הגדולה ליושנה: "הָאֱ-ל הַגָּדֹל הַגִּבֹּר וְהַנּוֹרָא."
ובשר ודם יש בו כח ליתן קצבה לדברים הללו? אמר רבי יצחק
בן אלעזר: יודעין הן הנביאים שא-לוהן אמיתי ואינן מחניפין לו.

It is written, "Ezra blessed the Lord, the great God... ."[543]
How did Ezra make him great? By pronouncing the
Tetragrammaton. Rabbi Mathnah said: He made Him great
with a blessing.

Rabbi Simon in the name of Rabbi Joshua ben Levi said:
Why were they called the Men of the Great Assembly?
Because they restored the greatness to its rightful place as
Rabbi Phinehas said: Moses established the formula for prayer,

---

[543] Nehemiah 8:6.

218

"...the God who is great, mighty and awesome... ."[544] Jeremiah said, "...the God who is great, mighty...,"[545] but did not say "awesome." Why did he say "the mighty"? Because it is fitting to call Him mighty for He sees the destruction of the Temple and is silent. [God is mighty because, so to speak, He controls His anger.] And why did he not say "awesome"? Because the expression "awesome" does not apply except to the Temple as it says, "Awesome is God from His sanctuary... ."[546] Daniel said, "the God who is great and awesome,"[547] but did not say "the mighty." His children are consigned to iron collars. Where is His might? And why did he say "the awesome"? Because it is fitting to call Him awesome for the awesome miracles he performed for us in the fiery furnace.[548] Once the Men of the Great Assembly arose, they restored the greatness to its rightful place by formulating the beginning of the silent prayer to read, "...the God who is great, mighty and awesome... ."

Does flesh and blood have the authority to place a limitation on these things? [What right did Jeremiah or Daniel have to "reduce" God's praises?] Rabbi Isaac ben Elazar said: The prophets knew that their God is truthful so they did not flatter Him.

---

[544] Deuteronomy 10:17.
[545] Jeremiah 32:18.
[546] Psalms 68:36.
[547] Daniel 9:4.
[548] King Nebuchadnezzar had Hananiah, Mishael and Azariah cast into a fiery furnace as punishment for refusing to worship an idol. Miraculously, they were not harmed. Daniel 3:19-25.

The Talmud states that anyone who alters the formula of the blessings specified by the sages does not fulfill his or her obligation.[549] *Moreover, as the "father of all prophets," surely Moses chose to glorify God by using a phrase which held profound meaning. Accordingly, it seems strange that Jeremiah and Daniel would deviate from Moses's usage even if they thought the historical events of their times justified it.*

The Talmud reports that a certain person who was leading the prayer service once said, "...the God who is great, mighty and awesome, the powerful, the sturdy, the feared, the strong, the stalwart, the constant, the honored..." When he finished, Rabbi Chanina said to him, "Have you completed all the praises of your Master? Why all this? As for these three which we normally recite, had Moses our master not said them in the Torah and the Men of the Great Assembly not come and established them in the prayer service, we could not say them. Yet you say all this and carry on? It resembles a flesh and blood king who possessed millions of gold dinarim, but they praised him that he owned silver. Is that not disgraceful?"[550]

Even the phrase "great, mighty and awesome" would be inappropriate to use in prayer had not the Torah itself authorized it by Moses's example. Since no praise of Hashem, even that of Moses, is truly complete, Jeremiah and Daniel felt justified in altering the traditional phrase when circumstances warranted.

---

[549] B.T. Brachoth 40B.
[550] B.T. Brachoth 33B and J.T. Brachoth 9:1.

220

A question still remains, however, as to why the rabbis of the Talmud raised an objection only when it came to adding to the phrase "great, mighty and awesome" in the silent prayer (עמידה). After all, Jews recite many other praises of God in other prayers.[551] Moreover, the very passage in the silent prayer which describes God as "great, mighty and awesome" continues, "Supreme Power, who bestows beneficent kindnesses and controls all, who remembers the kindnesses of the Patriarchs... ." In what sense, then, does the restriction apply?

Because God is omniscient, He has no trouble understanding or responding to prayers offered in any language or formulation. Nonetheless, the ancient Jewish sages composed the Amidah as the ideal prayer for everyone to use. Thus, whether one is learned or not, whether one is righteous or not, whether one is very pious or not, whether one is highly articulate or not, he or she can successfully use the special formulation of the sages to pray. Moreover, the rabbis designed this formulation for use under any and all circumstances. Whether explicitly or by way of implication, the silent prayer contains every possible supplication anyone could ever have.[552]

One reason the silent prayer has such potency is that it alludes to the merit of the Patriarchs. The very first words

---

551 Shulchan Aruch, Orach Chaim 113:9 specifically states that the restriction on adding to God's praises applies only to the silent prayer (עמידה).

552 Yad HaChazakah, Hilchoth Tefillah 1:4.

speak of "God of our fathers, God of Abraham, God of Isaac and God of Jacob." The Midrash points out that God did not answer the prayers of Moses himself until the latter said "Remember Abraham, Isaac and Jacob Your servants... ."[553] *Moreover, it was Abraham, Isaac and Jacob who established the three daily prayer services.*[554]

The expression "great, mighty and awesome" (הגדול הגבור והנורא) *actually alludes to the Patriarchs, thereby reinforcing this aspect of the silent prayer. Concerning Abraham, Scripture writes, "I will make your name great"* (אגדלה שמך).[555] *The Torah describes God as "the fear of Isaac"* (פחד יצחק)[556] *hinting at "mighty"* (הגבור). *Finally, upon awakening at the site of the future Temple, Jacob said, "how awesome is this place"*[557] (מה נורא המקום הזה).[558]

Adding to the phrase "great, mighty and awesome" (הגדול הגבור והנורא) *in the silent prayer would impair its effectiveness by interfering with its very powerful allusion to the Patriarchs. Therefore, the halachah specifically restricts adding praises there, but not elsewhere.*

An additional answer may flow from the Rambam's proposition that one cannot properly ascribe attributes to God because He is unknowable. Instead, one can only talk about God in terms of His actions. Even such descriptions as "great,

[553] Exodus 32:13. Shemoth Rabbah 44:1.
[554] See above J.T. Brachoth 4:1 and B.T. Brachoth 26B.
[555] Genesis 12:2.
[556] Genesis 31:42.
[557] Genesis 28:17.
[558] Otzar HaTefilloth, Dover Shalom p. 159.

mighty and awesome" merely describe God's actions, not His essence.[559] *Thus the term "great" refers to God's creating the world. The term "mighty" denotes His ability to punish those who disobey Him. "Awesome" alludes to how people fear His judgment.*[560] *None of these terms actually describes God Himself.*

Other praises in the silent prayer such as "remembers the kindnesses of the Patriarchs," "revives the dead," or "heals the sick," obviously describe God's actions, but a worshiper would not necessarily understand that adjectives such as "great, mighty and awesome" refer to actions rather than God's essence. The rabbis restricted the use of adjectives such as "great, mighty and awesome" so that worshipers not mistakenly think that they define God. They did not limit the use of other expressions which are clearly only descriptions of God's actions.

---

[559] Moreh Nevuchim Part I Chapter 59.
[560] Seder Eliyahu Zuta 23:1.

223

Brachoth 8:5 (Compare Breishith Rabbah 82:15)

האש והכלאים, אף על פי שלא נבראו מששת ימי בראשית, אבל
עלו במחשבה מששת ימי בראשית.
הכלאים: "[וְאֵלֶּה] בְּנֵי צִבְעוֹן וְאַיָּה וַעֲנָה הוּא עֲנָה אֲשֶׁר מָצָא אֶת
הַיֵּמִם בַּמִּדְבָּר [בִּרְעֹתוֹ אֶת הַחֲמֹרִים לְצִבְעוֹן אָבִיו]." (בראשית לו:כד).
מהו יֵמִם? רבי יהודה בן סימון אומר: המיונס. ורבנן אמרין: הַיֵּמִים;
חציו סוס וחציו חמור...
מה עשה צבעון וענה? זימן חמורה והעלה עליה סוס זכר ויצא
מהן פרדה. אמר הקדוש ברוך הוא להם, "אתם הבאתם לעולם דבר
שהוא מזיק, אף אני מביא על אותו האיש דבר שהוא מזיקו." מה עשה
הקדוש ברוך הוא? זימן חכינה והעלה עליה חרדון ויצא ממנה חברבר.
מימיו לא יאמר לך אדם שעקצו חברבר וחיה, נשכו כלב שוטה
וחיה, שבעטתו פרדה וחיה, ובלבד פרדה לבנה.
האש: רבי לוי בשם רבי בזירה: שלשים ושש שעות שימשה
אותה האורה שנבראת ביום הראשון. שתים עשרה בערב שבת ושתים
עשרה בליל שבת ושתים עשרה בשבת. והיה אדם הראשון מביט בו
מסוף העולם ועד סופו. כיון שלא פסקה האורה, התחיל כל העולם כולו
משורר, שנאמר, "תַּחַת כָּל הַשָּׁמַיִם יִשְׁרֵהוּ [וְאוֹרוֹ עַל כַּנְפוֹת הָאָרֶץ]."
(איוב לז:ג). למי שאורו על כנפות הארץ. כיון שיצאת שבת, התחיל
משמש החושך ובא ונתירא אדם ואמר, "אלו הוא שכתוב בו, '...הוּא
יְשׁוּפְךָ רֹאשׁ וְאַתָּה תְּשׁוּפֶנּוּ עָקֵב' (בראשית ג:טו), שמא בא לנשכני.
'וָאֹמַר אַךְ חֹשֶׁךְ יְשׁוּפֵנִי... .'" (תהלים קלט:יא).
אמר רבי לוי: באותו שעה שזימן הקדוש ברוך הוא שני רעפין
והקישן זה לזה ויצא מהן האור. הדא הוא דכתיב, "...וְלַיְלָה אוֹר בַּעֲדֵנִי."
(שם שם).

Fire and interbreeding of different species, although not created during the six days of Creation, nonetheless arose in Divine thought during the six days of Creation.

Respecting the interbreeding of different species, it is written, "These are the children of Zibeon and Aiah and Anah; that is Anah who found the yemim [ימים] in the desert while grazing the donkeys for Zibeon, his father."[561] What are yemim [ימים]? Rabbi Judah ben Simon says: freaks. The disciples say: crossbreeds, half horse and half donkey...

What did Zibeon and Anah do? They prepared a female donkey and caused a male horse to mate with it. A mule emerged from them. The Holy One, Blessed be He, said to them, "You brought into the world something which injures. I, too, shall bring upon you something which injures." What did the Holy One, Blessed be He, do? He prepared a snake and mated it with a lizard. A venomous lizard emerged from them.

[The Torah does not explicitly state that Zibeon and Anah interbred a donkey with a horse. Rather, it says that Anah *found* the hybrid yemim (ימים), implying that this "invention" was not entirely novel, but somehow inherent in the act of Creation.]

Never will a man say to you that a venomous lizard bit him and the wound healed, that a mad dog bit him and the wound healed, or that a wild mule kicked him and the wound healed, provided that it is a white wild mule.[562]

---

561 Genesis 36:24.
562 Actually only its feet are white. (P'nei Moshe)

Respecting fire, Rabbi Levi said in the name of Rabbi Bazera: The light which was created on the first day served thirty-six hours; twelve on the Sabbath eve, twelve on the Sabbath night [Friday night], and twelve on the Sabbath [day]. With that light, Adam saw from one end of the world to the other. When the light did not stop, all the world began to sing, as it says, "Beneath all the heavens His righteousness [extends]; His light upon the corners of the Earth."[563] [The expression "Beneath all the heavens His righteousness" (ישרהו) can be rendered "Beneath all the heavens they sing" (ישררו).] Once the Sabbath departed, darkness began to function. Adam grew afraid and said: Perhaps the one about whom it is written, "...he shall strike you [with his] head and you shall strike him [with your] heel,"[564] will come to bite me. "And I said, 'Indeed darkness strikes me... .'"[565]

Rabbi Levi said: At that moment, the Holy One, Blessed be He, prepared two tiles which Adam struck one upon the other, and fire emerged from them. Thus it is written, "...and night is light for me."[566]

The underlying symbolism of the prohibition against forbidden mixtures of species (כלאים) was discussed in the analysis of section 6:1 above.

---

[563] Job 37:3 translated according to Targum Yonathan ben Uzziel.
[564] Genesis 3:15.
[565] Psalms 139:11.
[566] Ibid.

An additional point can be made here. When people improve their surroundings in mundane ways such as growing food or weaving clothing, their actions are consonant with the natural order of the world. However, when they attempt to interbreed species, thereby "inventing" a "new" type of creature such as a mule, they can come to doubt the most basic tenet of Judaism: that there is a Creator.

The complex design of the universe implies the existence of a Creator. In particular, the presence of living organisms with highly complex characteristics suggests that an Intelligent Being must have created them. When people mimic the act of creation by interbreeding species and thereby apparently generating a "new" ones, they may come to question this premise. After all, if people can "create," perhaps the world came into being through some non-Divine means.

Such an attitude has gained popularity today. The fact that scientists can clone animals or alter genetic material, thereby changing the resulting offspring, has led some to think that creation was not a supernatural act, God forbid.[567] The passage under consideration counters this notion by pointing out that the potential for interbreeding species and producing supposedly new ones was already inherent in God's original act of creation. When people engage in such activities, they merely bring to fruition that which is already part of the

---

[567] This is not to suggest that the halachah forbids such scientific activities.

natural order God created. As King Solomon said, "There is nothing new under the sun."[568]

There is another negative aspect to crossbreeding (כלאים). The ancient rabbis teach that the evil inclination does not explicitly instruct a person to sin. Rather, the evil inclination gradually tempts one to sin. For example, Rabbi Yochanan ben Nuri says that an angry person who tears clothing, destroys things, or scatters money is tantamount to an idolater. "Such is the craft of the evil inclination. Today it says to him, 'Do thus!' Tomorrow it says to him, 'Do thus!' Finally it tells him, 'Worship idols!' And he goes and does so."[569] *Similarly, the first time a person commits a sin, he or she feels horrible about it. The second time, however, it appears like normal behavior because the individual has grown used to it.*[570]

A passage of the Jerusalem Talmud cited above proclaimed that it is worse to violate the words of the rabbis than to violate the laws of the Torah itself.[571] *This is because, initially, a person finds it easier to transgress rabbinical decrees than to disobey the very serious laws of the Torah itself. However, such "minor" violations gradually lead to much more serious ones and undermine the entire fabric of Torah observance. In support of this concept, the Talmud cites the verse, "One who digs a pit shall fall in it and a snake will*

---

[568] Ecclesiastes 1:9.
[569] B.T. Shabbath 105B.
[570] B.T. Yoma 86B.
[571] See J.T. Brachoth 1:4 above.

bite one who breaches a fence."[572] Digging a pit or damaging a fence appear to be relatively innocent actions. However, it is just such seemingly harmless activities which can produce the most dire consequences.

This idea of blurring the lines between good and evil, and the gradual descent to sin, is represented by mixing species together (כלאים) which, in turn, is associated with the snake, a symbol of the evil inclination. Although God commanded Adam, "But from the Tree of Knowledge of good and evil you shall not eat...,"[573] when Eve repeated the prohibition to the snake, she added, "...and do not touch it lest you die,"[574] either because Adam did not impart the commandment to her carefully or because she misunderstood him. This confusion as to the exact nature of what God had prohibited gave the snake a perfect opportunity to lead Eve astray. The Midrash teaches that he pushed Eve against the tree. When nothing happened, he told her that just as touching the tree was harmless, so eating its fruit would prove harmless.[575] Thus, a blurring of the distinction between good and evil caused the very first sin.

The Talmud teaches that if a person comes to purify himself or herself, Heaven helps. Conversely, if one seeks to defile oneself, Heaven opens the way.[576] The passage under consideration alludes to the same concept. When humans blur

---

[572] Ecclesiastes 10:8.
[573] Genesis 2:17.
[574] Genesis 3:3.
[575] Breishith Rabbah 19:3.
[576] B.T. Shabbath 104A.

the distinction between good and evil by producing crossbreeds (כלאים), God acts "measure for measure" by breeding the snake with a lizard to yield a venomous crossbreed. That is, God will permit the person to further obscure that vital distinction.

The Talmud continues this theme when it discusses the invention of fire. Initially, Adam and Eve had a clear perception of good and evil. The primordial spiritual light of Creation distinctly illuminated right and wrong for them. When they sinned, this light gradually dissipated. When it grew dark, Adam wondered whether the snake (evil inclination), with its power to deceive and confuse, would succeed in overwhelming him. God then showed Adam that people also have a good inclination (יצר טוב). They can make their own fire, their own means of illuminating and exposing the true evil of the snake no matter how deceptive it may be. That is the fire of the Torah which, the Talmud teaches, is the antidote to the evil inclination.[577]

Along these lines, the Talmud quotes the Torah's reference to the snake striking with its head to attack people whereas people crush it with their heels. The evil inclination often tries to lure people with twisted logic, in other words, it strikes with its "head." As an example, the evil inclination may say, "This food has only a minor kashruth problem involving a rabbinical decree. Why forego eating just for that? You need to eat to keep up your strength. Isn't it more

---

[577] B.T. Kiddushin 30B.

important to take care of your health? After all, that's a mitzvah too."

In Jewish thought, the heel symbolizes something callous and unfeeling. (In the English language also, an insensitive person is sometimes called a "heel.") One cannot rationalize with evil. Rather, when tempted by the twisted logic of the evil inclination, one must stamp it out with his or her heel, heedless and senseless to whatever explanations or excuses it may offer for violating halachah.

Brachoth 8:6 (Compare Breishith Rabbah 3:6)

[The sages of the Talmud discuss the derivation of the rule that one must see and benefit from the light of the Havdalah candle before reciting a blessing over it.]

דרש רבי זעירא בריה דרבי אבהו: "וַיַּרְא אֱ-לֹהִים אֶת הָאוֹר כִּי
טוֹב....," ואחר כך, "...וַיַּבְדֵּל אֱ-לֹהִים בֵּין הָאוֹר וּבֵין הַחֹשֶׁךְ." (בראשית
א:ד).
אמר רבי ברכיה: כך דרשו שני גדולי עולם, רבי יוחנן ורבי
שמעון בן לקיש: "וַיַּבְדֵּל אֱ-לֹהִים" אבדלה ודאי. רבי יהודה בי רבי
סימון אמר: הבדילו לו. ורבנן אמרין: הבדילו לצדיקים לעתיד לבוא.
משלו משל, למה הדבר דומה? למלך שהיו לו שני איסטרטיגין.
זה אומר, "אני משמש ביום," וזה אומר, "אני משמש ביום." קרא לראשון
ואמר לו, "פלוני, היום יהא תחומך." קרא לשני ואמר לו, "פלוני, הלילה
יהא תחומך." הדא הוא דכתיב, "וַיִּקְרָא אֱ-לֹהִים לָאוֹר יוֹם [וְלַחֹשֶׁךְ קָרָא
לָיְלָה]... ." (בראשית א:ה). לאור אמר לו, "היום יהא תחומך," ולחשך
אמר לו, "הלילה יהא תחומך."
אמר רבי יוחנן: הוא שאמר הקדוש ברוך הוא לאיוב, "הֲמִיָּמֶיךָ
צִוִּיתָ בֹּקֶר יִדַּעְתָּה שַׁחַר [יִדַּעְתָּ הַשַּׁחַר קרי] מְקֹמוֹ." (איוב לח:יב). ידעת
אי זה מקומו של אור ששת ימי בראשית, איכן נגנז?
אמר רבי תנחומא: אנא אמרית טעמא, "יוֹצֵר אוֹר וּבוֹרֵא חֹשֶׁךְ
עֹשֶׂה שָׁלוֹם... ." (ישעיה מה:ז). משיצא, עושה שלום ביניהן.

Rabbi Z'eira, the son of Rabbi Abahu, expounded: "God saw the light that it was good...,"[578] then afterwards, "...and

---

[578] Genesis 1:4.

God separated between the light and between the darkness."[579] [The sequence of this verse shows that one must see the light of the Havdalah candle before making the blessing.]

Rabbi Berachiah said: Thus expounded two eternally great figures, Rabbi Yochanan and Rabbi Shimon ben Lakish: "...and God separated..." means a literal separation [as will be explained further on].

Rabbi Judah the son of Rabbi Simon said: He separated it for Himself. And the sages said: He separated it for the righteous for the future.

They made a parable. To what may the matter be compared? To a king who had two managers.[580] This one said, "I will serve during the day," and this one said, "I will serve during the day." He summoned the first and said to him, "So and so, the day shall be your domain." He summoned the second and said to him, "So and so, the night shall be your domain." This is the meaning of what is written, "And God called the light day and darkness He called night... ."[581] To the light He said, "Day shall be your domain," and to the darkness He said, "Night shall be your domain."

Rabbi Yochanan said: This is what the Holy One, Blessed be He, said to Job, "Since you were born, did you command the day? Did you instruct the dawn to its place?"[582]

---

[579] Ibid.

[580] The word איסטרטיגין suggests "strategists," people who planned and managed for him.

[581] Genesis 1:5.

[582] Job 38:12.

This means, "Do you know the location of the light of the six days of Creation, where it is hidden?"

Rabbi Tanchuma said: I can give a Scriptural source for this concept. "The One who forms light, the Creator of darkness, Maker of peace... ."[583] Once they emerged, He made peace between them.

In Jewish theology, Hashem directs the course of the universe by means of two opposing approaches, chessed (חסד), kindness, and gevurah (גבורה), strength or judgment. These concepts signify, in part, the degree to which God reveals Himself in the universe. Hence, when God chooses to display His influence in the universe to a heightened degree, He is said to be acting through chessed (חסד), kindness. When, however, God limits the way in which humanity perceives Him, He is said to be acting through gevurah (גבורה), strength or judgment. "Light" represents the revelation of Hashem in the world, the aspect of chessed (חסד), kindness, while "darkness" represents restriction of this revelation, meaning gevurah (גבורה), strength or judgment.

The passage under consideration describes the cosmic struggle between these two modes of revelation. Rashi states in the beginning of his commentary to the Torah that Hashem initially planned to create the world only by means of the attribute of judgment. When He found that the world could not endure that way, He blended the attributes of judgment and

---

583 Isaiah 45:7.

mercy.[584] *If God were to strictly judge human behavior, no one could survive "for there is no man who does not sin."*[585] *Conversely, if God were to graciously forgive every wrongdoing, people would have no motive to restrict their behavior to what is right. Only through a balance of these two forces can humanity and the universe survive.*

The same applies to the revelation of Hashem in the universe in general. If Hashem's Divine influence were completely absent, the world could not survive and would revert to nothingness. On the other hand, a high degree of Divine revelation would overwhelm the physical universe because that which is physical can only exist when spirituality is, to some degree, withdrawn and hidden. Only by means of a perfect balance between revelation and hiddeness can the creation endure.

In a homiletic sense, both chessed (חסד), "light" and gevurah (גבורה), "darkness," "wished" to rule the universe, but God placed them in perfect equilibrium as symbolized by day and night. Throughout the year, at every latitude, daytime and nighttime fluctuate. During one season, days are long while nights are short. During another season, it is the reverse. The result is that during the course of an entire solar year at every location on Earth, there is exactly half nighttime and half daytime, a perfect balance. The same perfect balance exists between chessed (חסד), kindness, and gevurah (גבורה), strength or judgment.

---

[584] Rashi on Genesis 1:1.
[585] I Kings 8:46.

235

Brachoth 9:1 (Compare B.T. Brachoth 33B)

רבי יוחנן ורבי יונתן אזלין מיעבד שלמא באילין קורייתא
דדרומה. עלון לחד אתר ואשכחון לחזנא דאמר, "הא-ל הגדול הגבור
והנורא האביר והאמיץ..." ושיתקו אותו. אמרו לו, "אין לך רשות להוסיף
על מטבע שטבעו חכמים בברכות."

רב הונא בשם רב: "שַׁ-דַּי לֹא מְצָאנֻהוּ שַׂגִּיא כֹחַ... ." (איוב לז:כג).
לא מצינו כחו וגבורתו של הקדוש ברוך הוא.

רבי אבהו בשם רבי יוחנן: "הַיְסֻפַּר לוֹ כִּי אֲדַבֵּר אִם אָמַר אִישׁ כִּי
יְבֻלָּע." (איוב לז:כ). אם בא אדם לספר גבורותיו של הקדוש ברוך הוא,
מתבלע מן העולם.

אמר רבי שמואל בר נחמן: "מִי יְמַלֵּל גְּבוּרוֹת ה' [וַיַשְׁמִיעַ כָּל
תְּהִלָּתוֹ]" (תהלים קו:ב), כגון אני וחברי.

אמר רבי אבון "מִי יְמַלֵּל גְּבוּרוֹת ה' [יַשְׁמִיעַ כָּל תְּהִלָּתוֹ]." (תהלים
קו:ב). תרגם יעקב כפר נבורייא בצור, "לְךָ דֻמִיָּה תְהִלָּה אֱ-לֹהִים
בְּצִיּוֹן... ." (תהלים סה:ב). סמא דכולא משתוקא. למרגלית דלית לה
טימי, כל שמשבח בה פגמה.

Rabbi Yochanan and Rabbi Jonathan went to make peace
among certain villages in the south.[586] They entered a certain
locale and found the cantor reciting, "The God who is great,
mighty and awesome, the powerful, the bold..." and they
silenced him.[587] They said to him, "You have no permission to
add to the formula which the sages originated for blessings."

---

[586] The two rabbis hailed from Tiberias in northern Israel. (Perush
MiBa'al Sefer Chareidim).
[587] They did not interrupt him, but after he finished they instructed him
not to do so in the future. (Etz Yosef)

Rav Huna said in the name of Rav: "[As to] the Almighty, we do not find [sufficient ability to express His] exceeding might... ."[588] We do not find [expression for] the strength and might of the Holy One, Blessed be He.

Rabbi Abahu said in the name of Rabbi Yochanan: "[Is it necessary that] it will be told to Him when I speak; can a man speak that which will be hidden [from Him]?"[589] If a person comes to relate the mightiness of the Holy One, Blessed be He, he will be swallowed up from the world. [The phrase "that which will be hidden" (יבלע) can also mean "he will be swallowed up".]

Rabbi Samuel bar Nachman said: "Let one who can express the might of the Lord proclaim all His praise,"[590] by which King David meant, "for example, I and my colleagues."[591] However, Rabbi Avon said that Jacob of the village of Nivuraya in Tyre interpreted the verse, "Let one who can express the might of the Lord..." according to the following: "For You silence is praise, God Who is in Zion... ."[592] The best medicine of all is silence. God's glory is comparable to a priceless jewel. Whoever praises it, cheapens it. [Any attempt to describe God's true greatness will be an extreme understatement and, thus, actually amounts to an insult.]

See section 7:3 above for additional commentary.

---

[588] Job 37:23 according to Targum Jonathan ben Uzziel.
[589] Job 37:20 according to Metzudoth David.
[590] Psalms 106:2.
[591] P'nei Moshe.
[592] Psalms 65:2.

Brachoth 9:1

[The Torah sometimes calls God by the Hebrew word "E-lohim" (א–להים), using the plural form as a way of showing respect. Although it was customary even in ancient times to use a plural form when addressing or referring to royalty, this usage opened the door for certain unscrupulous people to claim that the Torah sanctions the view that there is more than one God.]

המינין שאלו את רבי שְׂמְלַאי, "כמה אלוהות בראו את העולם?"
אמר להן, "ולי אתם שואלין? לכו ושאלו את אדם הראשון,
שנאמר, 'כִּי שְׁאַל נָא לְיָמִים רִאשֹׁנִים [אֲשֶׁר הָיוּ לְפָנֶיךָ לְמִן הַיּוֹם אֲשֶׁר
בָּרָא אֱ-לֹהִים אָדָם עַל הָאָרֶץ]...' (דברים ד:לב). 'אֲשֶׁר בָּרְאוּ אֱ-לֹהִים
אָדָם עַל הָאָרֶץ,' אין כתיב כאן, אלא, 'לְמִן הַיּוֹם אֲשֶׁר בָּרָא אֱ-לֹהִים אָדָם
עַל הָאָרֶץ.'"
אמרו ליה, "והכתיב, 'בְּרֵאשִׁית בָּרָא אֱ-לֹהִים...'?" (בראשית א:א).
אמר להן, "וכי 'בָּרְאוּ' כתיב? אין כתיב אלא 'בָּרָא.'"
אמר רבי שְׂמְלַאי: כל מקום שפרקו המינין, תשובתן בצידן.
חזרו ושאלו אותו, "מה אהן דכתיב, '[וַיֹּאמֶר אֱ-לֹהִים] נַעֲשֶׂה אָדָם
בְּצַלְמֵנוּ כִּדְמוּתֵנוּ...'?" (בראשית א:כו).
אמר להן, "'וַיִּבְרְאוּ אֱ-לֹהִים אֶת הָאָדָם בְּצַלְמָם...' אין כתיב כאן
אלא 'וַיִּבְרָא אֱ-לֹהִים אֶת הָאָדָם בְּצַלְמוֹ...'." (בראשית א:כז).
אמרו לו תלמידיו, "לאלו דחיתה בקנה. לנו מה אתה משיב?"
אמר להן, "לשעבר אדם נברא מן העפר וחוה נבראת מן אדם.
מאדם ואילך, '...בְּצַלְמֵנוּ כִּדְמוּתֵנוּ... .' (בראשית א:כו). אי אפשר לאיש
בלא אשה ואי אפשר לאשה בלא איש. אי אפשר לשניהן בלא שכינה.
וחזרו ושאלו אותו, "מה ההן דכתיב, 'אֵ-ל אֱ-לֹהִים ה' אֵ-ל
אֱ-לֹהִים ה' הוּא יֹדֵעַ...'?" (יהושע כב:כב).
אמר להן, "'הֵם יֹדְעִים' אין כתיב כאן, אלא, 'הוּא יֹדֵעַ' כתיב."

238

אמרו לו תלמידיו, "רבי, לאלו דחית בקנה. לנו מה אתה משיב?"

אמר להן, "שלשתן שם אחד, כאיש דאמר, 'בָּסִילְיוֹס קֵיסַר אֲגוּסְטוֹס.'"

חזרו ושאלו אותו, "מה ההן דכתיב, '...אֵ-ל אֱ-לֹהִים ה' דִּבֶּר וַיִּקְרָא אָרֶץ...'?" (תהלים נ:א).

אמר להן, "וכי 'דיבְּרוּ וַיִּקְרָאוּ' כתיב כאן? אין כתיב אלא 'דִּבֶּר וַיִּקְרָא אָרֶץ.'"

אמרו לו תלמידיו, "רבי, לאלו דחית בקנה ולנו מה אתה משיב?"

אמר להן, "שלשתן שם אחד, כאיניש דאמר, 'וְאַמְנוֹן בַּנְיָין אַרִיכְטִיקַנְטֵן.'"

חזרו ושאלו אתו, "מהו דכתיב, '...כִּי אֱ-לֹהִים קְדֹשִׁים הוּא...'? (יהושע כד:יט).

אמר להן, "'קְדֹשִׁים הֵמָּה' אין כתיב כאן, אלא '...[כִּי אֱ-לֹהִים קְדֹשִׁים] הוּא אֵל קַנּוֹא הוּא... .'" (שם שם).

אמרו לו תלמידיו, "רבי, לאלו דחית בקנה, ולנו מה אתה משיב?"

אמר רבי יצחק: קדוש בכל מיני קדושות, דאמר רב יודן בשם רבי אחא: הקדוש ברוך הוא, דרכו בקדושה, דיבורו בקדושה וישובו בקדושה, חשיפת זרועו בקדושה, (א-להים) נורא ואדיר בקדושה.

דרכו בקדושה: "אֱ-לֹהִים בַּקֹּדֶשׁ דַּרְכֶּךָ [מִי אֵ-ל גָּדוֹל כֵּא-לֹהִים]." (תהלים עז:יד). הילוכו בקדושה: "[רָאוּ הֲלִיכוֹתֶיךָ אֱ-לֹהִים] הֲלִיכוֹת אֵ-לִי מַלְכִּי בַקֹּדֶשׁ." (תהלים סח:כה). מושבו בקדושה: "[מָלַךְ אֱ-לֹהִים עַל גּוֹיִם] אֱ-לֹהִים יָשַׁב עַל כִּסֵּא קָדְשׁוֹ." (תהלים מז:ט). דיבורו בקדושה: "אֱ-לֹהִים דִּבֶּר בְּקָדְשׁוֹ..." (תהלים ס:ח; קח:ח). חשיפת זרועו בקדושה: "חָשַׂף ה' אֶת זְרוֹעַ קָדְשׁוֹ..." (ישעיה נב:י). נורא ואדיר בקדושה: "[מִי כָמֹכָה בָּאֵלִם ה'] מִי כָּמֹכָה נֶאְדָּר בַּקֹּדֶשׁ [נוֹרָא תְהִלֹּת עֹשֵׂה פֶלֶא]" (שמות טו:יא).

חזרו ושאלו אותו, "מה אהן דכתיב, 'נכי[ן] מִי גוֹי גָּדוֹל אֲשֶׁר לוֹ אֱ-לֹהִים קְרֹבִים אֵלָיו [כַּה' אֱ-לֹהֵינוּ בְּכָל קָרְאֵנוּ אֵלָיו].'?" (דברים ד:ז).

אמר להן, "'כַּה' אֱ-לֹהֵינוּ בְּכָל קָרְאֵנוּ אֲלֵיהֶם' אין כתיב כאן, אלא, 'בְּכָל קָרְאֵנוּ אֵלָיו.'"

אמרו לו תלמידיו, "רבי, לאלו דחית בקנה. לנו מה אתה משיב?"
אמר להן, "קרוב בכל מיני קריבות. דאמר רבי פנחס בשם רב
יהודה בר סימון: עבודה זרה נראית קרובה ואינה אלא רחוקה. מה
טעמא? 'יִשָּׂאֻהוּ עַל כָּתֵף יִסְבְּלֻהוּ [וְיַנִּיחֻהוּ תַחְתָּיו וְיַעֲמֹד מִמְּקוֹמוֹ לֹא
יָמִישׁ אַף יִצְעַק אֵלָיו וְלֹא יַעֲנֶה מִצָּרָתוֹ לֹא יוֹשִׁיעֶנּוּ].' (ישעיה מו:ז). סוף
דבר, אלוהו עמו בבית והוא צועק עד שימות ולא ישמע ולא יושיע
מצרתו. אבל הקדוש ברוך הוא נראה רחוק ואין קרוב ממנו, דאמר לוי:
מהארץ ועד לרקיע מהלך ה' מאות שנה, ומרקיע לרקיע מהלך ת"ק שנה
ועביו של רקיע ת"ק שנה. וכן לכל רקיע ורקיע. ואמר רבי ברכיה ורבי
חלבו בשם רבי אבא סמוקה: אף טלפי החיות מהלך ה' מאות שנה
וחמש עשרה, מנין 'ישרה.'
"ראה כמה הוא גבוה מעולמו, ואדם נכנס לבית הכנסת ועומד
אחורי העמוד ומתפלל בלחישה והקדוש ברוך הוא מאזין את תפלתו.
שנאמר, 'וְחַנָּה הִיא מְדַבֶּרֶת עַל לִבָּהּ רַק שְׂפָתֶיהָ נָּעוֹת וְקוֹלָהּ לֹא יִשָּׁמֵעַ...'
(שמואל א א:יג), והאזין הקדוש ברוך הוא את תפילתה.
"וכן כל בריותיו, שנאמר, 'תְּפִלָּה לְעָנִי כִי יַעֲטֹף [וְלִפְנֵי ה' יִשְׁפֹּךְ
שִׂיחוֹ].' (תהלים קב:א). כאדם המשיח באוזן חבירו והוא שומע. וכי יש
לך א-לוה קרוב מזה, שהוא קרוב לבריותיו כפה לאוזן?"

Heretics asked Rabbi Simlai, "How many gods created the world?"

He answered them, "Do you ask me? Go and ask Adam, as it says, 'If you will ask about the first days which were before you, from the day God created Adam upon the earth... .'[593] It does not say, 'created [plural בראו] Adam upon the earth,' but rather, 'from the day God created [singular ברא] Adam upon the earth.'"

---

[593] Deuteronomy 4:32.

They said to him, "But is it not written, 'In the beginning God [א-להים plural] created... ?'[594]"

He responded, "Is it then written, 'they created [בראו]?' Rather, all that is written is "He created [ברא]!'"

Rabbi Simlai said: Any place where the heretics cast off tradition, the refutation of their position is right there.

The heretics once again asked him, "What is this that is written, '...we shall make man in our image, in our likeness...'?[595]

He said to them, " 'and God created [ויבראו plural] man in Their image [בצלמם]' is not written here, but rather, 'God created [ויברא singular] man in His image [בצלמו].'[596]" [This verse follows the one just cited by the heretics, thus showing that the refutation of their position can be found in the very place they cite to support it.]

His disciples said to him, "Those heretics you pushed away with a reed. As for us, how do you answer?" [The answer to the heretics is incomplete. Accepting the fact that there is only one God, why does the Torah use a plural form at all in this verse?]

He answered them: At first, Adam was created from dirt and Eve was created from Adam. From Adam onward, the Torah states, "...we shall make man in our image, in our likeness...,"[597] meaning that it is impossible for a man to

---

[594] Genesis 1:1.
[595] Genesis 1:26.
[596] Genesis 1:27.
[597] Genesis 1:26.

reproduce without a woman, nor for a woman to do so without a man, and it is impossible for both of them without the Divine Presence. [After the initial act of creating the first human beings, human reproduction requires a partnership of man, woman and God.[598] The expression "we" in the verse refers to this latter partnership.]

The heretics once again asked him, "What about that which is written, 'Most powerful of the powerful, the Lord, most powerful of the powerful, the Lord, He knows...'[599]?" [The Hebrew phrase employed in this verse uses several titles for God (א-ל א-להים י-ה-ו-ה), leaving room for heretics to imply that there is more than one deity.]

He said to them, " 'They know [הם יודעים]' is not written, but rather, 'He knows [הוא יודע].'"

His disciples said to him, "Those heretics you pushed away with a reed. As for us, how do you answer?"

He responded, "All three are actually one name, just as a person might say, 'Basilius Caesar Augustus.'" [The word "Basilius" means "king" in Greek. Roman emperors also called themselves "Caesar" in memory of Julius Caesar who ruled from 49 to 44 B.C.E. This custom became so popular that even hundreds of years later Russian rulers adopted the title "Czar" and German kings the title "Kaiser," both derivatives of Caesar. Thus, the word "Caesar" was no longer a proper name, but a title for the Roman emperor. "Augustus" was also the name of an early Roman ruler which later kings

---

[598] See B.T. Kiddushin 30B and B.T. Niddah 31A.
[599] Joshua 22:22.

adopted as a title.[600] Alternatively, the name may have been the equivalent of calling the ruler, "Your Majesty" since the word "august" in modern English means "majestic." In any event, the three terms were meant to be read together to denote only one person.]

The heretics once again asked him, "What about that which is written, 'Most powerful of the powerful, the Lord who spoke and called forth the world...'[601]?"

He said to them, "Is 'they spoke [דיברו]' and 'they called [ויקראו]' written here? Nothing is written here but, 'who spoke [דיבר] and called forth the world [ויקרא].'"

His disciples said to him, "Those heretics you pushed away with a reed. As for us, how do you answer?"

He responded, "All three are actually one name, just as a person might say, 'a master-builder architect.'"

The heretics once again asked him, "What about that which is written, '...for He is a holy [קדושים] God...'[602]

He said to them, " 'They [המה] are holy' is not written here, but rather, '...for He [הוא] is a holy God, a zealous God is he [הוא]... .'[603]"

His disciples said to him, "Those heretics you pushed away with a reed. As for us, how do you answer?"

Rabbi Isaac said: He is holy with all types of holiness for Rabbi Yudan said in the name of Rabbi Acha: The Holy

600 Ma'arecheth HeAruch.
601 Psalms 50:1 following Targum Jonathan ben Uzziel and P'nei Moshe.
602 Joshua 24:19.
603 Ibid.

One, Blessed be He, His way is with holiness, His speech with holiness, His sitting with holiness, the revelation of His might is with holiness. He is awesome and mighty in holiness.

His way is with holiness: "God, in holiness is Your way; who is a great power like God?"[604] His going is with holiness: "They saw Your goings, God; the goings of my God, my King, are in holiness."[605] His sitting is with holiness: "God rules over the nations; God sits upon His holy throne."[606] His speech is with holiness: "God spoke in His holiness... ."[607] The revelation of His might is with holiness: "God exposed His holy arm [i.e., might]... ."[608] He is awesome and mighty in holiness: "Who is like You among the mighty, Lord? Who is like You, mighty in holiness, awesome of praises, doing wonders?"[609]

The heretics once again asked him, "What about that which is written, "For which is a great nation to whom God is close [אֱ-לֹהִים קְרוּבִים]... ."[610]

He said to them, " '...as the Lord, our God, in all our calling to Them [אֲלֵיהֶם],' is not written here, but rather, '...as the Lord, our God, in all our calling to Him [אֵלָיו].'"[611]

---

604 Psalms 77:14.
605 Psalms 68:25.
606 Psalms 47:9.
607 Psalms 60:8 and 108:8.
608 Isaiah 52:10.
609 Exodus 15:11.
610 Deuteronomy 4:7.
611 Ibid.

His disciples said to him, "Those heretics you pushed away with a reed. As for us, how do you answer?"

He responded: The verse means that He is close with all types of closeness as Rabbi Phinehas said in the name of Rabbi Judah ben Simon: Idols appear close, but they are actually distant. What is the Scriptural support for this? "Let him lift it [an idol] upon a shoulder; let him bear it and set it down. Will it stand from its place? It will not stir. Even if he cries to it, it will not answer nor save him from his trouble."[612] In the end, his idol is with him in his house, he cries to it until he dies, but it does not listen or save him from his trouble.

But the Holy One, Blessed be He, appears distant, yet none is closer than He, as Levi said: From the earth to heaven is a journey of five hundred years and from heaven to heaven is a journey of five hundred years and the thickness of a heaven is five hundred years. So it is for each [of the seven] heavens. Rabbi Berachia and Rabbi Chelbo said in the name of Rabbi Abba the Red: Also the hooves of the angels are a journey of five hundred fifteen years corresponding to the numerical value of "straight" [ישרה].[613]

Observe how lofty God is from His world, yet a person enters the synagogue, stands behind a pillar, prays in a whisper and the Holy One, Blessed be He, listens to his prayer, as it says, "And Hannah spoke in her heart, only her lips moved, but

---

[612] Isaiah 46:7.
[613] Ezekiel described the angels saying, "Their legs are a straight [ישרה] leg" (Ezekiel 1:7). See above J.T. Brachoth 1:1.

her voice was not heard..."[614] and the Holy One, Blessed be He, heard her prayer.

So it is with all his creatures, as it says, "A prayer for one afflicted when he wraps himself and pours forth his speech before the Lord,"[615] meaning it is like a person who converses in the ear of his friend and he hears him. Do you have a god who is closer than this? For He is as close to His creatures as a mouth to an ear. [The point is that although Hannah was a prophet, God's willingness to listen to her was not exceptional. Rather, He hears the prayers of ordinary people as well.]

The discussion concerning the distance from earth to heaven and from heaven to heaven finds parallels in many sources.[616] The Maharal explains that such statements do not refer to physical dimensions, but to an unseen spiritual reality. Thus, the ancient sages meant to stress the extreme distance between humanity, which is a mixture of physical and spiritual elements, and the purely spiritual realms from which the physical world ultimately derives.[617]

The rabbis teach that the Tree of Life in the Garden of Eden was a journey of five hundred years in size.[618] The Tree of Life is actually the Torah.[619] Thus, the Talmud here means

---

[614] I Samuel 1:13.
[615] Psalms 102:1.
[616] See, e.g., B.T. Chagigah 13A, B.T. Pesachim 94B, J.T. Brachoth 1:1, Shir HaShirim Rabbah on verses 6:8 and 6:9.
[617] Be'er HaGolah, Be'er Shishi, p. 115.
[618] Tanna D'Bei Eliyahu Rabba 2:11 and J.T. Brachoth 1:1.
[619] Tanna D'Bei Eliyahu Rabba 1:1.

that one must possess tremendous Torah knowledge before one can begin to fathom the upper spiritual realms. Such profound understanding is impossible for an ordinary human being just as a journey of hundreds of years would be an impossible undertaking. Nonetheless, God does not require that people fully comprehend the spiritual essence of the universe in order to approach Him. Rather, He makes Himself readily available even to the simplest petitioner.

In another way as well, the expression "five hundred years" hints at Hashem's kindness in making Himself available to those who are unworthy. The Torah says not to worship idols for if one does, God "...will recall the sin of the fathers upon the sons unto the third and unto the fourth [generation] for My enemies. And I do kindness unto two thousand [generations] for those who love Me and those who keep My commandments."[620] Rashi explains that God punishes the descendants of wicked people if those descendants follow in the ways of their forebears. Such descendants are punished not only for their own wrongdoing, but for that of their ancestors as well. This attribute of punishment, however, lasts only to the third or fourth generation, whereas God's kindness towards the descendants of those who love Him lasts two thousand generations. Hence, the attribute of kindness exceeds that of retribution by a ratio of five hundred.[621] Likewise, in His kindness, God sets aside the barrier of many sets of five hundred years to welcome the prayers of all people.

---

[620] Exodus 20:5-6.
[621] Rashi on Exodus 20:5-6.

The extensive dialog with the "heretics" seems peculiar. It is axiomatic that Jews believe in only one God, a principle made clear over and over again in the Torah. The first two of the Ten Commandments state, "I am the Lord your God Who took you out of the Land of Egypt, from the house of bondage; you shall have no other gods except for Me."[622] *Furthermore, Jews recite the "Shema" twice each day which says, "Listen, Israel, the Lord is our God, the Lord is One."*[623]

If these "heretics" were Jews, how could they question such a fundamental tenet of the Jewish faith based on highly technical and forced readings of the text? On the other hand, if the "heretics" were polytheistic pagans, then why do they attempt to show that there is more than one god through Scriptural texts? It seems more likely that such people would try to prove their point using some other type of argument. In addition, how did idolatrous pagans become so familiar with Hebrew scriptures?

Apparently, these "heretics" were early Christians or members of related sects. Thus, they did not suggest that there is really more than one God. Rather, they were trying to find support for their belief that God has several "manifestations" or "offshoots" and that the founder of their sect was one of these.

The persistency of the early Christians in trying to convert Jews or, at least, justify their heretical position, may explain why the authors of this passage of the Talmud repeated

---

[622] Exodus 20:2.
[623] Deuteronomy 6:4.

so many arguments which so closely resemble one another. Because early Christianity was more prevalent in the Land of Israel than anywhere else, these issues were probably more frequently addressed by rabbis who wrote the Jerusalem Talmud than by their colleagues in Babylonia. The main point is that no forced or technical reading of Scripture can abrogate the fundamental principle that only one God exists Who is indivisible and does not have multiple manifestations.

This historical insight helps to explain the pronouncement of Rabbi Z'eira that it is forbidden to recite the first verse of the "Shema" repeatedly at one sitting.[624] Rashi explains that the reason for this prohibition is that one who repeats the first verse of the Shema appears to acknowledge more than one deity.[625] At first glance, such a proposition seems absurd. The verse itself says that there is only one God. How can repetition of it ever possibly be misinterpreted? The answer is that traditional Christianity recognizes the doctrine that there is only one God, but insists that the one God has different forms (a trinity). Such heretics might, indeed, even go so far as to twist the mere repetition of the verse, "Listen, Israel, the Lord is our God, the Lord is One"[626] to support their position.

The above interpretation also helps to explain why Rabbi Simlai gave a different explanation to the heretics than the one

---

[624] B.T. Brachoth 33B. Later codified in Shulchan Aruch, Orach Chaim 61:9.

[625] Rashi on B.T. Brachoth 33B, sub verba "Miltha miltha" (מילתא מילתא).

[626] Deuteronomy 6:4.

he offered to his students. Just as they do today, the Christians of ancient times denied the validity of the Oral Torah. Hence, they would have automatically rejected the type of homiletic interpretation Rabbi Simlai presented to his disciples. However, the heretics had no choice but to consider a refutation based upon the wording of the Tanach.[627] *As King Solomon said, "Answer a fool according to his folly lest he appear wise in his [own] eyes."*[628]

---

[627] See commentary of Rabbi Yaakov ibn Chaviv (HaKothev). He raises the same question but offers a different explanation.
[628] Proverbs 26:5.

Brachoth 9:1   (Compare Devarim Rabbah 2:29; Midrash Tehillim 4:3)

רבי יודן בשם רבי יצחק אמר בה ארבע שיטין:

בשר ודם יש לו פטרון. אמרו לו, "נתפס בן ביתך." אמר להן,
"אני מקיים עליו." אמרו לו, "הרי יוצא לידון." אמר להן, "אני מקיים
עליו." אמרו לו, "הרי הוא יוצא ליתלות." היכן הוא ואיכן פטרונו?
אבל הקדוש ברוך הוא הציל את משה מחרב פרעה. הדא הוא דכתיב,
"...[כִּי אֱ-לֹהֵי אָבִי בְּעֶזְרִי] וַיַּצִּלֵנִי מֵחֶרֶב פַּרְעֹה." (שמות יח:ד).

אמר רבי ינאי: כתיב, "...וַיִּבְרַח מֹשֶׁה מִפְּנֵי פַרְעֹה..." (שמות ב:טו).
ואפשר לבשר ודם לברוח מן המלכות? אלא בשעה שתפס פרעה את
משה חייבו להתיז את ראשו וקהת החרב מעל צווארו של משה ונשברה.
הדא הוא דכתיב, "צַוָּארֵךְ כְּמִגְדַּל הַשֵּׁן..." (שיר השירים ז:ה), זה צווארו של
משה.

רבי אמר רבי אביתר: ולא עוד, אלא שנתז החרב מעל צווארו
של משה על צווארו של קוסנתירו והרגתו. הדא הוא דכתיב, "וַיַּצִּלֵנִי
מֵחֶרֶב פַּרְעֹה" (שמות יח:ד), לי הציל, וקוסנתר נהרג. רבי ברכיה קרא
עליו, "כֹּפֶר לַצַּדִּיק רָשָׁע..." (משלי כא:יח). רבי אבון קרא עליו, "צַדִּיק
מִצָּרָה נֶחֱלָץ וַיָּבֹא רָשָׁע תַּחְתָּיו." (משלי יא:יח).

תני בר קפרא: מלאך ירד ונדמה להן בדמות משה ותפסו את
המלאך וברח משה.

אמר רב יהושע בן לוי: בשעה שברח משה מפני פרעה, נעשו כל
אוכלוסין שלו אילמין ומהן חרשין ומהן סומין. אמר לאילמין, "היכן הוא
משה?" ולא היו מדברים. אמר לחרשין, ולא היו שומעין. אמר לסומין,
ולא היו רואין. הוא שהקדוש ברוך הוא אמר לו למשה, "מִי שָׂם פֶּה
לָאָדָם אוֹ מִי יָשׂוּם אִלֵּם [אוֹ חֵרֵשׁ אוֹ פִקֵּחַ אוֹ עִוֵּר הֲלֹא אָנֹכִי ה']." (שמות
ד:יא). תמן קמת לך, וּהכא לית אנא קאים? הדא הוא דכתיב, "[כִּי] מִי
[גוֹי גָּדוֹל אֲשֶׁר לוֹ אֱ-לֹהִים קְרֹבִים אֵלָיו] כַּה' אֱ-לֹהֵינוּ בְּכָל קָרְאֵנוּ אֵלָיו."
(דברים ד:ז).

רבי יודן בשם רבי יצחק שיטה אוחרי: בשר ודם יש לו פטרון.

אמרו לו, "הרי נתפס בן ביתך." אמר, "הרי אני מתקיים עליו." אמרו לו,
"הרי יוצא לידון." אמר להן, "הרי אני מתקיים עליו." אמרו לו הרי,
"הוא מושלך למים." היכן הוא והיכן פטרונו? אבל הקדוש ברוך הוא
הציל את יונה ממעי הדגה. הרי הוא אומר, "וַיֹּאמֶר ה' לַדָּג וַיָּקֵא אֶת
יוֹנָה [אֶל הַיַּבָּשָׁה]." (יונה ב:יא).

רבי יודן בשם רבי יצחק אמר בשיטה אוחרי: הרי בשר ודם יש
לו פטרון. אמרו לו, "נתפס בן ביתך." אמר להן, "הריני מתקיים
תחתיו." אמרו לו, "הרי הוא יוצא לידון." אמר להן, "הריני מתקיים
עליו." אמרו לו, "הרי הוא מושלך לאש." היכן הוא והיכן פטרונו? אבל
הקדוש ברוך הוא אינו כן. הציל לחנניה מישאל ועזריה מכבשן האש.
הדא הוא דכתיב, "עָנֵה נְבוּכַדְנֶצַּר וְאָמַר בְּרִיךְ אֱ-לָהֲהוֹן דִּי שַׁדְרַךְ מֵישַׁךְ
וַעֲבֵד נְגוֹ [דִּי שְׁלַח מַלְאֲכֵהּ וְשֵׁיזִב לְעַבְדוֹהִי]... ." (דניאל ג:כח).

רבי יודן בשם רבי יצחק אמר בה שיטה אוחרי: הרי בשר ודם יש
לו פטרון וכו' עד הרי הוא מושלך לחיות. אבל הקדוש ברוך הוא הציל
את דניאל מגוב אריות. הדא הוא דכתיב, "אֱ-לָהִי שְׁלַח מַלְאֲכֵהּ וּסֲגַר
פֻּם אַרְיָוָתָא [וְלָא חַבְּלוּנִי]... ." (דניאל ו:כג).

רבי יודן אמר משמיה דידיה: בשר ודם יש לו פטרון. אם באת
לו עת צרה, אינו נכנס אצלו פתאום, אלא בא ועמד לו על פתחו של
פטרונו וקורא לעבדו או לבן ביתו והוא אומר, "איש פלוני עומד על
פתח חצירך." שמא מכניסו ושמא מניחו. אבל הקדוש ברוך הוא אינו
כן. אם בא על אדם צרה לא יצווח לא למיכאל ולא לגבריאל אלא לי
יצווח ואני עונה לו מיד. הדא הוא דכתיב, "...כֹּל אֲשֶׁר יִקְרָא בְּשֵׁם ה'
יִמָּלֵט... ." (יואל ג:ה).

אמר רבי פנחס עובדא הוה ברב דהוה עייל מחמתה דטיבריא.
פגעון ביה רומאי. אמרון ליה, "מן דמאן את?"
אמר לון, "מן דסופיינוס." ופנינה.
ברמשא, אתו לגביה. אמרין ליה, "עד אימתי את מקיים עם
אילין יהודאי?"
אמר לון, "למה?"
אמרין ליה, "פגעינן בחד. אמרין ליה, 'יהודאי.' ואמרינן ליה, 'מן

דמאן את?׳ אמר לן, ׳דסופייינוס.׳"

אמר לון, "ומה עבדתון ליה?"

אמר ליה, "דיו ליה פנינן יתיה."

אמר לון, "יאות עבדיתון."

ומה מי שהוא נתלה בבשר ודם ניצול, מי שהוא נתלה בהקדוש
ברוך הוא, לא על כל שכן? הדא הוא דכתיב, "...כֹּל אֲשֶׁר יִקְרָא בְּשֵׁם ה׳
יִמָּלֵט... ." (יואל ג:ה).

אמר רבי אלכסנדרי: עובדא בחד ארכון דהוה שמיה
אלכסנדרוס. והוה קיים דיין חד ליסטים.

אמר ליה, "מה שמך?"

"אלכסנדרוס."

אמר ליה, "אלכסנדרוס, פנה אלכסנדריה!"

ומה אם מי ששמו כשם של בשר ודם הוא ניצול, מי ששמו כשמו
של הקדוש ברוך הוא על אחת כמה וכמה. הדא הוא דכתיב, "...כֹּל אֲשֶׁר
יִקְרָא בְּשֵׁם ה׳ יִמָּלֵט... ." (יואל ג:ה).

רבי פנחס אמר בה תרתי, חדא בשם רבי זעירא וחד בשם רבי
תנחום בר חנילאי. רבי פנחס בשם רבי זעירא אמר: בשר ודם יש לו
פטרון. אם הטריח עליו ביותר, הוא אומר, "אשכח פלן דקא מטרחא לי."
אבל הקדוש ברוך הוא אינו כן, אלא כל מה שאת מטריח עליו הוא
מקבלך. הדא הוא דכתיב, "הַשְׁלֵךְ עַל ה׳ יְהָבְךָ וְהוּא יְכַלְכְּלֶךָ... ." (תהלים
נה:כג).

רבי פנחס בשם רבי תנחום בר חנילאי: בשר ודם יש לו פטרון.
ובאו שונאים ותפשו אותו על פתח חצירו של פטרונו. עד דצווח ליה, עד
הוא נפק, עברת חרבא על קדליה וקטלית יתיה. אבל הקדוש ברוך הוא
הציל את יהושפט מחרב ארם דכתיב, "...וַיִּזְעַק יְהוֹשָׁפָט וַה׳ עֲזָרוֹ וַיְסִיתֵם
אֱ-לֹהִים מִמֶּנּוּ." (דברי הימים ב יח:לא). מלמד שלא היה חסר אלא
חיתוך חראש, "וַיְסִיתֵם אֱ-לֹהִים מִמֶּנּוּ."

רבי זעירא בריה דרבי אבהו, רבי אבהו בשם רבי אלעזר: "אַשְׁרֵי
שֶׁאֵ-ל יַעֲקֹב בְּעֶזְרוֹ [שִׂבְרוֹ עַל ה׳ אֱ-לֹהָיו]." (תהלים קמו:ה). מה כתיב
בתריה? "עֹשֶׂה שָׁמַיִם וָאָרֶץ [אֶת הַיָּם וְאֶת כָּל אֲשֶׁר בָּם הַשֹּׁמֵר אֱמֶת

253

לְעוֹלָם].״ (תהלים קמו:ו). וכי מה ענין זה לזה? אלא, מלך בשר ודם יש
לו פטרון שולט באיפרכיא אחת ואינו שולט באיפרכיא אחרת. אפילו
תימר קוֹזְמוֹקְלָטוֹר שולט ביבשה, שמא שולט בים? אבל הקדוש ברוך
הוא שולט בים ושולט ביבשה. מציל בים מן המים וביבשה מן האש.
הוא שהציל את משה מחרב פרעה, הציל את יונה ממעי הדגה, חנניה
מישאל ועזריה מכבשן האש, לדניאל מבור אריות. הדא הוא דכתיב,
״עֹשֶׂה שָׁמַיִם וָאָרֶץ אֶת הַיָּם וְאֶת כָּל אֲשֶׁר בָּם [הַשֹּׁמֵר אֱמֶת לְעוֹלָם].״
(תהלים קמו:ו).

אמר רבי תנחומא: מעשה בספינה אחת של עובדי כוכבים
ומזלות, שהיתה פורשת מים הגדול והיה בה תינוק אחד יהודי. עמד
עליהם סער גדול בים ועמד כל אחד ואחד מהם והתחיל נוטל יראתו
בידו וקורא, ולא הועיל כלום. כיון שראו שלא הועילו כלום, אמרו
לאותו יהודי, ״בני! קום קרא אל א-להיך שהוא עונה אתכם
כשאתם צועקים אליו והוא גבור!״ מיד עמד התינוק בכל לבו וצעק
וקיבל ממנו הקדוש ברוך הוא תפילתו ושתק הים.

כיון שירדו ליבשה, ירדו כל אחד ואחד לקנות צרכיו. אמרו לו
לאותו התינוק, ״לית את בעי מזבין לך כלום?״

אמר להון, ״מה אתון בעי מן ההן אכסניא עלובה?״

אמרו לו, ״את אכסניא עלובה? אינון אכסניא עלובה! אינון
הכא וטעוותהון בבבל ואינון הכא וטעוותהון ברומי ואינון הכא
וטעוותהון עמהון ולא מהנון להן כלום, אבל את כל אהן דאת אזיל
א-להך עמך!״

הדא הוא דכתיב, ״[כִּי מִי גוֹי גָּדוֹל אֲשֶׁר לוֹ אֱ-לֹהִים קְרֹבִים אֵלָיו]
כַּה' אֱ-לֹהֵינוּ בְּכָל קָרְאֵנוּ אֵלָיו.״ (דברים ד:ז).

רבי שמעון בן לקיש אמר: בשר ודם יש לו קרוב. אם היה עשיר
הוא מודה בו ואם היה עני כופר בו, אבל הקדוש ברוך הוא אינו כן, אלא
אפילו ישראל נתונין בירידה התחתונה הוא קורא אותם, ״אַחַי וְרֵעָי.״
ומה טעם? ״לְמַעַן אַחַי וְרֵעָי [אֲדַבְּרָה נָּא שָׁ-לוֹם בָּךְ].״ (תהלים קכב:ח).

רבי אבון ורבי אחא ורבי שמעון בן לקיש: בשר ודם יש לו קרוב.
אם היה פילוסופוס, הוא אומר, ״ההן פלן מתקרב לן,״ אבל הקדוש ברוך

הוּא קוֹרֵא לְכָל יִשְׂרָאֵל קְרוֹבִים. הֲדָא הוּא דִּכְתִיב, "וַיָּרֶם קֶרֶן לְעַמּוֹ
תְּהִלָּה לְכָל חֲסִידָיו לִבְנֵי יִשְׂרָאֵל עַם קְרֹבוֹ הַלְלוּיָ-הּ." (תהלים קמח:יד).

Rabbi Yudan, in the name of Rabbi Isaac, made four
statements regarding this [concept that God is always close to
those who call him]:

One of flesh and blood has a patron. [In ancient Rome,
members of the lower class, called plebeians, used to associate
themselves with members of the upper class, called patricians
or patrons, who would exercise their influence for them,
usually for a fee.] If they say to him, "A member of your
household has been arrested," he responds, "I can exercise
influence for him." If they say to him, "A member of your
household is going to judgment," he responds, "I can exercise
influence for him." If they say to him, "Look, he's going to be
hanged," where is he and where is his patron? However, the
Holy One, Blessed be He, saved Moses from Pharaoh's sword
[when Pharaoh tried to seize Moses for killing an Egyptian who
had attacked a Jew[629]]. Thus it is written, "...for the God of my
father is my help and He saved me from the sword of
Pharaoh."[630]

Rabbi Yannai said: It is written, "...and Moses fled from
before Pharaoh... ."[631] Is it possible for flesh and blood to flee
from the government? [The Torah could simply have written
"and Moses fled," or that he "fled from Egypt." The

---

[629] Exodus 2:11-15.
[630] Exodus 18:4.
[631] Exodus 2:15.

expression "from before Pharaoh" (מפני פרעה) implies that he was actually standing in front of Pharaoh when he fled. As a powerful king, Pharaoh must have had soldiers and guards in his presence who would have easily prevented any escape. Hence, the verse cannot literally mean that Moses simply ran away.[632] Rather, at the time when Pharaoh arrested Moses, he condemned him to have his head stricken off, but the sword fell blunt upon Moses's neck and broke. Thus it is written, "Your neck is like a tower of ivory... ."[633] This refers to the neck of Moses.

A rabbi[634] said in the name of Rabbi Evyathar: Not only that, but the sword bounced from off the neck of Moses onto the neck of his executioner and killed him. Thus it is written, "...for the God of my father is my help and He saved me from the sword of Pharaoh,"[635] meaning, He saved *me*, but the executioner was killed. In support of this, Rabbi Berachiyah applied to Moses the verse, "The wicked one is an expiation for the righteous one... ."[636] Rabbi Avon applied to Moses the

---

[632] Etz Yosef points out that earlier on the verse says that Pharaoh "sought to kill Moses" (ויבקש להרג את משה) rather than saying Pharaoh "sought Moses to kill him" (ויבקש את משה להרגו), further implying that Pharaoh had already arrested Moses.

[633] Song of Songs 7:5.

[634] Although Rabbi Judah the Prince was often called simply "Rabbi," this cannot be not a reference to him because he would not have quoted Rabbi Evyathar who lived in a much later generation.

[635] Exodus 18:4.

[636] Proverbs 21:18.

verse, "A righteous person is rescued from trouble and a wicked one comes in his stead."[637]

Bar Kappara taught: An angel descended and appeared to them in the image of Moses. They arrested the angel while Moses fled.

Rabbi Joshua ben Levi said: At the time when Moses fled from before Pharaoh, some of Pharaoh's subjects became mutes, some of them deaf and some of them blind. He asked the mutes, "Where is Moses," but they did not speak. He asked the deaf ones, but they did not hear. He asked the blind, but they did not see. This is the meaning of what the Holy One, Blessed be He, said to Moses, "...who put a mouth for man, or who makes mute or deaf or able-bodied or blind? Is it not I, the Lord?"[638] [This was the response to Moses' complaint that he was incapable of appearing before Pharaoh because he had difficulty speaking.] In that situation I stood by you. Shall I not stand by you here also? Thus it is written, "For who is a great nation which has a god close to it as the Lord our God [is to us] whenever we call to Him?"[639]

Rabbi Yudan in the name of Rabbi Isaac made another statement: One of flesh and blood has a patron. If they say to him, "A member of your household has been arrested," he responds, "I can exercise influence for him." If they say to him, "Look, he is going to judgment," he responds, "I can exercise influence for him." If they say to him, "Look, he has

---

[637] Proverbs 11:8.
[638] Exodus 4:11.
[639] Deuteronomy 4:7.

been thrown into water [to drown]," where is he and where is his patron? However, the Holy One, Blessed be He, saved Jonah from the innards of the fish, as it says, "The Lord spoke to the fish and it spit out Jonah onto dry land."[640]

Rabbi Yudan in the name of Rabbi Isaac made another statement: One of flesh and blood has a patron. If they say to him, "A member of your household has been arrested," he responds, "I can exercise influence for him." If they say to him, "Look, he is going to judgment," he responds, "I can exercise influence for him." If they say to him, "Look, he has been thrown into fire," where is he and where is his patron? However, for the Holy One, Blessed be He, it is not so. He saved Hananiah, Mishael and Azariah from the fiery furnace. Thus it is written, "Nebuchadnezzar raised his voice and said, 'Blessed is the God of Shadrach, Meshach and Abed Nego, Who sent His angel and saved His servants who trusted Him... .'"[641]

Rabbi Yudan in the name of Rabbi Isaac made another statement: One of flesh and blood has a patron, etc. until they say to him, "Look, he has been thrown to wild animals." However, the Holy One, Blessed be He, saved Daniel from the den of lions. Thus it is written, "My God sent his angel and closed the mouth of the lions and they did not attack me... ."[642]

---

[640] Jonah 2:11.
[641] Daniel 3:28. Shadrach, Meshach and Abed Nego were the names given to Hananiah, Mishael and Azariah by Nebuchadnezzar. (Etz Yosef).
[642] Daniel 6:23.

Rabbi Yudan said on his own authority: One of flesh and blood has a patron. When a time of trouble arrives, he does not suddenly barge in upon him. Rather, he comes and stands at the doorway of his patron and calls to his servant or to a member of his household who then tells the patron, "Such and such a man is standing at the entrance to your courtyard." Perhaps he invites him in, perhaps he leaves him there. However, it is not so with the Holy One, Blessed be He. If trouble befalls a person, let him not cry out to [the angel] Michael nor to [the angel] Gabriel. Rather, let him cry out to Me and I will answer him immediately. Thus it is written, "Any who call in the name of the Lord shall be rescued... ."[643]

Rabbi Phinehas said: An incident took place when Rav entered a town after visiting the hot springs of Tiberias. Romans met him and said to him, "Whose are you? [Who is your patron?]"

He answered, "Suphinus," so they left him alone.

That evening the same Romans met Suphinus. They said to him, "How long shall you intervene for these Jews?"

He said, "Why do you ask?"

They responded, "We encountered one whom we heard being called a Jew.[644] We asked him, 'Whose are you?' and he responded, 'Suphinus.'"

"And what did you do for him?"

"It is enough that we let him alone."[645]

[643] Joel 3:5.
[644] Perush MiBa'al Sefer Chareidim.
[645] Etz Yosef suggests an alternative: The word "דיד" as used here may

"You behaved properly."

If one who depends on flesh and blood is saved, shall it not be all the more so for one who depends on the Holy One, Blessed be He? Thus it is written, "Any who call in the name of the Lord shall be rescued... ."[646]

Rabbi Alexandri said: An incident occurred with a certain judge whose name was Alexander who was trying the case of a certain robber.

The judge said, "What is your name?"

"Alexander."

He said, "Alexander, turn to Alexandria." [I.e., I will permit you to flee to Alexandria.[647]]

If one whose name is the same as flesh and blood is saved, shall it not be all the more so for one whose name is the same as the Holy One, Blessed be He? Thus it is written, "Any who call in the name of the Lord shall be rescued... ."[648] [This phrase (אשר יקרא בשם השם) can also be read, "Any who are called by the name of the Lord shall be rescued... ." The Midrash says that the word Israel (ישראל) can be read "upright

---

mean "tax," so that the response was that the soldiers had exempted Rav from paying a certain tax.

[646] Joel 3:5.

[647] This appears to be the plain meaning of the text. P'nei Moshe, however, comments that the judge let him off entirely because they had the same name. Etz Yosef agrees, stating that it would be an insult to the judge to punish someone with the same name since news would spread that "Alexander has been punished," and the public might not realize that it was another person.

[648] Joel 3:5.

ones of God" (ל–א ישרי). Thus, every Jew (ישראל) bears God's Name.[649]]

Rabbi Phinehas recited two expositions, one in the name of Rabbi Z'eira and one in the name of Rabbi Tanchum bar Chanilai.

Rabbi Phinehas in the name of Rabbi Z'eira said: One of flesh and blood has a patron. If he troubles him too much, he says, "I shall ignore so and so who bothers me." However, it is not so with the Holy One, Blessed be He. Rather, as much as you trouble Him, he accepts you. Thus it is written, "Cast upon the Lord your burden and He shall sustain you... ."[650]

Rabbi Phinehas in the name of Rabbi Tanchum bar Chanilai said: One of flesh and blood has a patron. If enemies come and seize him at the entrance of his patron's courtyard, by the time he cries out and by the time his patron emerges, a sword has traversed his neck and killed him. However, the Holy One, Blessed be He, saved Jehoshaphat from the sword of Aram as it is written, "...and Jehoshaphat cried out and the Lord helped him and God turned them from him."[651] This teaches that the only thing lacking was cutting off his head and God turned them away from him. [The verse could have simply said "and God turned them away." The additional phrase "from him" (ממנו) implies that the enemies were already upon Jehoshaphat and at the point of decapitating him.]

---

[649] MidrashTehillim 4:3.
[650] Psalms 55:23.
[651] II Chronicles 18:31.

Rabbi Z'eira, the son of Rabbi Abahu, said that Rabbi Abahu said in the name of Rabbi Elazar: "Happy is one for whom the God of Jacob is his aid, whose hope is upon the Lord his God."[652] What is written afterwards? "He makes the heaven and earth, the sea and all that are in them; the Guardian of truth forever."[653] What does one thing have to do with the other? Rather, a flesh and blood king has a patron who controls one province but does not control another province. Even if you say that the supreme Emperor of Rome[654] controls the dry land, does he then control the sea? But the Holy One, Blessed be He, controls both the sea and the dry land. He saves at sea from the water and upon the dry land from fire. He saved Moses from the sword of Pharaoh, Jonah from the innards of the fish, Hananiah, Mishael and Azariah from the fiery furnace, and Daniel from the pit of lions. Thus it is written, "He makes the heaven and earth, the sea and all that are in them; the Guardian of truth forever."[655]

Rabbi Tanchuma said: There was an incident involving a ship that belonged to heathens which set out to sea. A Jewish child was in the ship. A fierce storm engaged them at sea. Each one of the heathens stood, took his idol in his hands, and

---

[652] Psalms 146:5.
[653] Psalms 146:6.
[654] The word קוזמוקלטור is Greek. "Cosmos" means "universe" just as in modern English. The suffix "crat" means "ruler" just as in words such as "bureaucrat" or "autocrat" used today. (The ל and ר are sometimes exchanged when foreign words are used in the Talmud.) Thus, a "cosmocrat" is a "universal ruler."
[655] Psalms 146:6.

cried out, but it did not avail them at all. When they saw that nothing helped, they said to that Jew, "Arise, my son! Call to your God for we have heard that He answers you when you cry out to Him and that He is mighty." Immediately, the child stood and called with all his heart. The Holy One, Blessed be He, accepted his prayer and the sea became silent.

When they reached dry land, each one descended to purchase his needs. They said to that child, "Don't you want to buy something for yourself?"

He responded, "What do you want from this poor wanderer?" [As a stranger in this foreign land, I would not know where to go or what to buy?]

They said to him, "Are you a poor wanderer? They are indeed poor wanderers who are here but whose idols are in Babylonia, or who are here and whose idols are in Rome, or who are here and their idols are with them, yet do not help them at all! But as for you, wherever you go, your God is with you."

Thus it is written, "For who is a great nation which has a god close to it as the Lord our God [is to us] whenever we call to Him."[656]

Rabbi Shimon ben Lakish said: One of flesh and blood who has a relative, if that relative is wealthy, he acknowledges him, but if he is poor, he denies him. However, with the Holy One, Blessed be He, it is not so. Rather, even if Israel reaches the lowest degree, He calls them "My brothers and My friends." What is the Scriptural source for this? "For the sake

---

[656] Deuteronomy 4:7.

of my brothers and friends I shall speak peace for you."[657] [Although the speaker here appears to be King David,[658] since he spoke through a spirit of prophecy, it is as though God Himself is making this statement.[659] This shows the remarkable love God has for the Jewish people. Although Jews refer to Him as "our Father and our King," He calls them brothers and friends to show how dear they are to Him.]

Rabbi Avon, Rabbi Acha and Rabbi Shimon ben Lakish said: One of flesh and blood who has a relative, if that relative is a philosopher [someone wise and knowledgeable], he will say, "So and so is related to us." But the Holy One, Blessed be He, calls all Israel "relatives." Thus it is written, "He uplifts the glory of His people, [He is] the praise of all His pious ones, the Children of Israel, His close people; Hallelujah!"[660] [The term "His close people" (עם קרובו) implies "His relatives," since the word for "close" in Hebrew (קרוב) also means "relative."]

Throughout the centuries, Jews have been confronted with numerous situations involving vicious persecution. During such times, some may be tempted to modify or, at least, temporarily suspend their religious observance, hoping thereby

---

[657] Psalms 122:8.
[658] See Rashi ad loc.
[659] This seems to be the plain meaning. Rabbi Yaakov ibn Chaviv, however, offers an elaborate explanation that the psalm should be read as a colloquy among King David, the scoffers of the generation, the righteous of the generation, and God.
[660] Psalms 148:14.

to win favor among influential non-Jews. To such individuals, the rabbis of the Talmud point out that the favor of prominent non-Jews is often useless. The amount of assistance that friendly Gentiles are able or willing to offer is highly limited. They may not be willing to be "imposed upon" or to be identified with the downtrodden Jews. Moreover, their best efforts may simply not be effective. Accordingly, the proper response to religious oppression is not to relax or diminish religious observance, but, on the contrary, to augment one's attachment to God and His Torah, for only by doing so can one be truly assured of deliverance from evil.

Brachoth 9:1

אמר רבי יוחנן: "כִּי מִי אֲשֶׁר יְבָחַר [יְחֻבַּר קרי] אֶל כָּל הַחַיִּים יֵשׁ
בִּטָּחוֹן... ." (קהלת ט:ד). "יְבָחַר" כתיב. "...אֶל כָּל הַחַיִּים יֵשׁ בִּטָּחוֹן... ."
שכל זמן שאדם חי, יש לו תקוה. מת, אבדה תקותו. מה טעמא? "בְּמוֹת
אָדָם רָשָׁע תֹּאבַד תִּקְוָה... ." (משלי יא:ז).

...אמר רבי אחא: "כִּי מִי אֲשֶׁר יְבָחַר [יְחֻבַּר קרי] אֶל כָּל הַחַיִּים יֵשׁ
בִּטָּחוֹן... ." (קהלת ט:ד). אפילו אותם שפשטו ידיהן בזבול יש להם
בטחון. לקרבן אי אפשר שכבר פשטו ידיהן בזבול. לרחקן אי אפשר
שעשו תשובה. עליהן הוא אומר, "...וְיָשְׁנוּ שְׁנַת עוֹלָם וְלֹא יָקִיצוּ... ."
(ירמיה נא:נז).

רבנן דקיסרין אמרי: קטני עובדי כוכבים ומזלות וחילותיו של
נבוכדנצר אין חיין ואין נידונין. עליהן הכתוב אומר, "...וְיָשְׁנוּ שְׁנַת עוֹלָם
וְלֹא יָקִיצוּ... ." (ירמיה נא:נז).

Rabbi Yochanan said: "For whoever is associated with
all who are alive there is hope... ."[661] [The verse should be
read with the phrase "is associated" (יחבר), however the
phrase] "is chosen" (יבחר) is actually written in the verse,
meaning that for all who are living there is hope because as
long as a person lives there is hope. Once one dies, his or her
hope is lost. What is the Scriptural source for this? "With the
death of a wicked person, hope is lost... ."[662] [The point of
having the verse written with the phrase "is chosen" (יבחר) is
that no matter how one has conducted one's life as long as a
person lives, he or she may choose to change for the better.]

---

[661] Ecclesiastes 9:4.
[662] Proverbs 11:7.

...Rabbi Acha said: "For whoever is associated with all who are alive there is hope... ."[663] Even those who have set their hands against the Temple have hope. To draw them close is not possible for they have already set their hands against the Temple. To distance them is impossible for they have repented. Concerning them it is written, "...and they shall sleep an eternal slumber and they shall not awaken... ."[664]

The sages of Caesaria said: The children of the heathens and the soldiers of Nebuchadnezzar are not resurrected and are not judged. Concerning them Scripture says, "...and they shall sleep an eternal slumber and they shall not awaken... ."[665]

Rabbi Acha's statement seems self-contradictory. At first, he states that even one involved in the destruction of the Temple may repent and that such repentance works, yet he then goes on to say that repentance cannot really help.

The Talmud states that Nebuzaradan, the general of the Babylonian army which destroyed the first Temple, observed blood bubbling on the Temple floor. He discovered this to be the blood of the priest and Prophet Zachariah whom the people had murdered after he warned them of the Temple's impending

---

[663] Ecclesiastes 9:4.

[664] Jeremiah 51:57.

[665] Ibid. These rabbis apparently follow the view that only those who are very righteous or very wicked will be resurrected, the former to be rewarded and the latter to be judged. The soldiers of Nebuchadnezzar who did not actually participate in the destruction of the Temple and heathen children who are incapable of doing wrong will not be resurrected. See above J.T. Brachoth 5:2 with commentary thereon.

destruction. *Nebuzaradan then murdered tens of thousands of rabbis, schoolchildren and young kohanim inside the Temple to calm that blood, but it continued to froth. He then said, "Zachariah! Zachariah! The best among them I have slain. Would it please you that I should kill them all?" The blood then ceased bubbling.*

Upon further consideration, Nebuzaradan reasoned that if the consequences for the murder of one person were so serious, then he would surely face severe punishment for having murdered so many, so he fled from the army and converted to Judaism.[666] *Presumably, God accepted Nebuzaradan's repentance, contrary to what Rabbi Acha says in the instant passage.*

A similar question arises concerning Elisha ben Abuyah, a rabbi of the Talmud who had a vision of an angel sitting and recording the deeds of humankind. This rabbi had learned that angels never sit, so when he witnessed this vision, it occurred to him that perhaps more than one deity exists. Hashem considered this sin so egregious that a voice from Heaven announced that Elisha ben Abuyah could never repent.[667] *The Rambam rules that repentance always works, even if a person was a heretic throughout his or her life and repented only at the very end.*[668] *If so, how is it possible that Elisha ben Abuyah could not repent?*

---

[666] B.T. Sanhedrin 96B.
[667] B.T. Chagigah 15A.
[668] Yad HaChazakah, Hilchoth Teshuvah 3:14.

The answer appears to lie in the level of repentance required. The Talmud explains that one who fails to perform a positive commandment may repent and be immediately forgiven. However, one who violates a negative commandment must wait until Yom Kippur when the fasting, prayers and other activities of the day cause forgiveness. If one violates a commandment so serious that the punishment is spiritual excision or the death penalty, ordinary repentance and Yom Kippur do not suffice. For these, the person must suffer torment during his or her lifetime. Finally, one who desecrates God's Holy Name is not forgiven until he or she dies.[669] In addition, the Mishnah states that all of this works only with respect to sins against Hashem. If, however, one sins against a fellow human being, he or she cannot be forgiven without seeking forgiveness from that person.[670]

In light of the above, it appears that Elisha ben Abuyah could have repented, but that his repentance would require tremendous effort. Indeed, the Talmud relates a story about Elazar ben Dordaya, another rabbi who sinned so badly that he was told he could not repent. In contrast to Elisha ben Abuyah who simply gave up, Elazar ben Dordaya went to the mountains where he wept over his sins until his soul departed. A Heavenly voice then proclaimed that he merited a share in the world to come.[671] Hence, a pronouncement that one cannot

---

[669] B.T. Yoma 86A.
[670] Yoma 8:9.
[671] B.T. Avodah Zarah 17A.

repent is not absolute. It merely means that lower levels of repentance will not work.

The same principle applies here. Rabbi Acha evidently means that ordinary repentance cannot help a person such as Nebuzaradan who has destroyed the Temple. An exceptional repentance, however, could and did help.

Brachoth 9:1 (Compare B.T. Brachoth 58A)

הרואה אוכלוסין אומר, "ברוך חכם הרזים." כשם שאין פרצופין
דומין זה לזה, כך אין דעתן דומה זה לזה.

בן זומא, כשהיה רואה אכלוסין בירושלים, אומר, "ברוך שברא
כל אלו לשמשיני! כמה יגע אדם הראשון עד שלא אכל פרוסה. חרש,
זרע, ניכש, עידר, קצר, עימר, דש, זרה, בירר, טחן, הרקיד, לש, וקיטף,
ואפה ואחר כך אכל פרוסה. ואני עומד בשחרית ומוצא כל אלו לפני.

"ראה כמה יגיעות יגע אדם הראשון עד שמצא חלוק ללבוש. גזז,
וליבן, וניפס, וצבע, וטווה, וארג, כבס, ותפר ואחר כך מצא חלוק ללבוש.
ואני עומד בשחרית ומוצא כל אלו מתוקן לפני. כמה בעלי אומניות
משכימים ומעריבים ואני עומד בשחרית ומוצא כל אלו לפני."

וכן היה בן זומא אומר: אורח רע, מהו אומר? "וכי מה אכלתי
משל בעל הבית וכי מה שתיתי משל בעל הבית? חתיכה אחת אכלתי
לו. כוס יין שתיתי לו. וכל טורח שטרח לא טרח אלא בשביל אשתו
ובניו." אבל אורח טוב אומר, "ברוך בעל הבית! זכור בעל הבית
לטובה! כמה יין הביא לפני! כמה חתיכות הביא לפני! כמה טורח טרח
לפני! כל מה שטרח לא טרח אלא בשבילי!" וכן הוא אומר, "זְכֹר כִּי
תַשְׂגִּיא פָעֳלוֹ אֲשֶׁר שֹׁרְרוּ אֲנָשִׁים." (איוב ל״ו:כ״ד).

One who sees a large crowd of people should say,
"Blessed is the One who discerns secrets." Just as people's
faces do not match one another, so their minds do not match
one another [and yet God knows what each person is
thinking.[672]]

---

[672] Rashi on B.T. Brachoth 58A sub verba Chacham HaRazim
(חכם הרזים).

When Ben Zoma saw a large crowd in Jerusalem, he said, "Blessed is the One who created all these to serve me. Observe how much Adam exerted himself before he could eat a slice of bread. He plowed, sowed, weeded, hoed, harvested, piled, threshed, winnowed, screened, ground, sifted, kneaded, formed dough, baked and afterwards ate a slice of bread, while I arise in the morning and find all of this ready before me! Observe how much effort Adam exerted before he could find a robe to wear. He sheared wool, whitened, combed, dyed, spun, wove, washed, sewed and afterwards had a robe to wear, while I arise in the morning and find all this ready before me! How many skilled workers rise early and work late, while I arise in the morning and find everything ready before me!"

So also Ben Zoma used to say: What does a bad guest say? "What did I eat that belonged to the host? What did I drink that belonged to the host? One slice of his I ate. One cup of wine of his I drank. All the effort that he exerted, he exerted only for his wife and children." However, a good guest says, "Blessed is the host! May the host be remembered for good! How much wine he brought before me! How many servings he brought before me! How much trouble he went to for me! All the effort that he exerted, he exerted only on my account." So it says, "Remember how exalted is his work which men have seen."[673]

The Talmud stated earlier in this chapter, as well as in chapter eight, that human beings cannot even remotely

[673] Job 36:24 according to Rashi.

describe God's greatness. Because God is all powerful and created the world effortlessly, one may think it unnecessary to praise Him.

In response to this, Ben Zoma points out that a rude, self-centered person could argue that he has no obligation to thank a host on the grounds that the host really took no special pains on his account. After all, the host needed to prepare a meal anyway. However, it is not up to the guest to analyze how much effort the host has expended. Rather, the guest should simply look at what he or she has, in fact, received and express gratitude for it.

Rabbi Yisrael Salanter used to point out that, according to established halachah, poor people have a duty to avoid accepting charity and to show appreciation when they receive it.[674] Conversely, rich people have a duty to be generous and to give their donations with kindness and sympathy.[675] How would it work out if people would reverse these roles? The poor person, citing the rules which apply to the rich, might rudely demand support even if he or she could avoid it by foregoing certain relatively minor luxuries. The rich person, citing the rules which apply to the poor, would refuse to contribute unless the recipient were absolutely desperate and, even then, would do so only grudgingly. It is important for people to keep in mind that they must follow the halachoth which apply to **them** and not the halachoth that apply to their counterparts.

---

[674] Shulchan Aruch, Yoreh Deah 255:1-2.
[675] Shulchan Aruch, Yoreh Deah 249:3-4.

*Likewise, one should not think that because God created the world effortlessly, there is no obligation to show Him appreciation. That is looking at matters from the wrong perspective. The prayers and blessings people utter in this world are for **their** benefit, not God's. Such activities help people gain a greater awareness and appreciation of Hashem's existence and dominion. For this reason, Ben Zoma sought ways to enhance his feelings of gratitude. Even when it came to the ordinary necessities of life such as a loaf of bread or a simple garment, he pointed out how much went into providing them. Thus, he quotes the verse, "Remember how exalted is his work which men have seen."[676] Although God's work is effortless for Him, it is exalted from a human perspective. People must view creation from this point of view and render praise to the Creator accordingly.*

---

[676] Job 36:24 according to Rashi.

Brachoth 9:2 (Compare Breishith Rabbah 24:4 and VaYikra Rabbah 15:1)

אמר רבי יהושע בן חנניה: בשעה שהרוח יוצא לעולם, הקדוש
ברוך הוא משברו בהרים ומרשלו בגבעות, ואומר לו, "תן דעתך שלא
תזיק בריותי." מה טעם? "...כִּי רוּחַ מִלְּפָנַי יַעֲטוֹף... ." (ישעיה נז:טז).
משלהי ליה. כמה דאת אמר, "בְּהִתְעַטֵּף עָלַי רוּחִי... ." (תהלים קמב:ד).
כל כך למה? רבי חונא בשם רבי אחא: "...וּנְשָׁמוֹת אֲנִי עָשִׂיתִי"
(ישעיה נז:טז), בשביל נשמות שעשיתי.
אמר רבי הונא: בשלשה מקומות יצא הרוח שלא במשקל וביקש
להחריב את העולם כולו: אחת בימי יונה, ואחת בימי אליהו, ואחת בימי
איוב. בימי יונה: "וַה' הֵטִיל רוּחַ גְּדוֹלָה [אֶל הַיָּם וַיְהִי סַעַר גָּדוֹל בַּיָּם
וְהָאֳנִיָּה חִשְּׁבָה לְהִשָּׁבֵר]." (יונה א:ד). בימי איוב: "וְהִנֵּה רוּחַ גְּדוֹלָה בָּאָה
מֵעֵבֶר הַמִּדְבָּר [וַיִּגַּע בְּאַרְבַּע פִּנּוֹת הַבַּיִת וַיִּפֹּל עַל הַנְּעָרִים וַיָּמוּתוּ
וָאִמָּלְטָה רַק אֲנִי לְבַדִּי לְהַגִּיד לָךְ]." (איוב א:יט). בימי אליהו מניין?
"...וְהִנֵּה ה' עֹבֵר וְרוּחַ גְּדוֹלָה וְחָזָק מְפָרֵק הָרִים [וּמְשַׁבֵּר סְלָעִים לִפְנֵי
ה']... ." (מלכים א יט:יא).
אמר רבי יודן בר שלום נימר: אותו של איוב בשבילו היה ושל
יונה בשבילו היה. אין לך אלא של אליהו שהיה קוסמיקון. "...וְהִנֵּה ה'
עֹבֵר וְרוּחַ גְּדוֹלָה וְחָזָק מְפָרֵק הָרִים וּמְשַׁבֵּר סְלָעִים לִפְנֵי ה' לֹא בָרוּחַ ה'
וְאַחַר הָרוּחַ רַעַשׁ לֹא בָרַעַשׁ ה'. וְאַחַר הָרַעַשׁ אֵשׁ לֹא בָאֵשׁ ה' וְאַחַר הָאֵשׁ
קוֹל דְּמָמָה דַקָּה." (מלכים יט:יא-יב).

Rabbi Joshua ben Chanina says: When the wind goes
out into the world, the Holy One, Blessed be He, stymies it
with mountains and weakens it with hills. He says to it, "Pay
attention that you do not harm my creatures." What is the

Scriptural source for this? "...when the wind is subdued before Me... ."[677] He wears it out as you might say, "When my spirit is worn out... ." [The Hebrew word יעטף which means "subdued" in the first verse can also mean "worn out."]

Why is all this necessary? Rabbi Chuna said in the name of Rabbi Acha: [The end of the first verse reads] "...and souls I made,"[678] meaning "for the sake of the souls which I have made." [Thus, the verse can be read, "...when the wind is subdued before me for the sake of the souls which I made." If God did not weaken the wind, humanity could not survive.]

Rabbi Huna said: On three occasions the wind went forth without restraint and sought to destroy the entire world. Once in the days of Jonah, once in the days of Elijah, and once in the days of Job. In the days of Jonah: "And the Lord let loose a great wind upon the sea and it became a great gale in the sea and the ship was about to break up."[679] In the days of Job: "Behold a great wind came from across the desert and touched the four corners of the house and it fell upon the youths and they died; only I alone escaped to tell you."[680] In the days of Elijah, from where? "...and, behold, the Lord passes, and a great and mighty wind which takes apart mountains and breaks boulders is before the Lord... ."[681]

Rabbi Yudan bar Shalom of Nimar said: The one of Job was just for him and the one of Jonah was just for him. You

---

[677] Isaiah 57:16.
[678] Isaiah 57:16.
[679] Jonah 1:4.
[680] Job 1:19.
[681] I Kings 19:11.

have only the one of Elijah which was of worldwide proportions. Thus the verse says, "...and, behold, the Lord passes, and a great and mighty wind which takes apart mountains and breaks boulders is before the Lord; the Lord is not in the wind. And after the wind, earthquake; the Lord is not in the earthquake. After the earthquake is fire; the Lord is not in the fire. After the fire is a still, delicate sound."[682]

The Rambam taught that Hashem does not have any attributes. When the Tanach says that Hashem "is angry" or "pleased" or "kind," it is only describing God's behavior. For instance, if God brings destruction upon an evildoer, one might say that "God is angry," meaning that if a person would do something similar it would indicate anger. If God responds favorably to prayer, one might say that "God is kind," meaning that if a person would do something similar it would indicate kindness. However, Hashem does not actually have characteristics such as anger or kindness because God is immutable. He is not "angry" at one time and "kind" at another.[683]

Hashem has, however, created a system of spiritual forces which human behavior activates. Among these forces is the attribute of Divine judgment or justice which human wrongdoing can trigger.

---

[682] I Kings 19:11-12.
[683] Moreh Nevuchim, Part I, Chapters 52-54.

As used in the passage under consideration, the wind refers to this attribute of Divine justice.[684] *There have been certain times in history when, for various reasons, this spiritual force became aroused to the extent that God had to subdue it. For example, the Book of Job, tells how the Satan (the self-same attribute of justice), so to speak, provoked God against Job. "The Satan answered the Lord and said, 'Is it for nothing that Job fears God? Have You not safeguarded him and his household and all that are his from all about; the work of his hands You blessed and his possessions burgeon forth upon the land. However, send forth Your hand and touch all that are his [and see] if he will not curse You to Your face.'"*[685] *Although Hashem normally restrains the attribute of justice, He did not do so with Job. Rather, He permitted it to test Job's faith.*

The attribute of justice was again aroused when God commanded Jonah to admonish the people of Nineveh for their wicked ways, but Jonah fled to avoid fulfilling Hashem's command. The same phenomenon occurred again in the days of Elijah when the evil King Ahab and Queen Isabel tried to kill off God's prophets.

The Midrash says that "The King Messiah can never come until all the souls which arose in Divine thought to be created have been created and these are the souls which are mentioned in the Book of Adam."[686] *At the various stages of*

[684] See Zohar II, 203A.
[685] Job 1:9-11.
[686] Breishith Rabbah 24:4 and see B.T. Yoma 62A. The reference to the

history mentioned in the passage under review, the attribute of justice gained force to the point where an ultimate judgment, the judgment that will take place when the Messiah arrives, could have occurred. God, however, restrained the attribute of justice "for the sake of the souls which I have made." The Messiah cannot come and no final judgment can take place until all the souls Hashem planned to create have, indeed, come into being. Nothing can alter God's plan for how history will unfold.

One could raise the question: Why does God need to moderate the attribute of justice? Why not simply create it in a diluted form? The answer is that Hashem created the attribute of justice to be responsive to human activity. Thus, it was Jonah's evasion of God's will which triggered the release of a devastating wind. Likewise, the Talmud relates that Pharaoh had three advisors whom he consulted about his plans to destroy the Jews. The wicked Bilaam supported Pharaoh's scheme. The righteous Jethro counseled against it. Job, however, remained silent, a sin for someone of his stature. That silent failure to intervene activated the attribute of justice.[687]

In the time of Elijah, the efforts of King Ahab and Queen Isabel to eradicate the Jewish religion and replace it with the idolatrous Baal cult caused an unprecedented arousal of the attribute of judgment. The world might have come to an end,

Book of Adam probably means the Sefer Yetzirah, an ancient mystical work.
[687] B.T. Sotah 11A.

but that would have conflicted with Hashem's plans for the universe. No final scene of history, no ultimate judgment can occur, until all the souls God plans to bring into being have actually entered the world. Until God's plan is fulfilled, He "subdues the wind."

Torah from Jerusalem

Brachoth 9:2 (Compare B.T. Baba Bathra 109B-110A; J.T. Sanhedrin 11:5; Shir HaShirim Rabbah 2:5:3)

רבי חונא שמעון קמטריא בשם רבי שמואל בר נחמן: "[וַ]יָּקִימוּ
לָהֶם בְּנֵי דָן אֶת הַפָּסֶל] וִיהוֹנָתָן בֶּן גֵּרְשֹׁם בֶּן מְ[נַ]שֶׁה [הוּא וּבָנָיו הָיוּ כֹהֲנִים
לְשֵׁבֶט הַדָּנִי עַד יוֹם גְּלוֹת הָאָרֶץ]." (שופטים יח:ל). נון תלוי. אם זכה, בן
משה ואם לאו, בן מנשה.

חברייא בעון קומי רבי שמואל בר נחמן: כומר היה לעבודה זרה
והאריך ימים? אמר לון: על ידי שהיה עינו צרה בעבודה זרה שלו.

כיצד היתה עינו רעה בעבודה זרה שלו? הוה בר נש אתא
למיקרבה תור או אימר או גדי לעבודה זרה ואמר ליה, "פייסיה עלי."
והוא אמר ליה, "מה זו מועילה לך? לא רואה ולא שומעת ולא אוכלת
ולא שותה לא מטיבה ולא מריעה ולא מדברת."

אמר ליה, "חייך! ומה נעביד?"

ואמר ליה, "אזיל עביד ואייתי לי חד פינך דסולת ואתקין עלוי
עשר ביעין ואתקין קומוי והוא אכל מכל מה דאתי ואנא מפייס ליה
עלך." מכיון דאזיל ליה, הוה אכיל לון.

זימנא חדא, אתא חד בר פחין. אמר ליה כן. אמר ליה, "אם אין
מועילה כלום, את מה עביד הכא?"

אמר ליה, "בגין חיי."

כיון שעמד דוד המלך, שלח והביאו. אמר ליה, "אַתְּ בֶּן בְּנוֹ שֶׁל
אוֹתוֹ צַדִּיק וְאַתְּ עוֹבֵד עֲבוֹדָה זָרָה?!!"

אמר ליה, "כך אני מקובל מבית אבי אבא: 'מכור עצמך לעבודה
זרה ואל תצטרך לבריות.'"

אמר ליה, "חס ושלו-ם! לא אמר כן! אלא, 'מכור עצמך לעבודה
שהיא זרה לך ואל תצטרך לבריות.'"

כיון שראה דוד כך כך שהוא אוהב ממון, מה עשה? העמידו קומוס
על תיסבריות שלו. הדא הוא דכתיב, "וּשְׁבֻאֵל בֶּן גֵּרְשׁוֹם בֶּן מֹשֶׁה נָגִיד
עַל הָאֹצָרוֹת." (דברי הימים א כו:כד).

"שְׁבוּאֵל" שֶׁשָּׁב אֶל אֵ-ל בְּכָל לִבּוֹ וּבְכָל כֹּחוֹ. "נָגִיד עַל הָאֹצָרוֹת"

281

שמינוהו על תיסבורריות שלו.

מתיבין לרבי שמואל בר נחמן: והא כתיב, "...עַד יוֹם גְּלוֹת
הָאָרֶץ" (שופטים יח:ל)?

אמר לון: כיון שמת דוד, עמד שלמה וחילף סנקליטין שלו וחזר
לקילקולו הראשון. הדא הוא דכתיב, "וְנָבִיא אֶחָד זָקֵן יֹשֵׁב בְּבֵית
אֵ-ל... ." (מלכים א יג:יא). אמרין הוא הוה.

Rabbi Chuna quoted Simeon the Cabinetmaker, in the name of Rabbi Samuel bar Nachman: "The people of Dan established for themselves the idol and Jonathan the son of Gershom the son of Manasseh, he and his sons were priests to the Danite tribe until the day of the exile of the land."[688] The letter "Nun" (נ) in the name Manasseh (מנשה) is suspended. [In the Hebrew text, the letter "נ" is not written on the same line together with the other letters. Instead, it appears like this: מלֹשה.] If he merited he would be considered a son of Moses (משה) and if not, a son of Manasseh (מנשה). [The Jonathan in the verse is, indeed, the grandson of Moses. However, because he committed idolatry, Scripture inserted the letter "נ" to protect Moses's dignity and to hint that Jonathan was following the way of the notorious King Manasseh who tried to establish idolatry among the Jewish people.[689]]

The members of the academy asked Rabbi Samuel bar Nachman: Jonathan was a priest for idolatry, yet he lived so

---

688 Judges 18:30.
689 See Rashi on Judges 17:7 and 18:30.

long?[690]   He replied to them: Because he was stingy concerning his idols.

How is it that he was stingy concerning his idols? A person would come to offer an ox or sheep or goat to Jonathan's idol and say to him, "Appease him for me."

He would answer, "How does this benefit you? It does not see, nor hear, nor eat, nor drink, nor do good, nor do evil, nor speak."

"By your life, then what should we do?"

"Go prepare and fetch a dish of fine flour, set upon it ten eggs and place it before me. He [the idol] will eat from all that you bring and I will appease him for you."

Once the worshiper departed, Jonathan would consume the offering.

One time, a certain clever person showed up to whom Jonathan spoke as above. That person said, "If idolatry has no benefit at all, what are you doing here?"

He answered, "For a livelihood."

When King David ascended the throne, he sent for Jonathan and brought him before him. He said to him, "You

---

[690] The end of the verse states that Jonathan and his sons, "were priests to the Danite tribe until the day of the exile of the land." Seder Olam Rabbah 24:1 says that this refers to the exile of King Manasseh during the twenty-second year of his reign (see II Chronicles 33:11), approximately 1490 B.C.E. That would have been at least five hundred years after the events described in Judges 18. Moreover, as a grandson of Moses, Jonathan would already have been about three hundred years old even at the time of those events. Hence, the disciples question what caused Jonathan to merit living over eight hundred years.

are the grandson of that righteous man, yet you practice idolatry?"

He answered, "So I have received as a tradition from the house of my grandfather: 'Sell yourself to idolatry and do not become dependent upon people.'" [It is better to earn a living through practicing idol worship than to accept charity.]

"God forbid! He certainly did not say so! Rather, 'Sell yourself to a service which is strange to you and do not become dependent on people.'" [The Hebrew term for idolatry is "Avodah Zarah" (עבודה זרה) which literally means, "strange service." Therefore, Moses meant that one should engage in an occupation with which he is unfamiliar or which he considers beneath his dignity rather than accept charity. He was not suggesting that one stoop to promoting idolatry.]

Once King David saw that Jonathan loved money, what did he do? He appointed him as commissioner over his treasury. [As a Levite, Jonathan was entitled to receive tithes. In addition, the Jewish people would certainly have provided generously for the grandson of Moses. Accordingly, Jonathan's involvement with idolatry for the sake of money must have arisen from greed rather than need.[691]] Thus it is written, "And Shebuel son of Gershom son of Moses, minister of the treasuries."[692] He is called "Shebuel (שבואל)" because he returned to God (שב אל א-ל) with all his heart and all his strength. "...minister of the treasuries" because they appointed him minister over the treasury.

---

691 Korban HaEidah on J.T. Sanhedrin 11:5.
692 I Chronicles 26:24.

The students of the academy refuted Rabbi Samuel bar Nachman's premise [that Jonathan repented during the reign of King David]: Is it not written, "The people of Dan established for themselves the idol and Jonathan the son of Gershom the son of Manasseh, he and his sons were priests to the Danite tribe until the day of the exile of the land."[693] [The exile of King Manasseh did not occur until several generations after King David and the verse implies that Jonathan served as an idolatrous priest until that time.]

Rabbi Samuel bar Nachman answered them: Once King David died, King Solomon arose and changed his administration, so Jonathan [no longer minister of the treasury] returned to his original corruption. Thus it is written, "One elderly prophet dwelt in Beth El... ."[694] They say this was Jonathan.

It seems strange that King David would appoint as treasurer someone so greedy that he would promote idolatry in order to make money. One would think that he would go out of his way to prevent a person such as Jonathan from getting anywhere near his money. The explanation for King David's attitude may lie in the overall approach he adopted for trying to wean Jonathan away from idolatry.

The Talmud tells how Rabbi Judah the Prince once visited the town of Rabbi Elazar ben Rabbi Shimon after the

---

[693] Judges 18:30.
[694] I Kings 13:11.

*latter had died. "Did that righteous man leave a son?" he
inquired of the townspeople.*

*They answered, "He has a son and every harlot who is
hired for two dinarim is willing to hire him for eight!"
Although the young man had descended to such disgusting
behavior, Rabbi Judah the Prince located him and ordained
him a rabbi. He then sent the youth to live with Rabbi Shimon
ben Issi ben Lakunia, the boy's uncle. Every day the young
man complained that he wanted to return to his hometown. His
uncle responded, "They have ordained you, spread a gold
cloak upon you [as was customary when conferring ordination
in those days] and declared you a rabbi, yet you say, 'I want to
return to my hometown.'!?!"*

*The young man then announced: "I hereby abandon my
blemish!" Having repented, he later merited to become a great
Torah scholar.*

*Another time, Rabbi Judah the Prince visited the town of
Rabbi Tarfon after the latter had died. He again asked the
townsfolk if the renowned rabbi had any descendants. They
informed him that Rabbi Tarfon had a grandson who, like the
son of Rabbi Elazar ben Rabbi Shimon, had descended to the
depths of depravity, consorting with indecent women. Rabbi
Judah the Prince told that young man, "If you repent, I will
give you my daughter to wed," whereupon the boy repented.*[695]

*These stories sound quite remarkable. Certainly any
great rabbi who discovered that a young person had gone
astray, even far astray, would make an effort to influence that*

---

[695] B.T. Baba Metzia 85A.

person to return to the way of the Torah. However, it sounds incredible that Rabbi Judah the Prince would go to the extremes of giving such a person rabbinical ordination or offering him his daughter's hand. What he was really doing, of course, was to forcefully alert these young people to the depths to which they had fallen, and to demonstrate for them in the most powerful way possible the greatness they could attain if only they would abandon their evil ways. And it worked!

As king, it was largely David's duty to enforce the laws of the Torah. No one would have been surprised or critical of King David had he harshly denounced Jonathan or sought to severely punish his behavior. King David, however, chose a very different approach. By reminding Jonathan of who he was and what spiritual potential he had, King David was able to effect a complete reversal of Jonathan's attitude and behavior. Part of that approach included a practical demonstration of King David's faith in Jonathan's underlying goodness by specifically placing him, of all people, in charge of the treasury. The message was, "Look at what greatness you can have! Look at the position of trust I am giving you! Make sure you live up to it!"

The above explanation also resolves some other puzzling issues raised by this passage of the Talmud. First of all, the question of the disciples about how Jonathan could live so long despite serving idols seems odd. According to tradition, Og, the wicked king of Bashan, lived from before the Flood until after the Jews entered the Land of Israel, a period of more than five hundred years.[696] *Although the Torah says, "Joseph died and all his brothers and all that generation...And a new king arose over Egypt who did not know Joseph,"*[697] *the Midrash states that the Pharaoh who ruled during the time of Joseph was the same as the Pharaoh who enslaved the Jews and whose army later chased them to the Reed Sea. The Torah calls him "new" because he was deposed when he initially rejected the demands of his fellow Egyptians to enslave the Jews. When he later agreed to enslave and oppress the Jews, the other Egyptians reinstated him.*[698] *According to this view, Pharaoh lived for well over two hundred years. Although Pharaoh and Og were wicked, they lived a long time presumably because they played an important role in God's plans for the history of the world. If so, why were the disciples of Rabbi Samuel bar Nachman so surprised to learn that someone not righteous, such as Jonathan, lived a long time?*

Even more puzzling is Rabbi Samuel bar Nachman's answer. It may be true that Jonathan did not worship idolatry wholeheartedly. That would explain why God might not punish him. However, it does not explain why he merited an exceptionally long life. One would think that a person who deserved to live far beyond the limits of a normal human lifespan would have performed some outstanding deed. The mere lack of wrongdoing would not suffice.

---

[696] BaMidbar Rabbah 19:32.
[697] Exodus 1:6-8.
[698] Shemoth Rabbah 1:8.

288

The answer to these questions is that, in this case, Hashem granted long life to Jonathan to afford him an opportunity to repent, as he clearly had the potential to do. The Midrash says that God ordered Noah to take one hundred twenty years to build the ark in the hope that, in the meantime, the people would repent and He would not need to bring the Flood.[699] Even when the Flood started, the rains came softly at first so that, if the people repented, the rain would be a blessing.[700] Similarly, God granted Jonathan long life to give him every opportunity possible to repent.

The Talmud teaches, however, that when one causes the public to sin, Hashem does not help that person to repent. This is because it would be unjust for such a person to go to Heaven while his followers go elsewhere. Moreover, although one can regret and try to atone for his own sins, one has no sure way to cause those whom he has led astray to repent.[701] This explains the question of the members of the yeshiva: If Jonathan caused the public to sin by serving as a priest for idol worship, why would God give him a long life in which to repent? To this Rabbi Samuel bar Nachman answered that Jonathan did not lead anyone else astray. To the contrary, he denigrated idolatry and discouraged its worshipers. That is why his serving as an idolatrous priest did not prevent Hashem from granting him a lengthy opportunity to repent.

---

[699] Breishith Rabbah 30:7 and Rashi on Genesis 6:14.
[700] Breishith Rabbah 31:12 and Rashi on Genesis 7:12.
[701] Pirkei Avoth 5:18 and B.T. Yoma 87A.

Brachoth 9:2

רבי חזקיה בשם רבי ירמיה: כל ימיו של רבי שמעון בן יוחאי לא
נראתה הקשת בענן.

רבי חזקיה בשם רבי ירמיה: כן הוה רבי שמעון בן יוחאי אומר,
"בקעה! בקעה! התמלאי דינרי זהב!" והיתה מתמלאה.

רבי חזקיה בשם רבי ירמיה: כן הוה רבי שמעון בן יוחאי אומר,
"אני ראיתי בני העולם הבא ומיעוטין הן. אין תלתין אינון, אנא וברי
מנהון. אין תרין אינון, אנא וברי אינון."

רבי חזקיה בשם רבי ירמיה: כך היה רבי שמעון בן יוחאי אומר,
"יקרב אברהם מן גביה ועד גביי. ואנא מקרב מן גביי ועד סוף כל דרי.
ואין לא, יצרף אחיה השילוני עמי ואנא מקרב כל עמא."

Rabbi Hezekiah said in the name of Rabbi Jeremiah:
Throughout all the days of Rabbi Shimon bar Yochai a rainbow
never appeared among the clouds. [When Noah emerged from
the ark, God promised that he would never bring another Flood
to destroy the world and used the rainbow as a sign of that
promise.[702] Accordingly, when a rainbow appears, it signifies
that humankind has descended to the point where it should be
destroyed but God forebears from doing so because of His
promise. Rabbi Shimon bar Yochai had such great merit,
however, that no rainbow ever appeared during his lifetime.[703]]

Rabbi Hezekiah, in the name of Rabbi Jeremiah, said:
Thus did Rabbi Shimon bar Yochai say: "Valley, valley! Fill

---

[702] Genesis 9:9-14.
[703] P'nei Moshe.

yourself with gold *dinarim*!" And so it was. [The Midrash explains that Rabbi Shimon bar Yochai had a disciple who left his academy to go into business. He succeeded handsomely and became very wealthy. This caused the other students to grow discontent, so Rabbi Shimon bar Yochai took them to a valley which he miraculously filled with gold coins. He told his students that each one could take whatever he desired but that, in so doing, each would relinquish his future reward in the world to come. Hearing this, the students desisted.[704]]

Rabbi Hezekiah said in the name of Rabbi Jeremiah: Thus did Rabbi Shimon bar Yochai say: "I have seen those who merit the world to come and they are few. If they are thirty, I and my son are among them. If they are two, they are my son and I."

Rabbi Hezekiah said in the name of Rabbi Jeremiah: Thus did Rabbi Shimon bar Yochai say: "Let the merit of Abraham draw people close to God until my time and I will draw people close to God from my time until the end of all generations. If my merit is not sufficient, let that of Achiya the Shilonite join with mine and I will draw close all the nation."

How can so few people be destined for the world to come? The Talmud says that adequate reward for performance of a commandment cannot be had in this world.[705] This would suggest that whoever performs a commandment should, of necessity, receive reward in the next world. Furthermore, the

---

[704] Rabbi David Oppenheim (1664-1736) of Nicholsburg (Moravia).
[705] B.T. Kiddushin 39B.

Mishnah says that all Israel, with but a few unusual exceptions, have a share in the world to come.[706]

The Talmud also prescribes a prayer to be recited after Torah study which includes the phrase, "...I run to life in the world to come... ,"[707] implying that anyone who regularly spends time studying Torah earns a share in the world to come. Furthermore, a passage of the Talmud which has been incorporated into the prayerbook states that, "whoever recites halachoth daily is guaranteed to be a participant in the world to come."[708]

This problem can be solved by adopting the version of this passage found in the Babylonian Talmud, Tractate Sukkah 45B, which quotes Rabbi Shimon bar Yochai as saying that "men of distinction" (בני עליה) are few rather than "those who merit the world to come" (בני עולם הבא). These "men of distinction" were individuals who served God in a completely altruistic manner without desiring any reward for themselves, even spiritual reward.[709] Individuals possessed of such devotion would indeed be exceedingly rare. This also explains why Rabbi Shimon bar Yochai's merit was so great that no rainbow appeared during his lifetime and that his merit would suffice to draw people closer to God until the end of all generations.

---

706 Sanhedrin 10:1.
707 B.T. Brachoth 28B. This is codified in Shulchan Aruch, Orach Chaim 110:8.
708 B.T. Megillah 28B.
709 Rabbi Shneur Zalman of Liadi, Likutei Amarim Tanya Part I, Chapter 10.

In the alternative, perhaps Rabbi Shimon bar Yochai referred to a very special level of the world to come. Rabbi Chanina taught that in the future, Hashem will make a special canopy for each righteous person and that each such person will be "scorched" by the canopy of his neighbor, meaning that each will be put to shame by the merit of his neighbor.[710] Thus, there are many levels of reward awaiting even those who are righteous. Perhaps the greatest levels are reserved for Rabbi Shimon bar Yochai and his son.

---

[710] B.T. Baba Bathra 65A.

Brachoth 9:5   (Compare B.T. Brachoth 60B and VaYikra
Rabbah 24:2)

מתניתין: חייב אדם לברך על הרעה כשם שמברך על הטובה...

גמרא: רבי ברכיה בשם רבי לוי: על שם, "וְאַתָּה מָרוֹם לְעֹלָם
ה'." (תהלים צב:ט). לעולם ידך על עליונה. בנוהג שבעולם, מלך בשר
ודם יושב ודן. כשהוא נותן דימוס, הכל מקלסין אותו. וכשהוא נותן
ספקולה, הכל מרנגים אחריו. למה? ששטף בדינו. אבל הקדוש ברוך
הוא אינו כן, אלא, "וְאַתָּה מָרוֹם לְעֹלָם ה'." (תהלים צב:ט). לעולם ידך
על עליונה.

רבי הונא בשם רבי אחא: "לְדָוִד מִזְמוֹר חֶסֶד וּמִשְׁפָּט אָשִׁירָה לְךָ
ה' אֲזַמֵּרָה." (תהלים קא:א). אמר דוד לפני הקדוש ברוך הוא, "אם חסד
אתה עושה עמי, אשירה. ואם משפט אתה עושה עמי, אשירה. בין כך
ובין כך, לה' אזמרה."

אמר רבי תנחומא בן יהודה: "בֵּא-לֹהִים אֲהַלֵּל דָּבָר בַּה' אֲהַלֵּל
דָּבָר." (תהלים נו:יא). בין על מדות הדין, בין על מדות הרחמים, אהלל
דבר.

ורבנן אמרין: "כּוֹס יְשׁוּעוֹת אֶשָּׂא וּבְשֵׁם ה' אֶקְרָא." (תהלים
קטז:יג). "...צָרָה וְיָגוֹן אֶמְצָא וּבְשֵׁם ה' אֶקְרָא..." (תהלים קטז:ג-ד). בין
כך ובין כך, "וּבְשֵׁם ה' אֶקְרָא."

אמר רבי יודן בן פילה: הוא שאיוב אמר, "...ה' נָתַן וַה' לָקַח יְהִי
שֵׁם ה' מְבֹרָךְ." (איוב א:כא). כשנתן, ברחמים נתן. וכשלקח, ברחמים
לקח. ולא עוד, אלא כשנתן, לא נמלך בבריה וכשלקח, נמלך בבית
דינו.

אמר רבי אלעזר: כל מקום שנאמר, "וה'," הוא ובית דינו. בנין
אב שבכולם, "...וַה' דִּבֶּר עָלֶיךָ רָעָה." (דברי הימים ב יח:כב).

**Mishnah: A person is obliged to bless God for evil
just as he or she blesses Him for good...**

Gemara: Rabbi Berachia said in the name of Rabbi Levi: "You, Lord, are forever exalted"[711] means "You always have the upper hand." It is customary in the world that when a flesh and blood king sits and judges, if he grants clemency, everyone praises him, but if he metes out punishment everyone criticizes him. Why? Because his judgment is excessive. However, it is not so with the Holy One, Blessed be He. Rather, "You, Lord, are forever exalted"[712] meaning "You always have the upper hand." [Although the reason certain events occur in the world is unknown, whatever God does is for the benefit of humanity.]

Rabbi Huna said in the name of Rabbi Acha: "A song of David: Kindness and justice I will harmonize; to you, Lord, I will sing."[713] David said before the Holy One, Blessed be He, "If You do kindness with me, I will sing and if You do justice with me, I will sing. Either way, to the Lord I will harmonize."

Rabbi Tanchuma ben Judah said: "I shall praise a word of God; I shall praise a word of the Lord"[714] means "Whether respecting attributes of justice or whether respecting attributes of mercy, I will praise God's word."

The rabbis say: "A cup of salvation I shall raise and upon the Name of the Lord I shall call."[715] "...trouble and anguish I will find. And upon the Name of the Lord I shall call... ."[716] Whether this way or that way [whether I find

---

[711] Psalms 92:9.
[712] Ibid.
[713] Psalms 101:1.
[714] Psalms 56:11.
[715] Psalms 116:13.
[716] Psalms 116:3-4.

salvation or whether I find trouble and anguish], "And upon the Name of the Lord I shall call... ."[717]

Rabbi Yudan ben Pilla said: This is what Job meant, "...the Lord gave and the Lord took; may the Name of the Lord be blessed."[718] When He gave, He gave with mercy. When He took, He took with mercy. Not only that, but when He gave, He did not consult any creature, but when He took, He consulted His court [of angels].

Rabbi Elazar said: Wherever Scripture says, "And the Lord" ('וה) [as it does in the above verse in Job], it means He and His court. [The term "and" (ו) implies the addition of His court.] The primary source from which this rule derives is, "...and the Lord spoke evil about you."[719] [A few verses earlier, the prophet Michayahu said, "...I saw the Lord sitting upon His throne and all the host of Heaven standing at His right and left."[720] Since the Tanach explicitly states that God rendered judgment in conjunction with His court, one may conclude that the phrase "And the Lord" ('וה) means He and His court wherever it is used.[721]]

Classical Jewish literature repeatedly stresses the theme that whatever God does is for the best. For example, there are the famous stories of Nachum Ish Gamzo (נחום איש גמזו) who got his name because no matter what happened, he always

[717] Ibid.
[718] Job 1:21.
[719] II Chronicles 18:22.
[720] II Chronicles 18:18.
[721] See P'nei Moshe.

said, "This is also for the best." (גם זו לטובה).[722] Moreover, this belief is so fundamental to the Jewish religion that it is actually encoded in the Shulchan Aruch which says that, "A person is obliged to bless God for evil with perfect sincerity and a willing spirit just as he or she blesses God for good with joy, for evil is actually joyous and beneficial to those who serve God in that when one lovingly accepts what God has decreed, he or she thereby serves God and, hence, has joy."[723] Elsewhere, the code says, "A person should always be accustomed to say, 'All that the Merciful One does, He does for the best.'"[724]

In what sense does Hashem "consult His court?" If God is omniscient then what advice or insight can any Heavenly entourage add? One answer may be that God Himself judges with absolute truth. If Hashem would follow the results of such judgment, He would punish people severely. However, He consults His court, so to speak. From the point of view of lower beings, even spiritual beings such as angels, a person's actions may find justification. God is willing to be lenient and adopt such a point of view even though by the strict standard of absolute truth it would not be proper to do so.

A more profound explanation of how Hashem consults with his court is as follows. God Himself is purely merciful and good. The Rambam states that God does only good

---

[722] B.T. Ta'anith 21A. See also a popular story about Rabbi Akiva applying this principle in B.T. Brachoth 60B-61A.
[723] Shulchan Aruch, Orach Chaim 222:3.
[724] Shulchan Aruch, Orach Chaim 230:5.

because he creates existence itself and existence is, by definition, good. Evil is the lack of existence and does not emanate directly from the Creator.[725] In other words, God really does not want to punish nor to permit evil to occur. He does so only through an intermediary system of spiritual forces which constrict or hide His Divine influence. It is this absence of Divinity, or absence of existence, which produces evil. This system is called the "Heavenly Court."[726] Because a person's actions set into motion the spiritual forces of judgment, it cannot be said that Hashem directly causes evil. Instead, the metaphor of "consulting His court" applies.

---

[725] Moreh Nevuchim, Part III, Chapter 10.
[726] Rabbi Moshe Chaim Luzzatto, Derech HaShem 2:6.

Brachoth 9:5 (Compare B.T. Sotah 22B and J.T. Sotah 5:5)

עֲשֵׂה מאהבה וַעֲשֵׂה מיראה. עֲשֵׂה מאהבה שאם באת לשנוא, דע
כי אתה אוהב ואין אוהב שונא. עֲשֵׂה מיראה שאם באת לבעט, דע
שאתה ירא ואין ירא מבעט.

שבעה פָרוּשִׁין הן: פרוש שיכמי. ופרוש ניקפי. ופרוש קיזאי.
פרוש "מה הנכיי?" פרוש "אדע חובתי ואעשנה." פרוש יראה. פרוש
אהבה.

פרוש שיכמי, טעין מצוותא על כיתפא. פרוש ניקפי, "אקיף לי
ואנא עביד מצוה." פרוש קיזאי, עביד חדא חובה וחדא מצוה ומקזז חדא
בחדא. פרוש "מה הנכייה?" "מאן דאית לי מה נא מנכי עביד מצוה."
פרוש "אדע חובתי ואעשה," "הי דא חובתה עבדית, דאעבד מצוה
כוותה." פרוש יראה כאיוב. פרוש אהבה כאברהם.

אין לך חביב מכולם אלא פרוש אהבה כאברהם. אברהם אבינו
עשה יצר הרע טוב, דכתיב, "וּמָצָאתָ אֶת לְבָבוֹ נֶאֱמָן לְפָנֶיךָ... ." (נחמיה
ט:ח).

אמר רבי אחא: והפסידד? אלא, "...וְכָרוֹת עִמּוֹ הַבְּרִית (וְהַחֶסֶד)..."
(נחמיה ט:ח). אבל דוד לא היה יכול לעמוד בו והרגו בלבבו. מאי
טעמא? "...וְלִבִּי חָלַל בְּקִרְבִּי." (תהלים קט:כב).

Do from love and do from fear. Do from love so that if
you come to hate, know that you are one who loves and one
who loves does not hate. Do from awe so that if you come to
rebel, know that you are one who has awe and one who has
awe does not rebel. [If performance of a positive
commandment appears burdensome or uninviting, remember
that you love God and one who loves God should not despise
his or her responsibilities. If you seek to rebel against the
restrictions imposed by negative commandments, remember

that you respect God and one who truly respects God obeys the restrictions He has imposed.[727]]

There are seven types of ascetics: "the shoulder ascetic," "the waiting ascetic," "the offsetting ascetic," "the hedonistic ascetic," "the ascetic who says, 'Let me know my obligation and I will do it,'" "the ascetic of awe," "the ascetic of love."

The "shoulder ascetic" bears the commandments upon his shoulder [flaunting his piety].[728] The "waiting ascetic" says, "Wait for me while I do a mitzvah." [He has no time for anybody.] The "offsetting ascetic" commits a sin and then performs a mitzvah to compensate for it. The "hedonistic ascetic" says, "If I have a benefit from it, I will perform a mitzvah."[729] The ascetic who says, "Let me know my obligation and I will do it" means to say, "Let me know what sin I have committed and I will perform a compensating mitzvah." The "ascetic of awe" is like Job [who served God out of respect for God's greatness and majesty].[730] The "ascetic of love" is like Abraham.

There is none so precious as the "ascetic of love" like Abraham. Abraham our forefather converted the evil

---

[727] P'nei Moshe.

[728] Ma'arecheth HeAruch suggests that this may work in a literal fashion. For example, this ascetic carries a bundle of wood on his shoulder to show off how zealous he is to build a sukkah.

[729] Perush MiBa'al Sefer Chareidim. P'nei Moshe, however, states that the hedonist's attitude is "If I can manage to scrape together something from the little I possess, I will perform a mitzvah."

[730] Whether Job served God out of love or awe is the subject of a Tannaitic dispute in Sotah 5:5-6.

inclination to good as it is written, "You found his heart faithful before you... ."[731] [The Hebrew word for "his heart," לבבו, could have been written with only one "ב" as follows: לבו. By writing it with an extra letter, Scripture implies that Abraham found a way to serve God with both the good inclination and the evil inclination.[732]]

Rabbi Acha said: Did Abraham lose thereby? [Was his reward less because he no longer had to overcome temptation?] Rather, "...and He established with him His covenant..."[733] [734] However, King David was not able to withstand the evil inclination and killed it in his heart. What is the Scriptural source for this? "...my heart is void within me."[735]

The term "ascetic" (פרוש) here can also be translated "Pharisee" and, as used in the Talmud, bears the connotation of a hypocrite. In fact, the Babylonian Talmud even understands the "ascetic of awe" and "ascetic of love" to be hypocrites. Omitting the allusions to Abraham and King David

---

[731] Nehemiah 9:8.

[732] P'nei Moshe and compare B.T. Brachoth 54A.

[733] Nehemiah 9:8. The Talmudic text has the phrase "and the kindness" (והחסד) in parentheses, but this does not appear in the verse. Perhaps the phrase "the covenant and the kindness" (הברית והחסד) which appears a bit further on in verse 9:32 confused a copyist at some point.

[734] This translation accords with Perush MiBa'al Sefer Chareidim P'nei Moshe, however, based on the version of this passage found in J.T. Sotah 5:5 says that the word הפסיד, "lose," should be replaced with הפשיר, "compromise," meaning that Abraham forced the evil inclination to enter into a covenant with him.

[735] Psalms 109:22.

found in this passage, the Babylonian Talmud explains that these ascetics serve God for love of public recognition of their piety or out of fear of punishment.[736]

The Talmud explains elsewhere that a person should always perform the commandments even if he or she does so from ulterior motives because such performace will eventually lead that person to do so with proper motives.[737] *This rule holds true, however, only when one fulfills commandments which one has a duty to carry out. The hypocritical ascetics under discussion make an effort to display their false piety in ways which have nothing to do with the required performance of the mitzvoth, claiming, for example, that they have no time to speak with anyone.*[738]

The idea of co-opting the power of the evil inclination for good as Abraham did, "converting darkness to light and the taste of bitterness to sweetness,"[739] *is a popular theme in Kabbalistic and Chassidic literature.*[740] *However, this section*

---

[736] B.T. Sotah 22B. The Babylonian Talmud also offers some interesting alternative interpretations concerning what these ascetics do. For example, the "shoulder ascetic" acts as the people of Shechem did, a play on the term פרוש שכמי. The people of Shechem circumcised themselves to induce Jacob and his sons to intermarry with them rather than doing so for the sake of Heaven. The "waiting ascetic" (פרוש נקפי) is defined as one who deliberately bangs (מנקף) his feet against a wall so that he can show others how zealously he "ran to perform mitzvoth," supposedly injuring himself in the process.
[737] Ibid. and B.T. Pesachim 50B.
[738] Ben Yehoyada on B.T. Sotah 22B.
[739] Zohar I:4A.
[740] Likutei Amarim Tanya, Part I, Chapter 10.

of the Talmud teaches that only those who have developed their spiritual nature to the highest degree should engage in the religious activities necessary to perfectly achieve such a goal, such activities going far beyond those which the Torah requires of ordinary Jews. Even King David failed to attain this exalted state. Surely those of lesser stature should not attempt it lest they become mere hypocrites who appear pious outwardly but are quite different inwardly.[741]

The Talmud quotes Mar Ukba as saying, "With respect to this matter I am like vinegar compared to wine in comparison to my father, for when my father would eat meat on one day, he would not eat cheese until the same time the next day, whereas I do not eat cheese at the same meal with meat, but eat it at the next meal."[742] *Why did Mar Ukba think it so impressive that his father waited a full twenty-four hours between eating meat and milk instead of the standard six hours? Surely it would not have been too difficult for him to follow his father's custom. Mar Ukba's point, however, is that merely adopting the mechanical regimen of religious practices is meaningless. Anyone can stay up all night reciting Psalms or fast frequently, but it is not proper to engage in such activities unless one first attains the proper level of spiritual preparation, including proper performance of all the commandments for which he or she is already obligated in all their details and with sincere intentions.*

---

[741] See Maharsha on B.T. Sotah 22B sub verba "Parush Meduchah" (פרוש מדוכה).

[742] B.T. Chullin 105A.

Brachoth 9:5

אמר רבי יוסי בר בון: אם נתיישנו דברי תורה בפיך, אל תבוזה
עליהן. מה טעמא? "...וְאַל תָּבוּז כִּי זָקְנָה אִמֶּךָ." (משלי כג:כב).

אמר רבי זעירא: אם נזדקנה אומתך, עמוד וגדרה כשם שעשה
אלקנה שהיה מדריך את ישראל לפעמי רגלים. הדא הוא דכתיב, "וְעָלָה
הָאִישׁ הַהוּא מֵעִירוֹ [מִיָּמִים יָמִימָה לְהִשְׁתַּחֲוֹת וְלִזְבֹּחַ לַה' צְ-בָאוֹת
בְּשִׁלֹה]... ." (שמואל א א:ג).

"עֵת לַעֲשׂוֹת לַה' הֵפֵרוּ תּוֹרָתֶךָ." (תהלים קיט:קכו). רבי נתן
מסרס קראי: "הפרו תורתך, עת לעשות לה'."

רבי חלקיה בשם רבי סימון: העושה תורתו עתים, הרי זה מיפר
ברית. מאי טעמא? "הפרו תורתך עת [לעשות] לה'."

תני: רבי שמעון בן יוחאי אומר: אם ראית את הבריות
שנתייאשו ידיהן מן התורה מאד, עמוד והתחזק בה ואתה מקבל שכר
כולם. מאי טעמא? "הפרו תורתך, עת לעשות לה'."

הלל הזקן היה אומר: בשעה דמכנשין, בדר. ובשעה דמבדרין,
כנוש. וכן היה הלל אומר: אם ראית את התורה שהיא חביבה על
ישראל והכל שמחין בה, בדר. ואם לאו, כנוש.

אמר רבי אלעזר: מה התינוק הזה צריך לינק בכל שעה שביום,
כך כל אדם שבישראל צריך ליגע בתורה בכל שעות שביום.

רבי יונה בשם רבי יוסי בן גזירה: כל פיטטיא בישין ופיטטיא
דאורייתא טבין. כל כדבייא בישין וכדבייא דאורייתא טבין.

Rabbi Yossi bar Bon said: If words of Torah have
grown old in your mouth, do not despise them. [Although you
have repeated them frequently, do not stop studying them.[743]]

---

[743] Etz Yosef and HaKothev.

What is the Scriptural source for this? "...do not despise your mother though she has grown old."[744]

Rabbi Z'eira said: If your nation became old, stand up and fence it in just as Elkanah did when he directed all Israel to go up to Jerusalem on the pilgrim festivals. [This is a play on the word אמך, "your mother," which can be read אומתך, meaning "your nation." Elkanah set an example for the rest of the Jewish nation by ascending to the Tabernacle in Shiloh by a different route each time he went. When Jews who had become lax in observing the obligation to travel to the Tabernacle on the holidays of Pesach, Shavuoth and Sukkoth saw Elkanah performing this mitzvah, they were inspired to do likewise.[745]] Thus it is written, "And that man went up from his city seasonally to prostrate himself and sacrifice to the Lord of multitudes in Shiloh... ."[746] [The phrase "from his city" (מעירו) is superfluous. From where else would Elkanah be coming? The extra wording implies that he took a different route each time he went in order to publicize what he was doing.[747]]

"[It is] time to do for the Lord, [for] they have abrogated Your Torah."[748] Rabbi Nathan transposed the wording of the verse: "They have abrogated Your Torah because it is a time to do for the Lord." [Under certain very exceptional circumstances, the sages have authority to deviate from the laws of the Torah. For example, normally the Torah would

---

744 Proverbs 23:22.
745 Etz Yosef.
746 I Samuel 1:3.
747 Compare Perush MiBa'al Sefer Chareidim.
748 Psalms 119:126.

have forbidden Elijah to offer sacrifices outside the Temple at Mount Carmel. However, because so many Jews had abandoned the Torah in favor of worshipping Baal, Elijah did so to demonstrate the invalidity of that cult.[749]]

Rabbi Chilkiah said in the name of Rabbi Simon: One who restricts his Torah learning to specific times thereby abrogates the covenant. What is the Scriptural source for this? "They have abrogated Your Torah [by fixing] a time to do for the Lord." [Again switching around the wording of the verse.]

It is taught: Rabbi Shimon bar Yochai says: If you see people who have slackened greatly in Torah study, stand and strengthen yourself in it and you will receive the reward of all of them. What is the Scriptural source for this? "They have abrogated Your Torah [so it is] a time to do for the Lord."

[If one observes others scorning Torah study but is not drawn after them and, moreover, ignores their ridicule to do what is right, he deserves special reward.[750]]

Hillel the Elder used to say: At a time of gatherers, scatter and at a time of scattering, gather. [When others "gather in" by withdrawing and not disseminating Torah broadly, go out and teach it. However, when others "scatter," that is, publicize the Torah widely, remain humble and withdrawn.[751]]

Likewise Hillel used to say: If you see that the Torah is precious to Israel and all are rejoicing in it, scatter, and if not, gather in.

---

[749] Etz Yosef. See I Kings 18:20-39.
[750] Etz Yosef.
[751] P'nei Moshe and Perush MiBa'al Sefer Chareidim.

[This last statement does not necessarily contradict what Hillel said earlier. Even when there is a great need for scholars to spread Torah, they should only do so if such dissemination will be appreciated and respected. However, if people will, God forbid, ridicule the Torah, then it is better not to teach it even in circumstances where there is a strong need.]

Rabbi Elazar said: Just as a baby needs to nurse at every hour of the day, so a Jewish man needs to toil in Torah at every hour of the day.

Rabbi Jonah in the name of Rabbi Yossi ben Gezera said: All excessive talk is bad, but excessive talk of Torah is good. All falsehoods are bad, but falsehoods concerning the Torah are good.

When one discusses the Torah at length, one will discover new insights, as Ben Bag Bag says, "Reflect upon it and reflect upon it for everything is in it."[752] Hence, excessive talk of Torah is good. However, it is so wrong to show off one's accomplishments in Torah learning that he is allowed to deviate from the truth concerning them, denying that he has the level of scholarship which he, in truth, possesses.[753]

The Perush MiBa'al Sefer Chareidim has a version wherein this last statement is reversed: "All falsehoods are good, but falsehoods with respect to the Torah are bad." He explains that one may deviate from the truth in ordinary matters if it will create peace. Thus, for example, a person

---

[752] Pirkei Avoth 5:22.
[753] See B.T. Baba Metzia 23B-24A.

repeating an unflattering remark which one spouse made about another may alter it so as not to disturb marital harmony. This cannot be done with Torah, however, where truth must always be paramount.

Amudei Yerushalayim[754] has a third version: "All satiations (ברכיא) are good, but satiation of Torah is bad." One should never feel that he or she has done enough Torah learning.

The Babylonian Talmud rules that one should establish fixed times for learning Torah to ensure a minimum amount of Torah study.[755] However, this does not mean that when he has spare time he should think, "I already have set times for learning so I do not have to learn now." Rather, one should use as much spare time as possible for studying Torah as this passage of the Jerusalem Talmud states.[756]

Certainly the more mitzvoth a person performs, the better, but if a person failed to do a mitzvah such as, say, giving to charity on a certain occasion, it would not mean that he or she thereby nullified the covenant between God and Israel. Why does the Talmud teach that "One who restricts his Torah learning to specific times thereby abrogates the covenant?"[757]

---

[754] Rabbi Israel Eisenstein.

[755] B.T. Shabbath 31A and Shulchan Aruch, Orach Chaim 155:1.

[756] Mishnah Brurah on Shulchan Aruch, Orach Chaim 155:1.

[757] Similarly, Rabbi Nehorai taught that the verse, "For the word of the Lord he despised..." (Numbers 15:31) applies to one who has the opportunity to study Torah but fails to do so. (B.T. Sanhedrin 99A) Granted that it is wrong to miss a chance to learn, but why does the Tanna view it so harshly?

God wants the laws of the Torah to control every action a Jew takes. There is a Torah way of eating, a Torah way of getting dressed, even a Torah way of using the bathroom. When a person has the attitude that he must use every spare moment to learn Torah, he will think of Torah all the time because he must always evaluate whether each passing moment is one in which he could be learning. Having one's mind directed this way ensures that he will apply Torah teachings to everything he does. One who limits his learning to certain times, however, does not constantly think about the Torah and how it should guide his actions. This nullifies the covenant because it means that Torah does not always influence what he does.

Brachoth 9:5 (continued)

אמר רבי שמעון בן לקיש: במגילת חסידים מצאו כתיב, "יום
תעזביני ימים אעזבך." לשנים שיצאו, אחד מטבריא ואחד מציפורין
ופגעו זה בזה בחדא משכנא. לא הספיקו לפרוש זה מזה עד שהלך זה
מיל וזה מיל. נמצאו רחוקין זה מזה שני מילין. ואשה שהיתה יושבת
וממתנת לאיש. כל זמן שהיתה בדעתו להינשא לה, היתה יושבת
וממתנת לו. כיון שהפליג דעתו ממנו, היא היתה הולכת ונישאת לאחר.

Rabbi Shimon ben Lakish said: In the Scroll of the Pious they found written, "If you abandon me for a day, I will abandon you for two days." This is comparable to two people who went out, one from Tiberias and the other from Sepphoris. They met at a certain inn. They had hardly departed from one another when they each went a mile with the result that they were two miles distant from one another. It may further be compared to a woman who was waiting for a man to marry her. As long as it was apparent that he had in mind to marry her, she was sitting and waiting for him. When he diverted his attention from her, she went and married another.

These allegories reflect the Jewish belief that it is easy to have a close relationship with God. As the Torah says, "For this commandment which I command you today is not far from you, nor is it distant. It is not in Heaven that one should say, 'Who will ascend for us to Heaven and take it for us and cause us to hear it so that we may do it?' And it is not on the other side of the ocean that one should say, 'Who will cross for us to the other side of the ocean and take it for us and cause us to hear it so that we may do it?' For the matter is very close to you in your mouth and in your heart to do it."[758] *It is as simple to be close to Hashem as meeting an acquaintance at an inn. Moreover, even if one falls far short of the spiritual stature required to achieve closeness to God, He will patiently await the individual's improvement just as a young lady awaits her fiancee.*

However, God reacts to human behavior measure for measure. If a person "departs" from Him, God will depart in the opposite direction so that the distance will appear twice as great. Likewise, if there is no interest whatsoever in spiritual growth, Hashem will depart just as a lady will not await her intended if he no longer shows interest in marrying her.

---

[758] Deuteronomy 30:11-14.

Brachoth 9:5 (continued) (Compare B.T. Brachoth 64A)

אמר רבי אלעזר בשם רבי חנינא: תלמידי חכמים מרבים שלום
בעולם. מה טעם? "וְכָל בָּנַיִךְ לְמּוּדֵי ה' וְרַב שְׁלוֹם בָּנָיִךְ." (ישעיה נד:יג).

Rabbi Elazar said in the name of Rabbi Chanina: Torah
scholars increase peace in the world. What is the Scriptural
source for this? "All of your sons are learned of the Lord and
great is the peace of your sons."[759]

P'nei Moshe says that the redundant use of the term
"your sons" permits the homiletic conclusion that the verse
actually refers to scholars. The Babylonian Talmud, however,
says: Do not read "your sons" (בניך) *but rather "your*
builders" (בוניך),[760] *the idea being that Torah scholars "build"*
theories of Jewish law and philosophy from the premises set
forth in the written and oral Torah. Alternatively, Torah
scholars are "builders" because they build and strengthen
Torah institutions and observance among the Jewish people.[761]
Such scholars thus create peace between humankind and the
Creator. They also create peace among people because their
Torah learning enables them to make decisions concerning
Jewish law that help settle disputes.[762]

---

[759] Isaiah 54:13.
[760] B.T. Brachoth 64A.
[761] Rabbi Moshe Heinemann שליט"א.
[762] Iyun Yaakov, Rabbi Yaakov Reischer.

This fits in well with the theme of the Talmud that one must exert oneself to study Torah as much as possible. Failure to do so detracts from the cosmic harmony between humanity and Hashem.

תם ונשלם בעזרת הא–ל יתברך שמו

BIBLIOGRAPHY AND GLOSSARY

Abravanel, Rabbi Don Isaac: (1437-1508) In addition to his scholarly activities, Rabbi Abravanel was heavily involved in Spanish and Portuguese politics until the Jews were expelled from Spain when he fled to Italy.

Aggadah: Rabbinical interpretations of the text of the **Tanach** and related material which discusses the philosophical, theological and ethical aspects of the Jewish religion.

Amidah: A prayer Jews recite at least three times each day. During weekdays, the **Amidah** prayer consists of eighteen blessings. The word "**Amidah**" in Hebrew means "standing" because, if possible, one must stand while reciting it.

Amoraim: Sages who lived in the period after the **Mishnah** was reduced to writing. The debates of the **Amoraim** concerning the meaning of the **Mishnah** were reduced to writing in the sixth century C.E. as the **Gemara**. The Mishnah consists of the teachings of an earlier generation of sages called **Tannaim**.

Amudei Yerushalayim: Commentary on the Jerusalem Talmud by Rabbi Israel Eisenstein (Europe, 19th century).

Arizal: Acronym for **Rabbi Yitzchak Luria**, the foremost Kabbalist of the late Middle Ages. Rabbi Luria was born in Poland in 1534 and died in the Land of Israel in 1572.

Azulai, Rabbi Chaim Yosef David: Known by the acronym "**Chida**," Rabbi Azulai traveled widely and wrote voluminously on almost every aspect of the written and Oral Torah. He lived from 1724 to 1806.

B.T.: Babylonian Talmud

BaMidbar: The Book of Numbers. **BaMidbar Rabbah** is the portion of the **Midrash Rabbah** on the Book of Numbers.

Be'er HaGolah: Philosophical treatise written by the **Maharal** (Rabbi Yehudah Loewy of Prague, 1526-1609).

Ben Yehoyada: A comprehensive commentary on Aggadic material written by **Rabbi Yosef Hayyim** of Baghdad (1832-1909).

Bi'ur Halachah: An in-depth commentary on the **Orach Chaim** section of the **Shulchan Aruch** written by Rabbi Yisrael Meir Kagan who lived in Poland from 1838 to 1933. Rabbi Kagan has come to be known as the "**Chofetz Chaim**" after his most popular work.

Braitha: A teaching of the **Tannaim** which was not included in the **Mishnah**. Rabbi Chiya (Land of Israel, 3rd century C.E.) edited these teachings.

Breishith: The Book of Genesis. **Breishith Rabbah** is the portion of the **Midrash Rabbah** on the Book of Genesis.

Chanoch Zundel ben Yosef, Rabbi: Commentator who wrote extensively on **Ein Yaakov** and various collections of **Midrashim** (Poland, died 1867).

Chida: Acronym for **Rabbi Chaim Yosef David Azulai.** Rabbi Azulai traveled widely and wrote voluminously on almost every aspect of the written and Oral Torah. He lived from 1724 to 1806.

Chidushei Gaonim: An anthology of commentaries published in the Romm Vilna edition of **Ein Yaakov.** (The anonymous compilers were commissioned by the publisher.)

Choshen Mishpat: Section of the **Shulchan Aruch** written by Rabbi Yosef Karo who lived from 1488-1575 and died in the Land of Israel containing laws concerning business and financial matters.

Cordervero, Rabbi Moshe: Principal teacher of the Arizal and author of numerous Kabbalistic works (Land of Israel, 1522-1570).

Derech Hashem: Kabbalistic/philosophical work written by **Rabbi Moshe Chaim Luzzatto** who was born in Italy in 1707 and died in the Land of Israel in 1746.

Dessler, Rabbi Eliyahu Eliezer: Author of the ethical treatise called **"Michtav MiEliyahu."** (Russia and Great Britain, 1891-1954)

Devarim: The Book of Deuteronomy. **Devarim Rabbah** is the portion of the **Midrash Rabbah** on the Book of Deuteronomy.

Dinar (plural: **dinarim**): A silver coin commonly used in **Talmudic** times. Four **dinarim** equaled the value of the silver **shekel** referred to in the **Tanach**. The Talmud sometimes refers to the **dinar** as a **zuz**.

Dover Shalom: Commentary on the prayerbook by Rabbi Yitzchak Eliyahu Landau (Vilna, 1801-1876) found in **Otzar HaTefilloth**.

Ein Yaakov: A collection of Aggadic material compiled by **Rabbi Yaakov Ibn Chaviv** who lived in Spain and Turkey from 1445-1516.

Eisenstein, Rabbi Israel: Author of **Amudei Yerushalayim**, a commentary on the Jerusalem Talmud. (Europe, 19th century).

Esther Rabbah: The portion of the **Midrash Rabbah** on the Book of Esther.

Etz Yosef: Commentary on **Ein Yaakov** and various **Midrashic** collections by **Rabbi Chanoch Zundel ben Yosef**. (Poland, died 1867).

Even HaEzer: Section of the **Shulchan Aruch** written by Rabbi Yosef Karo who lived from 1488-1575 and died in the Land of Israel containing laws concerning marital law.

Fendel, Rabbi Zechariah: Contemporary author.

Fraenkel, Rabbi David: Author of the **Korban Ha'Eidah** commentary which gives a basic explanation of the Jerusalem Talmud and the **Shayarei Korban** commentary which delves into more complex issues raised by the Jerusalem Talmud (Germany, 1707-1762).

Gordon, Rabbi Aryeh Leib: Author of **Tikun Tefillah** and other commentaries on the prayerbook (Land of Israel, died 1913).

HaKothev: Commentary of **Rabbi Yaakov Ibn Chaviv** published with his collection of Aggadic material called **Ein Yaakov**.

Halachah (plural: **Halachoth**): Jewish law. Such laws may be ritual in nature, addressing the relationship between people and God, or civil in nature, addressing the relationship between a person and his or her fellows.

Havdalah: A ceremony performed at the conclusion of the Sabbath. The person who performs it recites four blessings: a) over wine; b) over fragrant spices; c) over a flame; d) acknowledging the distinction between the sacred and the profane.

Hayyim, Rabbi Yosef: Popularly known as **"Ben Ish Chai"** after his most popular work, Rabbi Hayyim flourished in Baghdad from 1832-1909. He wrote two commentaries on Aggadic material: **Ben Yehoyada** and **Sefer Benayahu**.

Heinemann, Rabbi Moshe: Major contemporary halachic scholar and decisor. (Baltimore, Maryland).

Heller, Rabbi Yom Tov Lipman: Author of the commentary on the **Mishnah** known as **Tosafoth Yom Tov** (Vienna, Prague, Poland, 1579-1654).

Ibn Ezra, Rabbi Avraham: Biblical commentator and scholar of Hebrew grammar. (Spain, 1089-1164).

Ibn Chaviv, Rabbi Yaakov: Editor of the **Ein Yaakov** anthology of Aggadoth who lived in Spain and Turkey from 1445-1516. Rabbi Ibn Chaviv also wrote a commentary on the Ein Yaakov anthology called **HaKothev.**

Isserles, Rabbi Moshe: Popularly known as the **Rama,** he flourished in Poland from 1530-1572. he is most famous for his glosses on the **Shulchan Aruch.**

Iyun Yaakov: Commentary on the **Ein Yaakov** collection of **Aggadoth** by Rabbi Yaakov Reischer (Prague, 1670-1733).

J.T.: Jerusalem Talmud

Kabbalah: Secret Jewish mystical tradition. Although the general outlines of this tradition are available to the public at large, its details are known only to select few students who have received them orally from their masters.

Kaplan, Rabbi Aryeh: A renowned Torah scholar and author who translated numerous works into English, including **Sefer**

HaBahir, Sefer Yetzirah and **Derech HaShem.** (United States, 1935-1983).

Kehati, Rabbi Pinchas: Author of a comprehensive modern commentary on the Mishnah called **Mishnayoth M'vuaroth.** Born in Poland in 1910, he moved to Israel where he died in 1976.

Kiddush: Blessing ideally recited over wine to sanctify the Sabbath and holidays.

Kohanim: Members of the priestly class who descended from Moses's brother, Aaron.

Korban Ha'Eidah: Commentary on the Jerusalem Talmud by Rabbi David Fraenkel (Germany, 1707-1762). **Korban Ha'Eidah** gives a basic explanation of the Jerusalem Talmud. Rabbi Fraenkel also wrote **Shayarei Korban** which delves into more complex issues.

Kimchi, Rabbi David: Commentator on the Tanach who lived in Spain and Southern France from 1160 to 1235.

Likutei Amarim Tanya: A Chassidic work which discusses a wide range of theological issues written by **Rabbi Shneur Zalman of Liadi**, founder of the Lubavitch Chassidic dynasty who lived from 1745 to 1812.

Luzzatto, Rabbi Moshe Chaim: Author of numerous Kabbalistic and philosophical works including **"Derech**

Hashem." He was born in Italy in 1707 and died in the Land of Israel in 1746.

Ma'avar Yabok: Prayerbook originally composed by Rabbi Aharon Berachiah ben Moshe (Modena, Spain, died 1639).

Ma'arecheth HeAruch: The **Aruch** was a seminal work on Hebrew lexicography written by Rabbi Nathan ben Yechiel (Rome, 1035-1110). The **Ma'arecheth HeAruch** published in the Romm Vilna edition of the Jerusalem Talmud contains excerpts from the **Aruch** which help explain words or phrases in the text. The editors also added material from the **Mussaf HeAruch**, a supplement written by Rabbi Benjamin Mussafia.

Maggid Devarav LeYaakov: A treatise of Chassidic theology and philosophy by the **Maggid of Mezeritch**.

Maggid of Mezeritch: Rabbi Dov Ber, chief disciple of Rabbi Yisroel Baal Shem Tov, the founder of the Chassidic movement. He lived in Poland from 1704 to 1772.

Maharal: Acronym for Rabbi Yehudah Loewy, 1526-1609, who was chief rabbi of Prague. Among his many works is an extensive commentary on the Aggadoth of the Babylonian Talmud.

Maharsha: Acronym for Rabbi Shmuel Eliezer Eidels of Poland, 1555 1632.

Maharzu: Acronym for Rabbi Ze'ev Wolf Einhorn of Vilna (died 1862) who wrote an extensive commentary on the **Midrash Rabbah**.

Marei HaPanim: Commentary on the Jerusalem Talmud by Rabbi Moshe Margolies of Amsterdam. In contrast to **P'nei Moshe**, a commentary by the same author, **Marei Panim** delves into complex Talmudic problems.

Me'Am Loez: An anthology of commentaries on the **Tanach** initiated by Rabbi Yaakov Culi (Turkey, 1689-1732) and completed after his death by other scholars.

Mechilta: Midrashic commentary on Exodus written by Rabbi Yishmael (Land of Israel, 2nd century C.E.) and his disciples.

Metzudoth David: Commentary on the **Tanach** by Rabbi David Altschuler (Poland, 18th century).

Michtav MiEliyahu: Ethical treatise written by Rabbi Eliyahu Dessler (Russia and Great Britain, 1891-1954).

Midrash: Homiletic interpretations of the **Tanach**. **Midrashic** works are often classified into **Halachic Midrash** which explains how religious law is derived from the text of the **Tanach** and **Aggadic Midrash** which discusses the philosophical, theological and ethical aspects of the text.

Midrash Rabbah: "The Great **Midrash**" is the most extensive collection of **Midrashic** interpretation. Almost all of the **Midrash Rabbah** is Aggadic in nature. The **Midrash Rabbah**

follows the text of the **Tanach** and so is identified as, for example, **Breishith Rabbah**, Midrashim on the text of **Breishith** (Genesis).

Mishnah: The Oral Law. A compilation of traditions passed down from generation to generation by word of mouth until committed to writing in the third century C.E.

Mishnah Brurah: A basic commentary on the **Orach Chaim** section of the **Shulchan Aruch** written by **Rabbi Yisrael Meir Kagan** who lived in Poland from 1838 to 1933. Rabbi Kagan is generally known as the "**Chofetz Chaim**" after his most popular work.

Mishnath D'Rabbi Eliezer: Midrashic commentary Rabbi Eliezer ben Yehuda of Pintchov (late 16th century to early 17th century) published in the Romm Vilna edition of the **Midrash Rabbah**.

Moreh Nevuchim: A philosophical treatise written by the **Rambam**. Among other issues, this work includes lengthy discussions of the use of allegorical expressions in the **Tanach**, Aristotelian philosophy and the rationale for **mitzvoth**.

Mussaf: Prayers recited on the Sabbath, New Moon and Festivals commemorating the special sacrifices which were offered in the Temple on those occasions.

Ne'ilah: Special additional prayer recited at the conclusion fast days such as **Yom Kippur**.

No'am Elimelech: Chassidic Torah commentary by Rabbi Elimelech of Lizensk (1717-1787).

Oppenheim, Rabbi David: Commentator on the **Jerusalem Talmud**. (Nicholsburg, Moravia, 1664-1736).

Orach Chaim: Section of the **Shulchan Aruch** written by Rabbi Yosef Karo who lived from 1488-1575 and died in the Land of Israel containing laws concerning everyday ritual practice.

Otzar HaTefilloth: Prayerbook containing an anthology of commentaries compiled by Rabbi Shalom Feigenson Sopher in the early 1900's and originally published in Vilna.

Perush MiBa'al Sefer Chareidim: Commentary on the Jerusalem Talmud by Rabbi Elazar Azkari of Turkey and the Land of Israel, 1533-1600.

Pesikta Rabbathai: A collection of **Midrashim** from the early Medieval period (probably 8th century C.E.).

Pirkei D'Rabbi Eliezer: A **Midrash** written by Rabbi Eliezer ben Hyrcanus (Land of Israel, 1st century C.E.) and his disciples.

Pirkei D'Rabbi Nathan: Also called **Avoth D'Rabbi Nathan**, this is an expanded version of **Pirkei Avoth** written by Rabbi Nathan (Babylonia, 2nd century C.E.) and his disciples.

P'nei Moshe: Commentary by Rabbi Moshe Margolies of Lithuania (died 1781) on the Jerusalem Talmud which provides a basic understanding of the text. Rabbi Margolies also wrote **Marei HaPanim** which delves into more complex issues raised by the text of the Jerusalem Talmud.

P'nei Yehoshua: Talmudic commentary by Rabbi Yaakov Yehoshua Falk (Germany, 1681-1756).

Rabbeinu Bachya: Rabbi Bachya ben Asher, 1263-1340.

Rabbeinu Tam: Rabbi Yaakov ben Meir who lived in France from 1100 to 1171 was a grandson of Rashi.

Rama: Acronym for Rabbi Moshe Isserles who flourished in Poland from 1530-1572. he is most famous for his glosses on the **Shulchan Aruch**.

Rambam: An acrostic for "Rabbi Moshe Ben Maimon," known in English as Rabbi Moses Maimonides. He was born in Spain in 1135 and died in Egypt in 1204.

Ramban: An acrostic for "Rabbi Moshe Ben Nachman," known in English as Rabbi Moses Nachmanides. He lived in Spain from 1194 to 1270.

Rashi: An acrostic for the name of **Rabbi Shlomo Yitzchaki** who lived in France during the 11th century.

Rashash: Acronym for **Rabbi Shmuel Strashun**, a Talmudic commentator who lived in Lithuania from 1794-1872.

Rosenblatt, Rabbi Samuel: Rabbi and scholar who translated several important texts of Medieval Jewish philosophy from Arabic into English. (Baltimore, Maryland, 1902-1982).
Rosh HaShannah: The Jewish New Year.

Saadia Gaon: Major Jewish philosopher and commentator. (Egypt and Babylonia, 882-942).

Salanter, Rabbi Yisrael: Founder of the Mussar Movement which stresses the study of ethical writings. (Lithuania, 1810-1883).

Scherman, Rabbi Nosson: Contemporary author and editor.

Seder Olam Rabbah: A history composed by Rabbi Yossi bar Chalafta (Land of Israel, 2nd century C.E.). (B.T. Yevamoth 82B)

Sefer Benayahu: A comprehensive commentary on Aggadic material written by **Rabbi Yosef Hayyim** of Baghdad (1832-1909).

Sefer Emunoth Ve'Deoth: Major philosophical exposition of the Jewish religion by **Saadia Gaon**.

Sefer HaBahir: A Kabbalistic text attributed to Rabbi Nechuniah ben Hakana (Land of Israel, 1st century C.E.).

Sefer Meirath Einayim: Commentary on **Shulchan Aruch, Choshen Mishpat** by Rabbi Yehoshua Falk, 1550-1614.

Sefer Ta'amei HaMinhagim: Anthology of traditional customs and commentary by **Rabbi Avraham Yitzchak Sperling.**

Sefer Yetzirah: A Kabbalistic work composed in its basic form by Abraham and later reduced to writing.

Sha'ar HaYichud: A section of **Likutei Amarim Tanya** written by **Rabbi Shneur Zalman of Liadi** (Russia, 1745-1812).

Shema: A prayer consisting of three paragraphs from the **Chumash** (Pentateuch) which Jews recite every morning and evening.

Shemoth: The Book of Exodus. **Shemoth Rabbah** is the portion of the **Midrash Rabbah** on the Book of Exodus.

Shir HaShirim: The Book of Songs. **Shir HaShirim Rabbah** is the portion of the **Midrash Rabbah** on the Book of Songs.

Shneur Zalman of Liadi, Rabbi: Author of numerous works including **Likutei Amarim Tanya,** a Chassidic work which discusses a wide range of theological issues. Rabbi Shneur Zalman founded the Lubavitch Chassidic dynasty. He lived from 1745 to 1812.

Shuchatowitz: Rabbi Mordechai: Contemporary scholar and head of the Baltimore **Beth Din** (rabbinical court).

Shulchan Aruch: A codification of Jewish law written by Rabbi Yosef Karo who lived from 1488-1575 and died in the Land of Israel. The Shulchan Aruch is divided into four sections: **Orach Chaim** concerning everyday ritual practice; **Even HaEzer** concerning marital law; **Choshen Mishpat** concerning business and financial matters; **Yoreh Deah** concerning several topics the author did not think fit conveniently into the other categories such as dietary laws and agricultural laws which apply to the Land of Israel.

Sifrei: A Midrashic commentary on the Books of Numbers and Deuteronomy written by Rabbi Shimon bar Yochai (Land of Israel, 2nd century C.E.). (B.T. Sanhedrin 86A).

Sifthei Kohen: Commentary on the **Yoreh Deah** section of **Shulchan Aruch** by Rabbi Shabbethai ben Meir HaKohen (1622-1663).

Sirilio, Rabbi Shlomo: Author of a commentary on the Jerusalem Talmud. (Spain and Jerusalem, 1485-1558).

Slichoth: Confessional prayers recited before the morning prayer service, especially during the month or week before **Rosh HaShannah** (Jewish New Year) and between **Rosh HaShannah** and **Yom Kippur** (Day of Atonement).
Sperling, Rabbi Avraham Yitzchak: Author of **Sefer Ta'amei HaMinhagim**, an anthology of traditional customs and commentary thereon. (Lvov, Ukraine, 1850-1920).

Sukkah: A hut Jews live in during the Festival of Tabernacles (**Sukkoth** in Hebrew) which falls in autumn.

328

Tanach: An acrostic for the Jewish Bible consisting the *Torah* (Pentateuch), *Neviim* (Prophets) and *Kethuvim* (Hagiographa).

Tanchuma: Midrashic commentary on the Torah written by Rabbi Tanchuma bar Abba (Land of Israel, 4th century C.E.) and his disciples.

Tannaim: Sages who lived during the time of the **Mishnah**.

Tanna D'Bei Eliyahu: A set of **Midrashim** which the Prophet Elijah taught to Rabbi Anan (Babylonia, 3rd century C.E.). The longer portion (**Tanna D'Bei Eliyahu Rabbah**) was taught to Rabbi Anan before he fell out of favor with Elijah. The shorter portion (**Tanna D'Bei Eliyahu Zuta**) was taught to Rabbi Anan after that. (B.T. Kethuboth 106A)

Targum Yonathan ben Uzziel: An Aramaic translation and commentary of the Tanach written by Rabbi Yonathan ben Uzziel (Land of Israel, 1st century C.E.).

Tikun Tefillah: Commentary on the standard prayerbook by **Rabbi Aryeh Leib Gordon** found in **Otzar HaTefilloth**.

Torah Temimah: A commentary on the Torah which quotes classical sources such as Talmud and Midrash on each verse and explains them. Written by Rabbi Baruch HaLevi Epstein of Poland in the 19th century.

Tosafoth: A group of approximately two hundred Talmudic scholars who flourished in Europe during the twelfth and thirteenth centuries. These scholars wrote and disseminated several versions of their commentaries on the Talmud.

Tosafoth Yeshanim: A collection of comments by various scholars of the **Tosafoth** period.

Tosafoth Yom Tov: Commentary on the Mishnah by Rabbi Yom Tov Lipman Heller 1579-1654.

Tosefta: A collection of traditional teachings organized by Rabbi Nechemiah (Land of Israel, 2nd century C.E.) and his disciples, paralleling the material of the Mishnah. (B.T. Sanhedrin 86A)

Tur Shulchan Aruch: Code of Jewish law written by Rabbi Jacob ben Asher (Germany and Spain, 1270-1340) which served as a model for the **Shulchan Aruch** written about two hundred years later by **Rabbi Yosef Karo**.

Turei Zahav: Commentary on the **Yoreh Deah** section of **Shulchan Aruch** written by Rabbi David ben Shmuel HaLevy (1586-1667).

VaYikra: The Book of Leviticus. **VaYikra Rabbah** is the portion of the **Midrash Rabbah** on the Book of Leviticus.

Yaakov Ibn Chaviv: Author of the "**Ein Yaakov**" collection of Aggadoth who lived in Spain and Turkey from 1445-1516.

Yad HaChazakah: A comprehensive codification of Jewish law written by the **Rambam** (Rabbi Moses Maimonides).

Yalkut Reuveni: Anthology of **Midrashim** and other classical Jewish literature edited by Rabbi Avraham Reuven Sopher Katz (Prague, died 1673).

Yalkut Shimoni: Anthology of Midrashim on the Tanach edited by Rabbi Shimon HaDarshan (Frankfort, 13th century C.E.).

Yeshiva: Academy

Y'feh Anaf: Commentary on **Ein Yaakov** and **Midrash Rabbah** by **Rabbi Shmuel Yafeh Ashkenazi** who lived in Turkey during the sixteenth century.

Y'feh Kol: Commentary on **Shir HaShirim Rabbah** by **Rabbi Shmuel Yafeh Ashkenazi** who lived in Turkey during the sixteenth century.

Y'feh To'ar: Commentary on parts of **Midrash Rabbah** by **Rabbi Shmuel Yafeh Ashkenazi** who lived in Turkey during the sixteenth century.

Yoreh Deah: Section of the **Shulchan Aruch** written by Rabbi Yosef Karo who lived from 1488-1575 and died in the Land of Israel containing laws

Yosef Tehilloth: Commentary on the Book of Psalms by the **Chida**.

Zohar: Kabbalistic commentary on the Torah attributed to Rabbi Shimon bar Yochai (Land of Israel, 2nd century C.E.) and his disciples.

INDEX